I'd like to dedicate this book to three people, who, in their own unique ways, made me want to write it: To Teresa Derichsweiler, early adopter, gadget lover, Internet trend spotter. It's great to have another addict in the neighborhood. To Larry Cohen, reluctant adopter, mocker of tech trends, devourer of blogs. It's great to have a skeptic there, too. And to Beverly Waters, my mother, whom I'm hoping, sincerely, will read this book and finally get online!

THE
EVERYTHING
GUIDE TO SOCIAL MEDIA

Dear Reader,

I've been covering the high-tech beat from Silicon Valley for a variety of terrific trade publications for almost two decades, and I've loved every minute of it. But I haven't had as many opportunities to write for a mainstream audience as I would have liked. I mean, how many people not working in seriously techie jobs really care about things like the fate of the Java Platform now that Oracle Corporation owns Sun Microsystems, or the government's apparent failure to publish significant research on public key cryptography? Hands?

But it's pretty clear that average, non-techie folks care about social media, which involve many of the technologies that I've been writing about over the years. This stuff isn't rocket science, but it is a tangle of blogs and wikis and social networks and hyperlinks and hashtags and web browsers, all interacting and intermingling on the Internet. And it could use a bit of explaining, not to mention some context.

I've done my best to provide that here. What you have in your hands is a guide for beginners who'd like to participate in social media, but need a few road signs to get started; for veterans who could use a broader map of the social media landscape; and for anyone who feels lost in this unfamiliar territory and just wants to understand what everyone is talking about.

All the best,

John K. Waters

Welcome to the EVERYTHING® Series!

These handy, accessible books give you all you need to tackle a difficult project, gain a new hobby, comprehend a fascinating topic, prepare for an exam, or even brush up on something you learned back in school but have since forgotten.

You can choose to read an *Everything*® book from cover to cover or just pick out the information you want from our four useful boxes: e-questions, e-facts, e-alerts, and e-ssentials.

We give you everything you need to know on the subject, but throw in a lot of fun stuff along the way, too.

We now have more than 400 *Everything*® books in print, spanning such wide-ranging categories as weddings, pregnancy, cooking, music instruction, foreign language, crafts, pets, New Age, and so much more. When you're done reading them all, you can finally say you know *Everything*®!

QUESTION

Answers to common questions

FACT

Important snippets of information

ALERT

Urgent warnings

ESSENTIAL

Quick handy tips

PUBLISHER Karen Cooper

DIRECTOR OF ACQUISITIONS AND INNOVATION Paula Munier

MANAGING EDITOR, EVERYTHING® SERIES Lisa Laing

COPY CHIEF Casey Ebert

ACQUISITIONS EDITOR Lisa Laing

ASSOCIATE DEVELOPMENT EDITOR Hillary Thompson

EDITORIAL ASSISTANT Ross Weisman

EVERYTHING® SERIES COVER DESIGNER Erin Alexander

LAYOUT DESIGNERS Colleen Cunningham, Elisabeth Lariviere, Ashley Vierra, Denise Wallace

Visit the entire Everything® series at *www.everything.com*

THE
EVERYTHING®
GUIDE TO
SOCIAL MEDIA

All you need to know about participating in today's
most popular online communities

John K. Waters

Foreword by John Lester

Avon, Massachusetts

An Everything® Series Book.
Everything® and everything.com® are registered trademarks of F+W Media, Inc.

Published by Adams Media, a division of F+W Media, Inc.
57 Littlefield Street, Avon, MA 02322 U.S.A.
www.adamsmedia.com

ISBN 10: 1-4405-0631-0
ISBN 13: 978-1-4405-0631-4
eISBN 10: 1-4405-0632-9
eISBN 13: 978-1-4405-0632-1

Printed in the United States of America.

10 9 8 7 6 5 4 3 2 1

Library of Congress Cataloging-in-Publication Data
is available from the publisher.

This publication is designed to provide accurate and authoritative information with regard to the subject matter covered. It is sold with the understanding that the publisher is not engaged in rendering legal, accounting, or other professional advice. If legal advice or other expert assistance is required, the services of a competent professional person should be sought.

—From a *Declaration of Principles* jointly adopted by a Committee of the American Bar Association and a Committee of Publishers and Associations

Many of the designations used by manufacturers and sellers to distinguish their products are claimed as trademarks. Where those designations appear in this book and Adams Media was aware of a trademark claim, the designations have been printed with initial capital letters.

This book is available at quantity discounts for bulk purchases.
For information, please call 1-800-289-0963.

Contents

18 Social Media and Education: Teaching the Digital Natives / 215

19 Social Media Marketing: Creating Buzz with the Social Web / 229

20 What's Next on the Horizon for Social Media / 240

Acknowledgments

I'd like to thank everyone at Adams Media for their support during the writing of this book, including Associate Development Editor Hillary Thompson, Copyeditor Richard Wallace, Proofreader Jennifer Robertson, Copy Chief Casey Ebert, Assistant Production Editor Jacob Erickson, Production Project Manager Michelle Roy Kelly, Cover Designer Erin Alexander, Director of Acquisitions and Innovation Paula Munier, and Publisher Karen Cooper.

I'd also like to thank my friends and family who persisted in checking on me after I disappeared off the face of the earth to work on this project, even though I often didn't return their calls, and couldn't talk about anything else on the rare occasions when I did. Thanks guys.

And I want to offer a special thanks to Lisa Laing, Managing Editor of the *Everything*® Series, who stuck by me during this project, despite some missed deadlines and un-kept promises. Your patience and perseverance were remarkable. Many, many thanks.

Top 10 Things Everyone Should Know about Social Media

1. "Social media" and "social networks" are not synonymous terms. Social media is the umbrella term for a range of online content that includes blogs, wikis, photo sharing services, social bookmarking sites, and social networks, such as Facebook and MySpace.

2. It's important to spend some time thinking about your settings on the social networks to which you belong, and to revisit those options regularly.

3. It's a good idea to use caution when meeting people on any social network. The safest social networking strategy is this: Network only with people you know in the real world.

4. A good rule of thumb to follow when you're considering the personal information options of any social network: Start by including things you wouldn't mind telling someone you just met at a party.

5. The blogosphere is the vast information network made up of the entire world's blogs, along with reader comments and any links or connections.

6. Tens of millions of people, from average joes to professional journalists and marketing gurus, are blogging every day.

7. Two issues that should concern you as a blogger are publishing statements that could be false or cause harm to someone's reputation, and violation of intellectual property laws by improperly linking to information, quoting from articles and other blogs, and/or using someone else's creative works.

8. Twitter is the world's most popular microblog, and its users generate about 600 tweets per second. But it's not the only microblogging service. Tumblr, Plurk, Squeelr, Beeing, Jaiku, and Indenti.ca are other examples.

9. A tag is a key word attached to a piece of web content, such as an online article, a blog posting, a digital photo, a video clip, or a website. Techies call it metadata, or data about data.

10. Virtually any crackpot with a bone to pick can badmouth your business online on one of the opinion-sharing sites. As long as it's not libelous, everybody's opinion is welcome. For this reason if for no other, companies can't afford to ignore social media.

Foreword

HUMAN BEINGS CRAVE AND create communities. As a species, we need each other to evolve and survive in this challenging and sometimes unforgiving world. So we eagerly seek each other out, looking for kindred spirits with whom to share knowledge, feelings, dreams, and goals. Together, we grow and thrive.

Human beings also crave and create tools. Again, it is part of our nature as a species. From the first time a human being picked up a stick and figured out how it might help him knock an apple out of a tree, to the creation of vehicles that can fly us beyond the surface of planet Earth, we've been creating tools that extend our abilities. With tools, we can touch the stars.

Communities and tools. Our brains are deeply wired for both of them. Which is why things gets *really* interesting when communities and tools intersect.

Social media is at the intersection of communities and tools. It gives people the ability to connect with each other across the planet, free from the tyranny of geography. It lets people communicate via the written and spoken word, but also gives them opportunities to go beyond that with the world of photo and video sharing. Finding the news that is important to us can be done by aggregating the shared ideas of people across the world as opposed to tuning in to a single controlled source of information. Mobile technology has replaced the now-antiquated concept of location-dependent communication ("I can be contacted at the office") with location-independent communication ("I can be reached anywhere"). Even our very concept of identity is evolving, as people explore different facets of their personality in virtual world environments for entertainment and work.

Traditional mass media has been turned on its head. Social media is giving every human being in modern society the tools to communicate and form communities in ways never seen before. And we face a serious challenge that has nothing to do with the technology of the tools themselves:

How can we learn to use social media in ways that improve the human condition and our quality of life? Our information-overloaded world can drive us away from wisdom and into mindless distraction if we are not careful.

It is my pleasure to provide the Foreword to *The Everything® Guide to Social Media*. In this book, you'll learn about the amazing variety of social media tools and how different communities are using them in innovative ways. You'll learn about the history of social media, where it started, where it is, and where it could be going in the future. When you're done reading, you'll have a deep understanding of the range of tools and how to best use them. Get ready for a fun ride, too!

When you put this book down, you'll do so with a sense of wonder at the magic of communities and tools coming together. And you'll have the critical knowledge you need to start exploring how to use social media wisely and thoughtfully, in ways that will ultimately improve your own life and the lives of others.

John Lester

Introduction

THERE WAS A TIME not that long ago when the World Wide Web was little more than a fancy online magazine stand full of static web pages—things like company profiles, personal home pages, and traditional media sites. Users went there for information that had been published by others. They read it and left. When those users began adding their own content to the web through a type of personal online journal called a "web log," the change was noted, but not widely appreciated, at least initially. When social networks first appeared, they were largely viewed as a teenage craze, not evidence of a changing web. And the first few wikis just looked like nutty experiments, nothing that would ever become a serious business tool.

How times change. You don't often hear the word "fad" these days when the discussion turns to blogs, social networks, and wikis, three types of the user-generated web content that we have come to call social media. You're much more likely to hear phrases like "paradigm shift" and "social media onslaught."

And an onslaught it is. You can barely pick up a newspaper or magazine, flip to a television show, or tune in to a radio station without bumping into a reference to Facebook, Twitter, or Wikipedia. Every other episode of *Law & Order* (pick your flavor) seems to include the discovery of a clue on the victim's "MyFace" page. Most national and local TV news programs now end with some version of, "And don't forget to follow us on Twitter." And there are so many bloggers out there that even traditional media types keep a watchful eye on the blogosphere.

Yet it's easy to sympathize with the doubters and the reluctant adopters who look at all this blogging and tweeting and "friending" with skepticism. "Facebook Shmacebook," they say, "I have real friends." Or "Step outside; the graphics are great." Snarky maybe, but understandable. There's almost a cultish quality to the social media hype, and enthusiasts can seem like true believers who chugged the Kool Aid.

What gets lost in the hype is the organic quality of the social media phenomenon. This isn't a techie trend driven by coders and gadget geeks, though they created the basic platforms and are now cranking out software to support and exploit it. And it's not a psuedo trend concocted by corporations to make money, though plenty of companies are now jumping on the social media bandwagon for that very purpose. Instead, social media grew and spread mostly unplanned in the hands of the end users.

Those end users have changed the web, dramatically and irrevocably. What was once primarily a publication platform is now a highly interactive environment full of user-generated content that trend watchers have dubbed "Web 2.0." And the end users are filling up this second generation of the web with their own ideas, reflections, and recommendations.

The result is exciting and compelling—and as confusing as a season of *Lost*. Seriously! Even the mainstream reporters who cover this stuff get it wrong all the time. What you have in your hands is my attempt to sort it all out and to get the Big Social Media Picture into focus.

The Everything® Guide to Social Media is a hybrid, a combination overview and how-to, covering just about everything in the social media space, from blogs to social networks, photo-swapping to wikis, review-and-opinion sharing to virtual worlds—and even the recent entries into the "location" category and emerging trends in social media marketing. You'll find some history, some current events, and some nuts and bolts.

This book gives readers a 50,000-foot view of social media, examining the origins of the phenomenon, and explaining the concept as it's understood today. It also provides examples of the types of social media services you'll find on the web, and describes in broad terms how they work.

Among the social media explored in this book are: blogs, including micro-blogging services such as Twitter; social networking services, such as Facebook, MySpace, and LinkedIn; photo-sharing services, such as Flickr, Webshots, and Photobucket; video sharing, including a close look at the YouTube phenomenon; social bookmarking, an increasingly popular social media niche; social news, a sub-category of social bookmarking that is also becoming popular; the opinion-sharing phenomenon, exemplified by services such as Yelp and Epinions; wikis, the collaborative websites that allow just about anyone to add content; location sharing, a hot new application of social media; and virtual worlds, which generate a unique type of social media in which "avatars" interact with each other in fully realized virtual environments.

This book also looks at the white-hot social media marketing phenomenon, and the ways in which companies and individuals are using social media to promote their products and services. And it offers a peek at what might be next in the evolution of the social media phenomenon.

The truth is, the topic of every chapter in this guide is worth its own book. But *The Everything® Guide to Social Media* pulls them all together. It gives Web 2.0 newbies a place to start, and it gives the social media savvy a broader navigation tool than they'll find anywhere else.

If you're new to social media, keep this in mind: This stuff isn't just for techies or sophisticated computer users or the tech-savvy digital natives for whom texting is as natural as breathing. If you've ever surfed the web, you've got just about all the basic skills you'll need to participate.

And keep this in mind, too: The social media phenomenon isn't a fad. Hundreds of millions of people now belong to social networks and log on every day. Tweets are flying around at the rate of about 600 per second. And blogging has become a real profession. It's clear that social media are here to stay, and they're affecting our lives in ways we're only just beginning to understand. The good news: they're accessible, interesting, useful, and fun.

Note: The dynamic nature of social media presented a few challenges during the writing of this book. The layouts of the social media websites in particular proved to be lively targets. Many made both big and small changes as this book was coming together. A few new features cropped up, as did rumors of changes yet to come. Most of those changes were incorporated into this book, but some were still underway at press time. Consequently, it made sense to avoid screenshots that might soon be inaccurate, even in the how-to chapters, and to provide generally applicable explanations that wouldn't be affected much by the changes.

CHAPTER 1

The Information Super-highway Becomes a Two-Way Street

The early critics called them all fads—blogging, social networking, twittering. But the growing collection of online services that allow people to create and publish web content and connect with each other in new ways over the Internet, known collectively as social media, is changing the way we consume information and entertainment, market goods and services, and connect with friends, family, and co-workers. It's a radical departure from traditional mass media and is turning a passive audience into a throng of active participants.

What Is Social Media?

"Social media" is one of those high-tech concepts, like "the cloud," that PR departments have jumped on like a pack of hungry dogs, and then slobbered over until its meaning has been blurred by hyperbolic drool. It's definitely a big-time IT-industry buzz phrase, but what does it actually mean?

Social media is an umbrella term that covers a group of web-based software applications, the content generated by users of those applications, and the services that make both accessible to just about anyone with a web browser. These include social networking (Facebook, MySpace, LinkedIn), wikis (web pages for collaboration), blogs (personal online diaries), video- and photo-sharing (YouTube, Flickr, Webshots), social bookmarking (Delicious, Digg), online reviews (Yelp, Epinions), and virtual worlds (*Second Life*, *World of Warcraft*).

User-Generated Content

Social media differ from traditional media (TV, radio, newspapers, etc.) in two radical ways. First, the users generate the content. You write the blog. You make and upload the video. You recommend the restaurant. Second, it's interactive. People don't just read your blog posting, your tweet, or your review; they *comment* on it. That interaction is, in fact, the essence of the form. And it can happen instantly—as the techies say, in real time, no waiting for a letter to the editor to be published in the paper, no languishing on hold until you're connected to the radio talk show host.

FACT

Tech book publisher Tim O'Reilly, a keen observer of bleeding-edge Information Age trends, believes that phenomena like user-generated content are sparking nothing less than a revolution. Speaking to attendees at the annual Web 2.0 Expo in 2008, he declared, "We're at a turning point akin to [the development of] literacy or the formation of cities. This is a huge change in the way the world works."

It would be hard to overstate the significance of these differences. Since Guttenberg invented movable type, most of us have been passive receivers of information. It has been generated by others and fed to us over what are essentially one-way communication systems. But social media are turning us into active participants in the generation and exchange of information. And that's a *huge* change.

You could say that social media has brought us something we've never had before: a media-delivery system that's a two-way street. Wikipedia expresses this idea succinctly: "Social media uses Internet and web-based technologies to transform broadcast media monologues (one to many) into social media dialogues (many to many)."

Perhaps more important, social media appears to be filling two basic human needs that often go unmet in our sprawling and increasingly complex society: to be connected with friends and relatives, and to be *heard*.

Types of Social Media Services

Lots of people have sought to sort the different services and technologies that swarm around the term "social media" into neat categories, but it's a constantly moving target. Not only are the technologies evolving, but the features provided by the various services increasingly overlap. MySpace, for example, provides a well-used blogging feature. Video hoster YouTube supports such social features as Ratings and Comments. And all the top social networking providers allow users to create online photo albums, which is the specialty of Flickr and Webshots.

However, most would probably agree to a handful of broad categories, including:

- **Messaging and communication:** Blogging services, video and photo blogging tools, podcasting, and micro-blogging.
- **Communities and social groups:** Essentially, all of the social, business, and special-interest networking services.
- **Photo and video sharing:** Specialty services that allow you to upload photos and videos to the web, and to manage those images.
- **Social bookmarking and tagging:** Services that allow users to identify online content with keywords, and share the links. You get the descriptions and some opinions, but not the actual content.

- **Collaboration and cooperation:** Websites that allow users to add and update content from their browsers. "Wiki" has become the generic term.
- **Opinion and reviews:** Services such as Yelp and Epinions, which provide user-generated reviews of everything from books to restaurants.
- **Virtual worlds:** Rich environments in which you interact with other users in real time through avatars. *Second Life* is the most famous, but online role playing games, such as *World of Warcraft*, fit this definition, too.

ESSENTIAL

In 2009, Google launched OpenSocial, a set of application programming interfaces (APIs) designed to provide common technical ground for developers of social networking applications. These APIs are what is known as "cross-platform" technology, which means that apps based on them work on just about any social network. By contrast, the Facebook Platform is a framework for apps that interact with core Facebook features.

Who Uses Social Media?

The demographics of social media are evolving quickly, and reacting to forces that are not always well-understood, so rock-solid numbers can be hard to get—especially if you want to know about users outside the United States. But there are some interesting statistics floating around the web.

For example: A non-profit group called the National Institute for Technology in Liberal Education (*www.nitle.org*) uses web crawlers, computer programs that relentlessly browse the web, to find active blogs and identify the languages they use. In a recent Blog Census, the group indexed 2.9 million blogs, nearly 2 million of which were believed to be active. Of the total, more than half were in English, but more than two dozen other languages were also represented, including those you might expect (Spanish, Japanese, French, German, and Chinese), and a few you might not, including Tagalog and even Esperanto!

Some social-media-usage demographics buck established trends. For example: Twitter's initial audience consisted mostly of older people (ages twenty-five to fifty-four), but in 2009 it began attracting a younger crowd. In fact, eighteen- to twenty-four-year-olds represent Twitter's fastest-growing demographic segment. That's unusual in the social media world. And when Facebook membership was approaching the 500-million mark in 2010, the fastest growing segment appeared to be fifty-five- to sixty-five-year-olds.

FACT

In 2007, social media began attracting more visitors than adult websites—an historic first. Since then, porn sites and social networking sites have been neck-and-neck in the unofficial competition for most popular activity on the Internet.

The demographic picture of social media users is still coming into focus, but one thing is already clear: The people who use all this stuff aren't just techies or trendy teens. Using social media services requires very little technical skill. Anyone who can master the basics of operating a computer and surfing the web can participate.

This might be one reason the growth of social networking in particular has been nothing short of astounding. The online competitive intelligence service Experian Hitwise (*www.hitwise.com/us*) found that, by December 2009, visits to social networking services accounted for 13 percent of all U.S. Internet visits, making it the single most popular online activity.

A Brief History of Social Media

Trend watchers claim that modern social media is a unique expression of the second generation of the web, which high-tech book publisher Tim O'Reilly famously dubbed "Web 2.0." The term came into popular use after his publishing company, O'Reilly Media, organized the first Web 2.0 Conference in 2004. Web 1.0 was about displaying web pages; Web 2.0 is about dynamic content, social mobilization, and user collaboration.

But you'll also hear IT old timers declare that social media is nothing new, that it was around in less sophisticated forms before there was a web. (Back when you had to walk miles in the snow to get to a network terminal, and you felt darned lucky just to be online!) The truth lies somewhere in the middle.

The Roots of Social Media

Before there was a web, there were Bulletin Board Systems (BBSs), Internet forums that allowed groups of users to log onto a computer network and interact with each other. They relied on phone lines and snail-slow modems to make the connection, and there were no pretty pictures. But you could upload and download software and data, read announcements, and exchange messages. The analogy here is the community bulletin board you might find in a laundromat or a grocery store.

BBSs emerged in the 1970s, and were originally operated mostly by hobbyists and corporate systems operators, who hosted them on their own machines. They covered a range of topics and interest areas, from politics to dating, music to the earliest incarnations of role-playing games. BBSs also played a role in early hacking activities, such as "phreaking," which involved breaking into phone systems.

With the arrival of the World Wide Web in the 1990s, BBS usage declined, and their role was eventually subsumed by a new model: online service providers. The earliest providers were CompuServe and Prodigy, later followed by America Online (AOL). The online services opened up the network, making it publicly available to a wide range of average-Joe subscribers.

Usenet, another early type of Internet forum, is still in widespread use. Made up of many special-interest "newsgroups," Usenet provides another digital meeting place for discussions of a range of topics, from video games to religion, sports to politics. The model differs from the BBS in that it's a distributed system, which means there is no central server running a newsgroup. Google Groups and Yahoo! Groups are examples of modern services providing access to collections of newsgroups.

The Well

One of the most successful BBSs in history is the Whole Earth 'Lectronic Link, better known as The WELL. This was by most accounts the first "virtual community," a term modern communication media critic and writer Howard Rheingold is credited with coining. The WELL was started by Stewart Brand and Larry Brilliant in 1985, and the name is a reference to Brand's famous counter-culture publication, *The Whole Earth Catalog*.

The WELL, which has been described as "the primordial ooze where the online community movement was born," actually survived the evolution of the technology and the fading of the BBS. In 1999, the publisher of the online magazine Salon.com bought The WELL and maintains it today, with membership available on a subscription basis.

The WELL might be best known as a meeting place for fans of the Grateful Dead; John Perry Barlow, who wrote the lyrics to several of the band's songs, served on the community's board of directors. Reportedly, Barlow met Mitch Kapor on The WELL; the two later founded the nonprofit digital rights advocacy group, the Electronic Frontier Foundation.

Early Social Networks

Founded in 1995 by Boeing engineer Randy Conrads, Classmates.com was one of the earliest services that might be considered a social network by modern standards. The service aims to help its members connect with long-lost friends from school, work, and even the U.S. military.

Like other social networking services, Classmates.com allows you to build a profile, see other profiles, and post to a public message board for free, but full access to all its capabilities requires users to pay a subscription fee. Direct messaging, event planning, and other features require the subscription. It's this subscription fee, at least in part, that has caused critics to argue that Classmates.com isn't a true social networking service, and that it has more in common with an online dating service. On the other hand, it gives the service a clear business model, which is not something you can say for all social networks. It's also worth noting that it's the oldest service of this type in continuous operation.

FACT

Classmates.com was sued in 2008 by Anthony Michaels for false advertising. According to *Wired* magazine's Ryan Singel, Michaels alleges that the service sent him an e-mail claiming friends from high school were looking for him, but when he purchased a Gold Membership and logged on, he found no one he knew. Critics of the service have asserted that this is a common practice.

The service has also been criticized for its marketing practice of sending e-mails to potential members, which may distinguish it from other social networks, but hardly disqualifies it from the category. Classmates.com claims a current active membership of around 40 million, which earns it a spot among the top social media providers.

Some social media mavens point to Classmates.com as the first social network, but others feel that SixDegrees.com better fits the current definition. This service was launched two years later than Classmates.com, and shut down in 2001. Its format was very similar to what we see on today's social networking sites, and the features offered are now considered core capabilities, including the ability to make lists of friends and family members, send direct messages, and post to other users' message boards. Founded by Andrew Weinreich, the free service was named for the idea, popularized by the game "Six Degrees of Kevin Bacon," which was based on the idea that no more than six people separate us from everybody else. Current social networking services use the social-circles network model pioneered by this service. In its heyday, SixDegrees.com reportedly had about a million registered members.

ALERT

SixDegrees.com, the now deceased social networking service, should not be confused with SixDegrees.org, which is a charitable group founded by actor Kevin Bacon. SixDegrees.org (*http://sixdegrees.org*) is a web-based network of celebrities, who promote their favorite charities and provide an online connection to promote giving.

LiveJournal was another early example of a social network. It came online in 1999 and became the first blog-based virtual community. Founded by computer programmer Brad Fitzpatrick, it was organized as a self-contained community (like The WELL). The free service was bought by Russian media company SUP in 2007, and is now the most popular social networking service in that country, with nearly 3 million Russian-speaking subscribers.

Russian president Dmitry Medvedev posted his first blog on the LiveJournal .com website in 2009. In the live video blog posting, he talked about the how "the Internet has grown into a fully fledged self-regulating system, and one that strongly influences all aspects of our life." The LiveJournal blog is an extension of his blog on Kremlin.ru.

The Modern Lineup

What we think of as modern Web 2.0-type social media services began emerging in the early 2000s. Friendster, which was founded in 2002, is today one of the most popular social networking services in Asia. The Hi5 social network appeared in 2003, and now claims more than 60 million active members, mostly in Latin America. LinkedIn became the first business-oriented social networking service that same year. MySpace joined the party that year, too. Facebook, the leading social network, existed at Harvard in 2004, but wasn't available to the public until 2006.

A number of media-sharing sites also came online during this same time period. Photobucket, widely considered the first big photo-sharing service, was founded in 2003. Flickr, the most popular online photo-sharing service, was launched a year later; today, the company claims to host more than 4 billion images. And the first video-hosting website, YouTube, began its reign as the top site for posting videos in 2005. What started out as a destination for little more than your funniest home videos now has the horsepower (thanks to its acquisition by Google) to host high-definition videos, TV shows, and serious political content.

ESSENTIAL

It has been argued that massively multiplayer online games (MMOGs) are, in effect, a type of social network, because they provide what are called "persistent worlds." Games like *World of Warcraft* provide virtual environments in which the events of the games take place, but also offer social networking tools, such as forums and chat rooms.

Around the same time, a new information-sharing model emerged with the launch of an awkwardly named service called Del.icio.us (these days, simplified as "Delicious.") Founded in 2003, Delicious added what is known as *social bookmarking* to the social media mix. The service allows users to bookmark virtually any content they find on the Internet, tag that link with a searchable keyword, and save or share it. Another bookmarking service, Digg, founded a year later, added a feature that allows users to cast a vote for or against specific pieces of online content, such as news stories. Reddit added its take on social news in 2005.

In 2006, the world's first microblogging service, Twitter, launched a social media tsunami that flooded the world with real-time updates, 140 characters at a time. According to the company, Twitter was publishing its users' short text messages at the rate of 5,000 a day in 2007; by 2008, that number had grown to 300,000; by 2009, Twitter users were sending 2.5 million tweets every day.

Social Media Goes Mainstream

By 2005, the world was beginning to take social media seriously. The December 12 issue of *BusinessWeek* told corporations and enterprises about the potential marketing value of the emerging "MySpace Generation" of college students and teens.

But if there was a tipping point at which the techie and teeny-bopper image of social media shifted, it probably came in the summer of 2009. On June 16 of that year, the U.S. State Department asked Twitter to delay its announced plans to take the micro-blogging site offline for an hour of routine maintenance. Why? So that the citizens of Iran would be able to communicate following a highly contested presidential election. The Iranian government had banned other media, and the stream of Twitter postings known as "tweets" had become a critical source of real-time news and images of the violence that erupted following the election.

Celebrities and Social Media

A potent force in the evolution of social media from techie toy to mainstream info channel was celebrity adoption. When actor Ashton Kutcher became the first Twitter user to attract a million followers in 2009, even CNN took notice—largely because Kutcher had challenged the news organization to beat him to the million-follower mark with its own Twitter breaking-news feed. The mainstream media was all over this friendly duel, and it sparked a lively conversation about the social media phenomenon.

Twitter co-founder Biz Stone called the Kutcher-CNN rivalry "another big moment for us." And people in social media circles began talking about "the Kutcher effect" (a play on words inspired by his movie, *The Butterfly Effect*).

Just as Ashton Kutcher was claiming his millionth Twitter follower, Oprah Winfrey was sending her first tweet. She sent it from the set of her TV show. It read, "HI TWITTERS. THANK YOU FOR A WARM WELCOME. FEELING REALLY 21st CENTURY." Not the most tech-savvy message, but a social media milestone nonetheless. Oprah had actually attracted more than 73,000 followers to her Twitter account before she sent that first tweet.

In 2010, the twittersteam—that ever-rushing river of tweets—practically boiled with a much-publicized rant by movie director Kevin Smith against Southwest Airlines. It seems the carrier had thrown him off a stand-by flight because of his size—after he'd already buckled in. "Dear @SouthwestAir," Smith wrote, "I know I'm fat, but was Captain Leysath really justified in throwing me off a flight for which I was already seated?" Smith's tweets generated a gush of reactions—pro and con—and gave late night talk show hosts several days of material. Few instances of user-generated web content have, to date, gotten as much mainstream publicity.

Today, it's hard to imagine a celebrity who cares about his or her career not maintaining some kind of social media presence. Actors, musicians, and performers of all kinds maintain fan pages on Facebook and MySpace, and some twitter like maniacs. Actor Vin Diesel, singer Britney Spears, Olympic gold-medal winner Michael Phelps, musical performer Lady Gaga, actress Megan Fox, and yes, Ashton Kutcher, all maintain a robust Facebook presence.

So omnipresent are celebs on social networking sites today that most include "Celebrities" on their lists of page-type browsing categories. So-called fan pages reportedly attract millions of new users to social networking.

Social Media on the Move

By and large, social media users log onto the web from their desktop or laptop computers. But it's worth noting that a growing number do it from their cell phones. A recent survey by the digital marketing intelligence experts at comScore (*www.comscore.com*) found that the number of people accessing Twitter from mobile platforms in January 2010 was up

347 percent from the previous year. That's 4.7 million people twittering with their thumbs! Mobile Facebook users numbered more than 25 million in the survey, which is an increase of 112 percent from the previous year.

These numbers actually say more about how people use computers than social media. They reflect a much larger trend: cell phones are rapidly becoming the dominant computing platform.

Mark Donovan, senior vice president of comScore's mobile group, summarized the phenomenon in a press release: "Social networking remains one of the most popular and fastest-growing behaviors on both the PC-based Internet and the mobile web," he said. "Social media is a natural sweet spot for mobile since mobile devices are at the center of how people communicate with their circle of friends, whether by phone, text, e-mail, or, increasingly, accessing social networking sites via a mobile browser."

ALERT

In 2010 a Dutch website called Please Rob Me began to use Twitter posts and a GPS-based gaming site called Foursquare to figure out who wasn't home, and then publish the names and addresses of those people. The site's developer, Boy Van Amstel, said he did it to raise awareness of "the danger of publicly telling people where you are."

Social Media and Politics

Websites are nothing new in political circles, but Barack Obama's use of social media in the 2008 presidential campaign changed politics in America forever. Mr. Obama used social networking platforms such as Facebook and Twitter, and media services such as YouTube, so effectively to build support and raise money for his campaign that it's already become standard practice.

He or his campaign signed up for all the major social media brands in 2007, including MySpace, Facebook, YouTube, Twitter, Flickr, Digg, LinkedIn, and even the virtual world of *Second Life*. Social networking, it has been said, became the organizing principal of his campaign effort.

What sometimes goes unsaid about why social media worked for the Obama campaign is that although they used it very effectively to connect with and nurture relationships with supporters in cyberspace, it also got those supporters to do things to help the campaign in the real world.

President Obama was the first politician to fully exploit the potential of social media, both for his campaign, and to reach out to the people he governs, but he won't be the last. The thing to keep in mind here is that social media are making it possible for more people than ever before to gain access to, and interact with, their leaders.

FACT

As of this writing, Barack Obama's Facebook page boasts 7.8 million fans; he has nearly 200,000 pages of friends on MySpace. And 3.4 million people are following him on Twitter. The White House Facebook page counts 500,000 fans; its Twitter account is followed by 1.7 million.

Need more evidence that the most powerful government in the world is taking social media seriously? Here's one: The White House now has a Director of New Media. Macon Phillips is responsible for developing and managing the administration's "online agenda." That includes the White House's website, WhiteHouse.gov.

Business Learns to Deal with Social Media

The enterprise is definitely paying attention to social media. The prospect of tapping into online communities made up of millions of potential customers has become downright mouthwatering to companies of every stripe. "Social media marketing" has entered the business lexicon now, and a lot of companies are taking it very seriously. Social media "branding" has emerged as another popular buzzword.

But social media also provide businesses and professionals with a new way to maintain their relationships with existing customers and clients. And because they're providing a two-way street, social media can give companies something that's almost better than new customers: feedback from existing customers. People who wouldn't complain to your face feel freer to express their disappointments online. This capability alone makes the new information channel potentially invaluable to a wide range of companies.

The downside of social media for the enterprise is that it spreads bad news, fast. This isn't a bad thing for consumers if the news is true, but because reliable gatekeepers don't usually vet the negative reviews and information that sometimes gets circulated via social media, it's not necessarily good, either. Virtually any crackpot with a bone to pick can bad-mouth your restaurant, beauty salon, or dentist's office online. As long as it's not libelous, everybody's opinion is welcome. For this reason, if for no other, companies can no longer ignore social media.

The growing impact on businesses of the review-sharing sites hasn't made everyone happy. In 2010, Yelp, which features consumer-driven reviews of restaurants, retailers, and products, was hit with a lawsuit claiming that its reviews are bogus. According to the *Wall Street Journal*, the suit alleged that Yelp employees offered to remove negative reviews of a store in San Mateo, California, if the owner bought some advertising. Yelp issued a statement to online technology news and reviews site *TechCrunch*, saying, in part, that the claims were "demonstrably false, since many businesses that advertise on Yelp have both negative and positive reviews," which the businesses realize "provide authenticity and value."

Social media also presents a unique opportunity for professional networking. And not just on business-focused networking services such as LinkedIn. Facebook has, for some people, become a critical business networking platform. And some companies are even using social media for internal networking.

CHAPTER 2

Blogs: The Voice of the People

They started as obscure, personal online diaries, but grew to become genuine mainstream media competitors. "Blogs" and "blogging" are now as much a part of our lexicon as "online" and "e-mail," and this unique form of social media represents an increasingly important information source for an ever more web-centric world. The proliferation of blogging services and simple-to-use blogging tools has made it easier than ever for anyone to join the blogosphere. But there are some tricks to this trade. Here's what you need to know to get the most from your blogging experience.

What's a Blog?

Short for "weblog," a blog is a type of shared online journal. It's written by an individual, published on a web page, and usually available to anyone with access to a web browser. It contains the blogger's thoughts, observations, recommendations, reflections, opinions, and feelings on whatever he or she wants to write about. And the entries are displayed in reverse chronological order, with the most recent posting at the top.

The credit for coining the term "blog" usually goes to Peter Merholz, president and co-founder of Adaptive Path. According to the oft-reported story, in 1999 he shortened the term "weblog," which had been coined by Jorn Barger, editor of early blog site Robot Wisdom, in 1997. Evan Williams, co-founder of Pyra Labs (which started Blogger) gets the credit for first using "blog" as a verb.

Blogs can include photos, audio clips, and video, and they frequently contain links to other blogs or websites. Blogs can be publicly viewable, or tucked safely behind a company firewall. Both public-facing and "internal" company or organizational blogs are often focused on particular topics or issues.

True blogs as we define them today include a feature that makes them unique in the annals of information distribution: a place for potentially instantaneous, generally uncensored reader feedback. Seconds after a blog post hits the web, legions of readers could be posting their reactions to it, good and bad. Consequently, what begins as a journal-like entry can blossom rather quickly into a rich, global conversation.

ESSENTIAL

One of the most exciting—make that headline-grabbing—developments in the blogging world in recent years is the appearance of the microblog. The service that put microblogging on the map, of course, is Twitter, whose 140-word missives are flooding the blogosphere. But Twitter isn't the only microblogging service. Tumblr, Plurk, Squeelr, Beeing, Jaiku, and Indenti.ca are other examples.

Nowhere in the world of social media is the info highway's new two-way street carrying more traffic than the blogosphere. Tens of millions of people, from average joes to professional journalists and marketing gurus, are blogging every day. Together, they have generated the vast information network known as the *blogosphere*. The blogosphere is the entire world's blogs taken as a whole, along with reader comments and any links or connections. It's the totality of all blogs, including traditional blogs, video blogs, and microblogs (so Twitter is included). Here are some additional blogging terms worth knowing:

- **Blog search engines:** Used to surf the blogosphere. Technorati is one of the most popular. Google and Yahoo! also provide blog search engines.
- **Blogroll:** A list of links to other blogs, typically shown in a sidebar on a blog index page.
- **Permalink:** A link that points to a specific blog posting. The link is permanent because it remains intact even after the posting has slipped off the front page and into the blog archive.
- **TrackBack:** A system that notifies you that another blogger has mentioned your blog posting in his or her blog.
- **Ping:** A notification to another blogger that you have linked to, or commented on, something in that person's blog. ("Ping" is an acronym for Packet Internet Grouper.)
- **Linklog:** A blog that is mainly a collection of hyperlinks to other websites.

Personal Blogs

Personal blogs most closely resemble the original online diaries or journals that evolved into the modern blog. They're created and maintained by average people with something to say. These bloggers might hold forth on the issues of the day, offer tips for hobbyists, publish their poetry, recommend books, chronicle their vacations, gossip about celebrities, advocate for causes, or just share the memorable events of their lives.

Some blogs offer windows into the personal lives of the bloggers, sometimes in excruciating detail; others are more like newspaper or magazine columns filled with insightful, focused comments on a topic or the issues of the day; and some are strictly about business, taking the form of intra-company blogs, public-facing executive blogs, or "expert" blogs maintained by individuals promoting their personal brands.

Relatively few personal blogs ever build a large enough audience to have much influence, but that doesn't necessarily diminish their power as a medium of personal expression and reflection. Fame and fortune aren't always the goal. Still, some do rise above the crowd to reach a worldwide audience. For example, San Francisco writer and editor Maggie Mason's engaging blog, Mighty Girl (*www.mightygirl.net*), which chronicled the trials and tribulations of her more-or-less normal life, won a huge following. So popular was Mason's blog—especially her non-sponsored recommendations of products she personally liked—that it got the attention of the likes of Oprah Winfrey, and spawned a shopping blog called Mighty Goods. Both *Forbes* and *BusinessWeek* recognized that blog as a top shopping site.

Corporate Blogs

Corporate blogs have spread across the blogosphere like a plague of locusts in recent years, and the results have been a mixed bag. On the one hand, a blog provides a company with what amounts to a news channel that bypasses the traditional-media gatekeepers. On the other, a corporate blog gives consumers a direct line to a company spokesperson, whether it's really the CEO or someone from the marketing department.

And not all corporate blogs are useless PR generators. One of the most critically successful corporate blogs is The Official Google Blog (*http://googleblog.blogspot.com*), which *Time* magazine has described as "a self-serving site dedicated to advancing the viewpoints of a multi-billion dollar company," quickly adding, "And guess what? It's great." The blog works, *Time* opined in 2009, because so many people use Google's search engine (so many that "google" has become a verb), and the site offers genuinely useful tips on how to make the most of it.

Political Blogs

Political blogs also abound these days, ranging across the breadth of the political spectrum. Both individuals and organizations maintain these online soapboxes, which typically advocate for a distinct position or cause. News tends to drive political blogs, with events igniting posts that bristle with hyperlinks to the traditional media articles and video clips that inspired them. And there's always lots of reader feedback. Political blogs shouldn't be confused with the blogs that now appear on mainstream news sites, or such online-only publications as Politico.com and Daily Kos, which are written by reporters and professional commentators.

Actually, you could argue that those blogs constitute a fourth category: blogs written by traditional media pros and next-generation online reporters. Online news publications, such as *The Huffington Post*, *Talking Points Memo*, and *The Daily Beast*, general interest sites, such as LifeHacker, and tech news sites, such as CNet, publish blogs that are often more like traditional newspaper and magazine columns.

FACT

During the 2004 presidential campaign, the Democratic and Republican parties issued press credentials to bloggers covering their respective conventions. A year later, Garrett M. Graff, who was blogging at the time for the website FishbowlDC, became the first blogger to receive a daily White House press pass.

And then there are the fake blogs, marketing screeds masquerading as real blogs written by individuals, but actually penned by PR pros to advance the interests of an organization or company. These marketing vehicles aren't necessarily evil, they're just not the real thing.

Few technology trends have shaken up the world of journalism quite as profoundly as blogging. It has been, in the true sense of the term, disruptive technology, something akin to what digital photography did to film and the copy machine did to printing. The ability of individuals of modest means to publish online has started a wave of citizen journalism. Non-professionals are using their blogs to point out factual errors and bias in traditional media reporting, to publish their own views of events and issues, and even to break a few stories.

Starting Your Own Blog

The past decade has seen incredible growth in the blogosphere. Tens of millions of mostly non-techie, non-professional bloggers now keep the Internet buzzing, thanks in no small part to the emergence of easy-to-use blog-building tools and affordable blog-hosting services that handle all the heavy lifting. It's safe to say that it has never been easier to start your own blog. But where do you start?

For most neophyte bloggers, the answer to that question is with a blog-hosting service. Even if you're a web-savvy dude, the sheer convenience of a service that maintains a website designed especially to host multiple bloggers makes it the logical place to start. Once you've dipped your toe into the blogosphere and played around with some of the popular, user-friendly tools and features, then you might decide you want something more sophisticated, and crank up your own blog site using some of the more powerful blog-publishing software.

Blog-Hosting Services

Blog-hosting services provide a range of features and capabilities. You won't necessarily need all of them, but here are a few you should look for:

- **Comments controls:** A big part of blogging is user feedback. You'll want a system that gives you control over the way your readers can respond to your blog, and how you can respond to them.
- **Access management:** Although blogs are generally open to the public at large, you might prefer to restrict your blog to a smaller audience. Access management capabilities allow you to keep your blog in the family, or share it with the world.
- **Design templates:** Your blog page won't need the visual impact of a full-on web page, but it still needs to look good, and the elements need to be well organized. Look for a gallery of pre-defined page layouts. Look, too, for catalogs of widgets, which are small graphical elements that jazz up your page with added functionality and links.
- **Photo posting features:** Photos are common blog elements nowadays, and even if you don't think you'll be posting any, you might want to make sure you have the option. Also, consider support for audio and video clips.
- **Stats tracker:** Speaking of stats, at some point, you're going to want to know how many people are reading your blog. Some hosting services provides tools for measuring things like pageviews per post, referrals, and the like inside the app tracking the traffic you generate.
- **Support for your favorite blogging tools:** If you love WordPress, be sure you sign up with a hosting service that supports it. In general, look for

services that seem to be aware that there's a world of third-party tools out there.

- **Mobile posting capabilities:** It's amazing how much we do nowadays from our cell phones. We e-mail, shop, surf the web—and, yes, blog. A mobile posting capability is essential for active bloggers who really want to keep their blogs up to date.
- **Mobile publishing capabilities:** You're not the only one using your iPhone more than your desktop computer, so it might improve your readership stats if you sign up with a hosting service that publishes to mobile platforms.
- **Blogging from social networking sites:** This feature lets you post to your blog from, say, Facebook or MySpace.
- **Spam protection:** Yup, it's even a problem on blog sites. Look for a service that deals with spam, and while you're at it, check out its overall security posture.
- **Ad revenue sharing:** Some blog hosting services post advertising on their site, and if your blog is driving traffic to the site, you might be able to get a cut of the revenue.
- **Free versus fee:** Many blog-hosting services are free, which is great, but services that charge a small monthly fee shouldn't be struck from your list out of hand. Consider what's provided; it might be worth it.

Also, look for a blog-hosting service that is search engine optimized (SEO). This means that it has employed techniques to improve your ranking on the popular search engines, which improves your chances of being found by web surfers. SEO is not achieved with so-called search engine marketing (paid ranking upgrades), but rather with technology and web know-how.

The number of services that host multiple blogs on the web is growing. Here are a few of the better known services and what they provide:

- **Blogger:** a free hosting service maintained by search engine giant, Google. Launched in 1999, it's one of the best-known blog-hosting services. Its feature list includes: a simple user interface, customizable templates, photo and video support, comment controls, reader notification, mobile support, group blogging, and a search feature, among others. (*www.blogger.com*)

- **WordPress.com:** from the maker of the world's most popular blog publishing platform, this service is also free, with premium features available for a fee. Its feature list includes design templates, a widget gallery, three gigabytes of file storage, support for photos, and stat-tracking tools, among others. It's currently hosting more than 300,000 bloggers. (*www.wordpress.com*)
- **LiveJournal:** the service offers free blog hosting, but with an emphasis on the personal journal aspect of blogging. Provides design templates, privacy controls, integration with YouTube, Photobucket, and Slide. Launched the same year as Blogger. Fee-based upgrades are available. (*www.livejournal.com*)
- **Typepad:** a fee-based, blog-hosting service, it provides customizable design templates, mobile support, a widget catalog, podcasting support, spam control, revenue opportunities, and traffic tracker, among others. Offers a fourteen-day free trial. (*www.typepad.com*)
- **Xanga:** more of a community/journaling model, but a very user-friendly blogging service. Offers free and fee-based premium services. Provides templates, comments, photo manager, videoblogs, tracking, and other features. (*www.xanga.com*)
- **Vox:** a free, personal blog-hosting service with a neighborhood feel. Provides a built-in blog editor, privacy controls, e-mail, and support for photos and videos. (*www.vox.com*)

Blogging Tools

Another trend that has driven the rapid growth of blogging over the past decade is the advent of a new generation of blogging tools, with which you can build and manage your own blog. Why would you want to host your own blog? If you want a blog to promote you or your company's brand identity, hosting your own blog gives you your own web address (URL). Also, you're free of the hosting site's design templates.

Self-hosting isn't for everybody, but if you've got the technical know-how to go it alone, you'll have plenty of tools to do it right. And many of the most popular blog-development tools are open source, which usually means free, but more importantly, they're maintained by a committed developer community. WordPress is an example of an open-source project, and it's widely considered the most popular blogging software.

FACT

The proliferation of blogging has been helped by a data format known as a "news feed" or "web feed," which is used to channel frequently updated web content to users via e-mail or through newsfeed readers. RSS (Really Simple Syndication) is one of the best known and most widely used news feed format; Atom is another.

Here are just a few examples from the growing selection of blog-development tools you'll want to check out:

- **WordPress:** This is one of the blogging world's most popular publishing platforms. Free and available on WordPress.org (not to be confused with WordPress.com, see above), it's open-source software powered by the popular dynamic scripting language, PHP, and the open source MySQL database management system. Features include: workflow, a plug-in architecture, and a templating system.
- **Movable Type:** This is another free, open-source blog-publishing system. Provides customizable templates, tagging features, access management, TrackBack, and supports multiple blogs. Comes with a dashboard, a WYSIWYG editor, and features for managing photos, audio, and video. (The developers of this system, Six Apart, also created the TrackBack feature.)
- **ExpressionEngine:** Billed as a content-management system, not strictly a blog-development tool. But it's worth mentioning as another flavor of tooling you might want to consider. This is a powerful web-publishing solution that bundles plenty of features into its weblog module, including custom data fields, multiple nested categories, sticky topics, workflow, publish and expiration dates, and other features. The system supports an unlimited number of blogs, RSS and Atom syndication, a template library, mobile blogging support, and more.
- **Google Analytics:** One of the top web-traffic tracking tools, and it's free. Provides reports in detail about the visitors to your blog.

Risks of Blogging

Before you plunge into the blogosphere, consider the risk involved. It's not an especially dangerous place, and this isn't meant to discourage participation, but keep in mind that it's not immune from defamation and liability laws.

According to the Electronic Frontier Foundation (*www.eff.org*), the leading civil liberties group focused on digital rights, the two issues that should concern you most as a private blogger are: 1) publishing statements "that could be false or cause harm to someone's reputation," and 2) violation of intellectual property laws by improperly linking to information, quoting from articles and other blogs, and/or using someone else's creative works.

Before you begin your blogging adventure, jump on the EFF site and check out "Bloggers' FAQ on Online Defamation Law" (*www.eff.org/issues/bloggers/legal/liability/defamation*), and "The Bloggers' FAQ on Intellectual Property" (*www.eff.org/issues/bloggers/legal/liability/IP*).

For corporations, employee blogging activity poses a new kind of enterprise security threat that should be considered when developing policies. The source of the risk: disgruntled or malicious employees, and simple carelessness. Your employees don't necessarily have to have bad intentions to do some damage to your company's brand and reputation.

In a corporate environment, blogging presents an opportunity for deliberate or accidental breaches of confidentiality that can be just as damaging as corporate espionage. Bloggers can also become unwitting accomplices to spyware distributors and hackers.

But you don't have to ban the blog. The solution is to establish a clear, well-communicated set of acceptable blog-use policies as part of the company's overall security posture. Employers should establish best blogging practices, including a blogging code of ethics. With these kinds of policies in place, such high-profile, blogging-related firings as the dismissal in 2004 of a Delta Airlines flight attendant for posting "inappropriate pictures in uniform," or the Googler bounced for blogged comments about life at work, can be avoided.

Blogging to Promote Your Business

Blogs have been compared to e-mail in terms of their potential impact on commercial enterprises. Before you scoff, consider instant messaging (IM), which started out as irrelevant teeny-bopper tech and evolved into an essential business tool. Ask a hard-working exec or a busy professional which she'd rather give up, her phone or her ability to text, and the answer might surprise you. The reason these technologies found their way into the enterprise is simple: they provided non-technical users with uniquely accessible tools for fast and easy information publication, interpersonal communication, and collaboration.

If you want to build a big audience, getting noticed by the blog search engines is essential. Technorati is one of the most famous of these. Making it to the Technorati 100 List is not only prestigious, but a real measure of success, because Technorati counts the number of unique blogs linking to your blog over a specified period.

The Company Blog

Company blogs are all but an enterprise commonplace today. Because they're inexpensive to set up and maintain, companies of virtually all sizes have them. These days a company website looks naked without at least one executive blog. High-tech executives at companies such as Microsoft, Apple, and Oracle have been blogging for years, but so have top execs from other industries. Mark Cuban, owner of the Dallas Mavericks basketball team, blogs several times a week on a site called Blog Maverick (*http://blogmaverick .com*). Wholefoods CEO John Mackey isn't as prolific a blogger as Cuban, but he posts every couple of months on his company's website (*www2.whole foodsmarket.com/blogs/jmackey*). Caroline Shaw, CEO of The Christie, one of Europe's leading cancer centers, blogs regularly to get the word out about the work of her company (*www.christie.nhs.uk/blogs/cs*).

The Benefits of a Company Blog

In marketing circles, a company's blog is as important today as the company's website on which it appears. The practice of issuing press releases, though it hasn't gone away, is beginning to look dated. Blogs are immediate, dynamic, and much easier to update than the content on the website itself. Perhaps most important, a blog is uniquely designed to generate reader responses and comments. The result is a kind of conversation that can provide a company with invaluable information about how the public sees its products and services.

The most obvious benefit derived from a company blog is its ability to communicate the organization's position or message to the public. Through blogs, companies can also share expertise and experience in a way that positions the organization as an authority and a resource, and ultimately promotes the brand. Microsoft, for example, uses its blogs to provide tips and technical information to its customers, to answer customer questions, and to host conversations among product users.

Internal company blogs can serve as useful communication tools that link members of distributed project teams—especially when the team members are in different time zones. They can save time by substituting for face-to-face meetings among employees with crowded schedules. And they can create a sense of community within a company.

The Voice of the Company

The most popular blogs are conversational, personal, newsy, and friendly. Individuals blog about the things they're passionate about. A company blog should have the same feel. No one visits a blog that sounds like a press release or an annual report. And direct sales pitches are simply off-putting to blog readers.

Some companies encourage their employees to blog because of the buzz that a wide-ranging conversation can generate for the company. More bloggers mean more hits, which means more people are talking about the company. Many consultants even warn against establishing a corporate blog culture in which only executives post.

However, company blogs must exist within boundaries established by management that aren't necessary for the free-range blogger. You don't want a company blog to become a spigot from which your organization's proprietary information gushes into the wide world. Neither do you want your employees posting embarrassing photos or making untoward comments. Without a clearly defined corporate blogging policy, this very useful tool can become a source of trouble.

CHAPTER 3

Twitter: The Microblog with the Macro Impact

On March 5, 2010, the microblogging service known as Twitter (*www.twitter.com*) published its 10 billionth tweet. The company claimed that the short text messages were now flowing at the rate of about 600 per second. Not bad for a service not far from its fourth birthday. Today, people use Twitter for everything from publishing personal musings to pushing products, tracking trends to circumventing the censorship of repressive governments. The Twitter stream is flowing fast these days; if you're ready to jump in, here's what you need to know to enjoy the swim.

What Is Twitter?

Twitter is a web-based messaging service that allows its users to share short text updates about the moments of their lives. The company describes itself as "a service for friends, family, and co-workers to communicate and stay connected through the exchange of quick, frequent answers to one simple question: What are you doing?"

Twitter is a microblog. Microblogging, as the name suggests, is like blogging, only the messages are shorter. In Twitter's case, a lot shorter. Twitter messages, which are called tweets, are limited in 140 characters. Like a blog, Twitter is a one-to-many information distribution system: one person posts a message that lots of people read.

It's useful to keep in mind that Twitter is not a social network, like Facebook or MySpace, but an *information* network. This is an important distinction, because Twitter isn't really about building communities, but about sharing news, knowledge, opinions, and ideas (and what you had for breakfast). It's really not so much a place to hang out as *listen in*.

QUESTION

Is the act of posting on Twitter called twittering or tweeting?
Looks like it's both. Initially "twitter" was the verb and "tweet" was the noun. Twitter co-founder Biz Stone said during a 2009 appearance on The View that he preferred that form. But the public has since come down on the side of "tweet" as a verb. Cable news reporters, characters on TV shows, and a growing number of the tech-savvy are now tweeting.

Twitter's Origins

Twitter reportedly evolved from a 2006 employee brainstorming session at a San Francisco podcasting company called Odeo Inc. That company was founded by Evan Williams and Noah Glass. At the time, Williams was best-known as the co-founder of Pyra Labs, a company he started with Meg Hourihan in 1999, and for creating the enormously popular Blogger web-publishing tool, now owned by Google.

Odeo engineer Jack Dorsey usually gets the credit for coming up with the idea for Twitter. Software developer Dom Sagolla, who was on Dorsey's brainstorming team on that fateful day, recalls on his website *140 Characters*: "His idea was to make it so simple that you don't even think about what you're doing, you just type something and send it." Dorsey and Odeo employees Biz Stone and Florian Weber built the first version, Sagolla says. The first version was used only by Odeo's employees to send status updates to each other.

Later that year, Dorsey, Williams, Stone, and other Odeo employees formed a new company, called Obvious Corporation, which acquired Odeo's assets, including Twitter. Obvious spun Twitter into its own company in 2007. Dorsey was the first chief exec; Williams is the current CEO.

Twitter's Coming out Party

Many people point to the 2007 South by Southwest Interactive (SXSWi) tech conference in Austin (not the famous music and film festivals) as the moment Twitter exploded onto the scene. Williams and company used the event as a platform for the official launch of the service, and it was a splashy debut. Sixty-inch plasma screens mounted in conference center hallways carried a constant stream of tweets, which surged during the event from 20,000 per day to 60,000.

QUESTION

Why 140 characters?
The notorious 140-character limit on Twitter messages was imposed at first simply because the microblogger was originally designed to run on cell phones, which rely on the Short Message Service (SMS) text-messaging standard. Cell phone companies typically limited the length of SMS messages to around 160 characters. Limiting tweets to 140 characters leaves room for the user name.

Twitter's marketing maneuver worked, and even earned the company the SXSWi Web award in the Blog category for that year. A Twitter crew was on hand at the show, including Williams, Stone, Dorsey, and others, and they accepted the award with a tweet that read: "We'd like to thank you in 140 characters or less. And we just did!" Twitter's messages may be short, but the service has become a towering citizen of the blogosphere.

How Twitter Works

Twitter is a free service. All you need to sign up is an e-mail address. To send and receive messages, all you need is a computer with a web browser and an Internet connection, or a mobile phone.

The messages you post on Twitter—your tweets—go into the great twitter stream, where they can be found by other twitterers through a search engine, hash tags, or a trend tracker (more on these later). Tweets are even showing up in Google searches these days, thanks to the search engine giant's decision to add so-called real-time search to its capabilities.

But Twitter users access most of the content in the twitter stream by following people. When you add someone to your follow list, you chose to have the system post that person's tweets automatically on your home page. Those tweets arrive virtually as soon they're posted, in more or less real time, and they're displayed in reverse chronological order, just as in a standard blog.

People who follow you receive your tweets in the same way, but following someone doesn't guarantee that they'll follow you. This is another way in which Twitter differs from social networks like Facebook and MySpace, where interactions among members are more reciprocal. In fact, you can add and remove people from your follow list at will, without generating e-mail notifications and hard feelings. And you can block people from following you with a mouse click.

How People Use Twitter

Even though it's a microblog, Twitter's content isn't necessarily small stuff. It's true that lots of people twitter about the mundane details of their lives—what they ate for breakfast, what they're watching on television, and worse—but Twitter isn't just for people with way too much time on their hands.

Local Information Channel

Neighbors have used Twitter to circulate information in times of crisis. For example: The service emerged as a real-time news channel for San Diego residents during the 2007 wildfires disaster. The local news was overwhelmed, but a local twitterer, Nate Ritter, kept the information flowing. His updates kept the locals informed about evacuations, meeting spots, where to pick up supplies, and help for pets. Ritter is credited with popularizing the hashtag, a

Twitter convention for grouping tweets. He used *#sandiegofire* to identify his updates about the disaster.

During a 2008 gas shortage in Atlanta, Twitter became a resource for people looking for fuel. Tessa Horehled created the hashtag *#atlgas* that allowed people to track updates on where gas was available in the city. "While driving around in search of gas," she wrote at the time, "I would insert the #atlgas hashtag in my tweets with the station name, street inter-section, and what grade gas they had available, if any."

FACT

Twitter is a trend buster in at least one respect: most of its initial users were not web-savvy young people. According to comScore, people between ages twenty-five and fifty-four made up 65 percent of all tweeters in December 2008, with eighteen- to twenty-five-year-olds making up just 9 percent. Now that their elders have paved the way, the younguns are following in droves.

Eye-Witness Accounts

In 2008, Twitter was used to break the news of terrorist attacks in Mumbai, India. Just moments after the first shots were fired, the twitter stream was flowing with reports from Twitter users in India, who provided instant eyewitness accounts of events as they unfolded. And as was mentioned earlier, Twitter played a key role in the 2009 Iranian elections. It became virtually the only local source of real-time news and images of the violence that erupted following the election.

When a US Airways flight executed an emergency landing in the Hudson River in 2009, the first pictures of the downed plane and its lucky passengers were seen on Twitter; a member of the team aboard the rescue ferry upload-ing the photos from his iPhone to TwitPic. The twitterer, Janis Krums, was interviewed on MSNBC 30 minutes after his tweets hit the blogosphere.

Sending Up a Red Flag

Twitter may have helped to get an American photojournalist out of an Egyptian jail. In 2008, James Karl Buck, a graduate student from the University of California at Berkeley, was in Mahalla, Egypt, covering an anti-government protest over rising food prices and decreasing wages when he and his translator were arrested. As the story goes, on the way to jail, Buck pulled out his Blackberry and sent a one-word tweet: "Arrested." His followers picked up the message and spread the word that Buck was in trouble. A lawyer was hired on his behalf, and Buck was released in less than twenty-four hours. As he left the police station, he sent another one-word tweet: "Free."

Drumming up Disaster Relief

Twitter has become a tool for raising funds for disaster relief efforts, too. Many of the groups seeking to help victims of the earthquake in Haiti used Twitter to call for contributions. The American Red Cross maintains a Twitter presence; its profile reads in part, "Follow us for disaster and preparedness updates." And of course, Twitter updates helped to keep people inside and outside the country informed about events, even after the news began to slip from the front page.

Politics

Politicians are using Twitter to promote causes and themselves. Barack Obama is the first president to have his own Twitter account (@BarackObama). By 2010 at least forty-seven members of Congress had Twitter accounts.

Profits

Twitter has also become a hot marketing medium. In fact, a quick scan of Amazon.com and the web reveals that most of the current writing about Twitter is focused on its potential as a place to promote your company, your products, and yourself. And it's not just big companies who are twittering for dollars. Speaking at the 2009 TED Conference, Twitter CEO Williams showed his audience photos of a block-long line of customers queuing up at LA's popular Kogi Korean BBQ taco truck; a constant Twitter feed keeps Kogi's customers informed about where and when it will stop next.

Twitter Basics

As Twitter co-founder Evan Williams has described it, Twitter is based on a "seemingly trivial concept: you say what you're doing in 140 characters or less, and people who are interested in you get the updates."

Sending a tweet is easy. You just type your message into the box at the top of your Home page under the "What's happening?" heading. A counter on the right starts at 140 and counts down as you type. Spaces and punctuation count. If you go over, you can't send the tweet until you whittle it down.

Your Home page displays all of the tweets from you and the people you are following in a large central window, last-posted first. Your Profile page displays your profile and your tweets only. Both pages show the number of people you are following, the number following you, the total number of tweets you've sent to date, and the number of lists you maintain.

Getting your point across in 140 characters or less can be a little tricky. Remember that scene in *A River Runs Through It* where the dad makes his home-schooled son rewrite his essay over and over again, saying "cut it in half" each time he hands it in? Had he been born a couple of decades later, that kid would have been a great twitterer.

ESSENTIAL

If you want to make it easier for people to find you on Twitter, be sure to pick a user name that is as close to your own name as possible. "JaneDaily" is going to show up on a search engine when they type in "Jane Daily." "JaneyD2010" probably won't.

Finding and Following

Twitter will offer you a list of Suggested Users when you first sign up. ("Suggested" is a little misleading; it's just a list of popular twitterers.) And the service will ask to have a look at your e-mail contacts to see if anyone you already know is on Twitter. If you do decide to import your contacts list (and you don't have to), you can sort out the people you want to follow, or dump the whole thing and start from scratch.

The easiest way to follow someone on Twitter is to simply click on the "Follow" button under their profile picture or next to a tweet they've posted. Twitter allows its users to guard their accounts and requires permission to follow them, so some people might make you ask to follow them, but most won't. Unfollowing people is just as easy: just click the "Unfollow" button that now appears next to the profile or tweet of the person you're following.

You can also invite friends and colleagues you already know are using Twitter through an e-mail invitation. That capability is provided on the Find People page.

Why does Twitter limit the number of people I can follow?
In late 2008, Twitter decided to limit the number of people any one member can follow to 2,000 to "alleviate some of the strain on the behind-the-scenes part of Twitter, and reduce downtime and error pages." The system also limits the number of tweets you can post (1,000 per day) and the direct messages you can send (250 per day).

A search engine on Twitter allows you to look for people by name, and a list of topics—things like business, travel, entertainment, health—organizes some members you can follow. Clicking on "Entertainment," for example, opens a list of tweet-savvy celebrities. Click on "Politics" and you get accounts like the ACLU, Newt Gingrich, and the Capitol Hill newspaper, *Roll Call*. This list really isn't a bad way to get started; if you chose topics that interest you, you'll automatically have something in common with the people you follow. Twitter limits the number of people you can follow to 2,000, but there's no limit to the number of people who can follow you—just ask Ashton Kutcher.

Those who are starting from scratch but want to build a following need to have realistic expectations about that process. Keep in mind that the people with the most followers on Twitter leveraged their existing popularity to build a large Twitter audience. People like long-time social networking maven Robert Scoble and TechCrunch founder Michael Arrington command high numbers because they were already well known in tech circles. Ashton Kutcher and other actors attract followers because they're in the movies and on TV. Best-selling authors have no trouble building a large following. President Obama has a huge number of followers, which is no surprise because he's the president.

Retweets

Sometimes you see a tweet that you just have to share with your follow-ers, all of whom may not have seen it because they may not be following that guy. That's where retweets come in. A retweet is a tweet that amounts to a "What he said." You're also giving credit where credit is due. It's simple to send a retweet: Just click the "Retweet" button next to the tweet in question. The original tweet will come up with "RT" at the beginning.

Replies

On Twitter, a reply is a tweet that is aimed directly at another Twitter user in response to a specific tweet. Reply messages start with the @ sign, followed directly by the user name, and then the message. They look like this: "@johnkwaters wow, thank you so much." You start a reply by clicking on the "Reply button" next to the tweet in question. Keep in mind that replies are public; everyone else can read them.

Replies are an example of a Twitter convention that was not originally part of the system. It became popular in the user community, and Twitter embraced it later. (It's also a sign of the company's responsiveness.)

Direct Messages

If you want to keep your reply just between you and the twitterer, you can send her what Twitter calls a "direct message." Where a reply can go out to anyone whose tweet you've come across, direct messages can only go to the people on your follow list.

How Tweet It Is: Advanced Twittering

To get the most from your Twitter experience, you'll want to master just a few more conventions of the platform. There's no heavy lifting here, just some odd jargon and a few tricky moves.

Hashtags

A hashtag is a form used on Twitter to group tweets around an event, news item, issue, or topic. It's called a "hashtag" because the keyword is literally tagged with the hash or pound sign (#). A hashtag looks like this: *#nowplaying, #rsa, #followfriday*. But you can also just add the hash sign to the beginning of any keyword to create one, as in: "I'm hoping to finish this meeting soon and grab some #pizza." If you include a hashtag with your tweet, it gets included in the category represented by the word or acronym that follows the hash sign. So in this case, any other messages that have #pizza in them show up in search of that hashtag.

This is another innovation of the Twitter community, which the service has embraced. In fact, Twitter recently purchased the Summize real-time search engine that supports hashtag searches. Some hashtags have become standards. And using more than one in a tweet is considered bad form.

A number of third-party services track Twitter hashtags. The best known is probably Hashtag.org, but the list also includes TwitterGroups, Tweet-Chat, TweetGrid, and Twitterfall, among others.

Lists

In late 2009, Twitter added a new Twitter Lists feature, which made it possible to sort the people you follow into groups. This was a frequently-asked-for feature (though most people thought of it as "groups"), and it adds a great deal to the usability of the service. Here's how it works:

You create a list by clicking on "New List" on the sidebar, which opens a dialog box. Just fill in the name of the list (say, "family" or "authors"), decide whether you want it to be public or private, and click "Create list." Now you can add the people you follow—and even the people you don't, by clicking on the "Follow" button on their Profile page. A list of your lists appears in the sidebar. Twitter allows you to group up to twenty people in a list.

Location Sharing

In 2010 Twitter finally launched a new feature it had been promising for a while. Called "Tweet with Your Location," it allows you to annotate your tweets with information about your physical location. You can share exact latitude and longitude, or a more general location, such as your city. You have to turn on this feature by going to the Settings page and clicking on "Add a location to your tweets." Even if you decide to turn on this feature, you can still turn it off for specific tweets.

Why would you want to include your location with a tweet? Twitter explains it this way: "Tweeting with your place or coordinates can add con-text to your updates and help you join the local conversation, wherever you are." But the service also includes a bunch of language cautioning twitterers to do this carefully.

Twittering Apps

The creators of Twitter made it easy for other people to build applications for the Twitter platform. Software developers have responded with hundreds of applications, from tools that help you manage tweet traffic to plug-ins for your browser, and from search apps to data bases. The list is massive (70,000 by one recent count), and growing every day. Here are just a few examples to get you started:

Desktop Twitter Clients

So-called client software on your desktop computer allows you to access a service from a server somewhere else, usually through the Internet. Microsoft's Outlook is one of the best known examples of an e-mail client. If you have a Twitter client, you can read and write tweets without having to log onto the main Twitter website.

Twitter clients are among the most useful applications for this platform. They can make a huge difference in your experience with the microblogging service, and the most tech-savvy twitterers use them. Some of these tools even combine news feeds from Twitter and a social network, such as Facebook.

There are dozens of Twitter clients on the market today. Here are some of the most popular:

- TweetDeck
- twhirl
- Seesmic
- Twiteriffic

Mobile Twitter Clients

Mobile phone support has always been part of the Twitter game plan, and a host of clients for your smartphone have emerged in the last couple of years. Here are some examples:

- Tweetie (for the iPhone)
- OpenBeak (formerly Twitterberry for the Blackberry)
- MoTwit (for the Palm)
- Tiny Twitter (for any Java-enabled device and Windows Mobile Pocket PC or Smartphone)

Twitter is one of the technologies that are accelerating the transformation of mobile phones into real computing platforms. According to webtrend gurus at comScore, the number of mobile users of the microblogging service in January 2010 reached 4.7 million—that's up from just over a million users twelve months earlier.

Browser Plug-Ins

Some Twitter applications don't take you away from your desktop web browser, but are designed to enhance the experience. Here are some examples:

- Twitterfox (updates status of follow list on the Firefox browser)
- Twippera (a Twitter widget for the Opera browser)
- Twitterbar (allows you to post to Twitter via the address bar of your web browser)
- Twitterline (displays the public timelines of the people you follow on your browser toolbar)

Photo and Video Tools

When you're stuck with 140 characters, consider including a picture (which is rumored to be worth eighty-six more). Microblogging isn't just about text these days, and Twitter provides a way to include pictures in your updates. But several app makers have also added some interesting tools to the photo-support mix.

- Twitpic (probably the most popular; some Twitter clients have built-in support)
- Snaptweet (for sharing Flickr photos on Twitter)
- Twiddeo (it's Twitter with video)
- MobyPicture (for sharing photos, audio, and video)

Twitter Directories

Twitter gives you tools to search its membership that are hard to beat. But a number of third-party software makers are giving it a shot. Here are some examples that put unique spins on the process:

- Twits like Me (a search engine that finds "other users that twitter about the same things that you do")
- Twellow (billed as yellow pages for Twitter)
- Just Tweet It (searches for twitterers with common interests in database of subject-specific directories)
- Twittie Me (billed as "a place for twitter users to advertise their profiles and get followed by other people who share their interests")

Search Tools

Twitter improved its search capabilities recently, but a number of third-party search tools aimed at the platform are worth trying. Here are some examples:

- Twitdir (searches for words in usernames, locations, or descriptions)
- Twittertroll (a real-time search engine)
- Tweet Scan (keyword searches on Twitter)
- Twitterment (topics-based search engine)

Tracking the Trends

Twitter gives you some pretty good tools for trend watching, but it's such a popular activity that third-party developers have jumped in with their own offerings. Here are some examples:

- Twitscoop (billed as "Twitter's interface for the rest of us" tracks Twitter trends, but also events)
- Tweetmeme (a service that aggregates popular links on Twitter)
- Twitturly (tracks and ranks links on Twitter)
- Twitterholic (scans Twitter public timeline a few times a day and calculates individual statistics "for each twittering twit in our database")

CHAPTER 4

It Takes a Village:
Social Networks

Everyone knows what a social network is. It's your family, friends, and neighbors. It's your co-workers, customers, and business contacts. It's the fabric of your community and the common threads that connect you to the people in it. But in our increasingly web-centric world, the terms "social network" and "social networking" have taken on another shade of meaning. Nowadays, when someone says "social network," chances are they're referring to a relatively new generation of online communities, such as Facebook, MySpace, and LinkedIn.

What Is Social Networking?

"Social networking" is one of those buzz-word blankets that gets thrown over a lot of things. So let's get specific: An online social network is a kind of computer-mediated community. That's a mouthful of tech talk, but all it means is that members of a social network interact primarily through computers connected to the Internet. Those computers might sit on a desk (your Mac Pro), in a lap (your ThinkPad), or in the palm of a hand (your Blackberry).

The web is the medium in which these communities live, and the content created by their members—the messages they exchange, the pictures they share, the web-page links they pass around—is part of the Web 2.0 world of social media.

Social networking services, such as Facebook, host the website where members meet and interact. They also provide the digital tools and features that enrich those interactions. A social networking service typically provides its members with tools for creating and editing a personal profile, for searching for friends and colleagues, for sending and receiving messages, for posting pictures, for reminding you about upcoming birthdays and anniversaries, for recommending someone professionally, and an array of other capabilities. And for the most part, social network membership is free, though there are some online communities that require paid subscriptions.

QUESTION

If membership is free, how do social networks make money?
That's a question the networks themselves are still trying to answer. One obvious way they generate revenue is through advertising. The home pages of many social networks feature at least a window or two of sales pitches with links to products or shopping websites.

The New Community

In effect, these web-based networking services are re-defining "community" and what it means to be a part of one, because they can encompass a much broader range of relationships than just your immediate family, friends, and co-workers. They allow you to add old classmates, distant relatives, and long-lost *compadres* to your current circle of friends. People who haven't seen each other in decades are re-connecting today on social networks. And they're not restricted by geography, so friends and family strewn across time zones can interact as though they live on the same block.

Social networks can also foster new relationships. Although most members tend to use their networks to enhance existing associations, this is a place where new social connections, both personal and professional, are made.

Like any community, social networks post codes of conduct that include basic courtesies we would extend to each other in any civilized social environment. And because these communities are hosted on the web by a service provider, it's a lot easier to enforce them. Bad actors, when they are discovered, can be banned from the website. But along with conventions meant to keep members from stepping on each other's digital toes, social networks add boundaries that are unique to the online world. Most, for example, prohibit the posting of copyrighted material.

Don't Call Them Social Networks

Mainstream media reporters and news readers throw around the term "social network" like a Frisbee at the dog park. But a social network is a specific type of social media service, and it shouldn't be confused with other types of social media (blogs, microblogs, wikis, etc.) or other kinds of online services with a social component. Here's a list of online services that are commonly—and incorrectly—referred to as social networks, along with brief explanations of the difference.

- **Blogs:** Blogs are definitely part of the Web 2.0 world of social media, but blogging services are not social networks. Blogs and microblogs generate the content of the information network known as the blogosphere. Some social networks include blogging capabilities, but a blog is about publishing an individual's opinions, ideas, and observations, not about building communities.
- **Internet Forums:** Internet forums and message boards generate user content, so include them in your list of social media, but leave them off the social network list. These forums, which are analogous to public bulletin boards, are the granddaddies of social networks, but they're different animals.

- **Wikis:** Wikis are web-based applications that allow multiple users to create and edit documents online. They're tools of collaboration, so they do bring people together and they fit solidly in the social media world, but they're not social networks.
- **Bookmarking and Tagging Services:** Another form of social media that gets lumped in with the networks. There are great tools out there for tagging and bookmarking in a social context, but those tools are not themselves social networks.
- **Social News Sites:** Websites like Digg, Reddit, and Slashdot contribute significantly to the social networking "conversation," but they're not social networks. They're valuable social news services that allow users to post links to, and rank, Internet content.
- **Photo and Video Sharing/Hosting:** Social media services like Flickr, Picasa, and YouTube have allowed the Internet to come alive with pictures and video, and they have enriched the experience of social networking greatly. But they're media-sharing and image-hosting services, not true social networks.
- **Dating Services:** There's certainly no doubt that dating is a social activity, and the many online services designed to facilitate a romantic connection definitely bring people together. But they're not true social networks. These are matchmaking services that usually charge a fee. But even the free ones aren't about community. Once you've met the guy or gal of your dreams, there's really no reason to continue your membership.

It might help to remember that "social media" is the umbrella term for all the services covered in this book, and that a "social network" is just one type of social media.

How Do People Use Social Networks?

These days so many of us spend so much time in front of computers, both at work and at play, that it's hard to imagine a computer-based social application *not* emerging. Given how busy our lives are and how spread out our families have become, this thing we call social networking seems kind of . . . well . . . inevitable. And the way people are using these social networks shouldn't surprise anyone. It's all the same stuff we do offline, but with a tech assist. Members of social networks share personal news, send birthday greetings, and pass around pictures of the new baby. They seek the advice of friends and colleagues, promote their careers, and share their professional expertise. They advocate for causes, round up supporters, and solicit contributions. And along the way, they make a few new friends.

Staying Connected to Family and Friends

One reason people are flocking to social networks is that their busy lives and far-flung families have made it difficult, if not impossible, to stay meaningfully connected with all the people they love. It's a modern combination of too few hours and too many miles that has put an historic strain on our family ties. Social networks create an online space for nurturing those connections.

The military has recognized the value of this capability. In 2010, the *New York Times* reported that the Department of Defense issued a new policy that essentially allowed troops to access social networking sites from the military's non-classified computer network.

Even people whose friends and family are within spitting distance are using social networks as convenient places for everyone to touch base, check in, and catch up. Access to the web isn't yet universal, but just about anyone can find a terminal with a browser and an Internet connection, so a social network makes sense as a family touchstone.

Professional Networking

Remember what an impact e-mail had on the business world? We forget sometimes because e-mail is ubiquitous, but it was *huge*. Suddenly you could reach out to clients, customers, and co-workers without interrupting their busy day with yet another annoying phone call. Social networking adds a significant refinement to that groundbreaking communication model.

Business people and professionals use social networks to connect with others in their industries. They do it on sites like Facebook and MySpace, but they also take advantage of the specialized bells and whistles offered by such business-oriented social networking services as LinkedIn and Xing. They use the services to stay connected with industry colleagues, enhance professional relationships, and share best practices.

They also use them to expand their reach. People who don't know you and would be unlikely to return your phone call might be happy to respond to a query sent within a professional network to which you both belong. These kinds of networks also give you a chance to share your own expertise and become someone others reach out to.

Organizing

Social networks are all about spreading the word, so they're perfect for organizers of every stripe, who use them to coordinate social events, to manage political gatherings, to direct civic meetings, to synchronize fund raisers, and a host of other things.

But the same environment that makes life easier for the organizers of the big stuff also helps with the small stuff. Individual members use their social networks to organize parties, coordinate class reunions, synchronize "meet ups," and even to plan family vacations.

Promotion

People use social networks to promote their businesses, their political causes, and themselves. Actors use them to hype their movies; pop stars use them to push their CDs; politicians use them to promote their campaigns; and experts use them to market their latest books.

Civic groups use social networks to promote local events. Nonprofit groups use them to support fundraisers. Grass-roots organizers use them to nurture movements. Businesspeople and professionals use social networks to promote their careers by spotlighting their accomplishments in their profiles, and by offering their expertise to other members.

Socializing

And yes, people do use social networks to *socialize*. Amid all the hype about the marketing potential and personal promotional opportunities, it's easy to forget that social networks, at their core, are about people hanging out with each other. The popular networks fairly roar with virtual conversations among old friends and new, talking shop, comparing notes, sharing gossip, and just catching up.

The Social Networking Landscape

The social networking landscape is a shifting terrain of services. They're old and new, large and small, and ever evolving. Some of the bigger players are pretty well established now, and some old-school networks have proved to be remarkably resilient. But social networking services do come and go. And even the networks we now consider mainstream are constantly adding new capabilities and integrating with complementary social media.

Consequently, it can be tough to slap a label on these things, and any list of social networks is going to have an expiration date. It's best to view anything billed as a "definitive list" with skepticism and to take any categories with a grain of salt. However, this shifting landscape needs at least a few landmarks, and the following partial list of social networks should help you find your way around.

General-Interest Networks

You could also call them all-purpose networks, or maybe popular networks, or even mainstream networks, but those labels aren't much better. Whatever you call them, these are the social networks that most resemble Facebook and MySpace.

FACT

In 2010, Internet search giant Google launched its second social networking service: Google Buzz. (Its first was Orkut.) The new service bundled the usual social networking features, made popular by Facebook and MySpace, but also integrated tools from Google's growing roster of web-based apps, including Gmail, Picasa, Google Reader, and Blogger.

Facebook (*www.facebook.com*)

Founded in 2006, this is the largest social network in the world today with more nearly 500 million members. The service is free, and its membership includes a broad range of people, many celebrities, and a growing list of political figures. Members create profiles, upload pictures and video clips, send and receive messages, chat live, and play games. Lots of apps have been created by third-party developers for the site. Includes news feeds of your friends' posts. Facebook supports more than 500 groups in twenty-three categories. The network also supports fan pages and profiles, but it's mostly friend-focused.

MySpace (*www.myspace.com*)

Established in 2003, this free service was the largest social network from 2006 to 2008. Today it claims more than 100 million users. MySpace gets the credit for popularizing social networking. The service attracts a younger audience, and it has served as a popular platform for singers and bands. Members create profiles, upload and share photos and videos, send and receive messages, chat, blog, and play games. (In 2010, it announced a new focus on gaming.) The network has a huge music database and supports some 10,000 groups in twenty categories.

Friendster (*www.friendster.com*)

One of the first of the modern social networks, Friendster was founded in 2002, and was reportedly the model for MySpace. This free service claims approximate 115 million members, and 90 percent of its traffic comes from Asia. Members create customizable profiles, upload multimedia, chat, and send and receive message. Friendster provides access to hundreds of apps written for the network.

Bebo (*www.bebo.com*)

This free social network is owned by AOL and is popular in the UK. Members create profiles; search for friends; send and receive messages; share photos, videos, and music; blog; and chat. Bebo provides a Lifestream Platform, designed to deliver real-time, chronological updates from all of your friends—including updates from Facebook, MySpace, YouTube, Flickr, Twitter and Delicious. The network is also integrated with Skype, so that real-time interactions can use that service. There are lots of third-party applications.

Orkut (*www.orkut.com*)

This free social network is maintained by Google, and is very popular in India, Estonia, and Brazil. (Google Brazil now manages the service.) Members must have a Gmail account. Orkut allows members to create profiles, and provides features for friend finding, search, uploading photos and video, sending messages, and blogging. It also provides the Google Talk plug-in for voice and video chat.

hi5 (*www.hi5.com*)

Founded in 2003, this social network claims around 50 million active members, most of them in Latin America. Members create profiles, browse groups and categories by keyword, and search for other friends. Members can give each other virtual high fives. The network supports chat rooms and profile customization, and it launched a new game-developer program in 2010.

Badoo (*www.badoo.com*)

Founded in London in 2006, and now owned by a Greek company, this free, multi-lingual social network is popular in Europe. It claims more than 50 million users. Members create profiles, chat, blog, and share photos. Badoo charges for a feature called Rise Up, which gives user profiles more prominence. Critics charge that it resembles a dating site.

Business Networks

Lots of people and companies do business on Facebook and MySpace, but some social networks were created specifically with business networking in mind. These networks—and there are a couple dozen of them—provide what you might call a professional context for the social networking they host. And their members also make a few friends.

LinkedIn (www.linkedin.com)

Launched in 2003, LinkedIn is the biggest network in the business category, with more than 60 million registered users around the world. It's most popular in the United States (about half its membership), but it has millions of users in Europe and India. This free service is all about professional contacts. Member profiles include job histories and recommendations from employers and colleagues. Users grow their contact lists by harvesting from their contacts' contact lists. (Each member has to be asked to join a new list.) Members also use it to network during a job search.

Xing (*www.xing.com*)

Billed as the leading business network in Europe, this service claims more than 8 million members. Users develop resume-like profiles on personal homepages, as well as "online business cards." They maintain their address books, send and receive messages, schedule appointments, and plan events. A power search feature includes intelligent search filters. Xing also supports company profiles.

ESSENTIAL

Salesforce.com, the company that popularized the concept of software as a service, jumped on the social-networking bandwagon in 2010 with a new "Facebook for the enterprise" service called Chatter. Billed as a collaboration application and social development platform, Chatter aims to allow developers to bring Facebook- and Twitter-like capabilities to the company's Force.com enterprise cloud-computing platform. Developers use Chatter to add social features, such as profiles, status updates, and real-time feeds, to any of the applications built on Force.com

Ryze (*www.ryze.com*)

Ryze is a free, business-focused social network that was founded in 2001, and now claims a global membership of 500,000. It was one of the first networks designed specifically with business pros in mind, and it maintains a special focus on entrepreneurs. Members get a free home page, and have access to specialized, industry-hosted sub-networks. The site features the usual social-networking features, and offers additional capabilities with a paid membership.

eBay Neighborhoods (*http://neighborhoods.ebay.com*)

eBay is a very popular online marketplace that brings together a huge range of buyers and sellers. You often hear those folks described collectively as the eBay community, but eBay itself is not a social network. However, eBay's Neighborhoods feature, which the company introduced in 2007, does fit the definition. The company bills it as a "place to connect with others who share the same passion for products and topics."

Niche Networks

The second generation web is also home to a burgeoning species of social networks with a special focus or theme. The members of these networks do their socializing around movies, music, and games, or they share a common background, such as schools, workplaces, and ethnic orientations. Here are a couple of examples:

Buzznet (*www.buzznet.com*)

This is a music-focused network that boasts about 10,000 members. Fans interact in thousands of music communities. Members share photos, videos, and blog posts about their favorite bands. Buzznet is definitely youth-oriented, with lots of information about new CDs and band tour dates. Its list of celebrity bloggers includes pop star Britney Spears, reality TV stars Kim and Khloe Kardashian, Brody Jenner of *The Hills*, and actress Mischa Barton, among others.

deviantART (*www.deviantart.com*)

As the name implies, deviantART is a social network for art lovers (not, however, deviants). Founded in 2000, it claims more than 11 million members. It provides a gallery where members display their art, everything from photography and digital art to Adobe Flash applications and "skins" for software applications. Members create profiles, display their work, and network with other artists. Membership is free, and provides access to 80 million pieces of art in 2,000 categories. Artists may upload an unlimited number of pieces, and members add comments.

Flixter (*www.flixter.com*)

A social network for movie lovers, Flixter was founded in 2006. The service allows members to create profiles, chat with friends, and rate movies. It features movie clips and celebrity photos.

Blackplanet (*www.blackplanet.com*)

A social network aimed at African Americans, Blackplanet was founded in 1999, making it one of the oldest on the list. Billed as the largest black community online, it's a free service that allows members to create profiles, find members, search, upload photos and video, share music, send messages, chat, participate in forums, coordinate community events, and blog.

Social Security

It won't surprise you to learn that the bad guys have the social networks in their sights. The popular social nets are bursting with opportunity for all kinds of mischief from spammers, phishers, cybercriminals, and garden-variety burglars. The networking services take security very seriously, and generally speaking, they have their defenses up. Along with the usual industrial strength spam filters and firewalls, they're employing systems that track unusual surges in message flows, spot questionable behavioral trends, and scan user-generated pages for malicious content.

Your Privacy

It's almost counterintuitive to talk about the privacy concerns of social network members, who, after all, are publishing their personal details on the Internet. But most network services actually provide their members with quite a bit of control over who sees their information. The problem is, members often fail to exercise that control, and the network's default privacy settings aren't always on high.

Virtually all social networking services provide their members with privacy tools, usually somewhere on the home page under "Settings." And it's generally up to the user to manage those settings. You can and should use these tools to tune you level of transparency—in other words, to decide how much of your information you want to be viewable by the public, and how much you want to keep between you and your networking friends.

Corporate Security Risks

Among the hot topics at the 2010 RSA Security Conference, the huge annual trade show for hardcore cyber-security pros, was the risks of social networking in corporate networks. Employees can open up a big hole in the company's defenses when they access their social networking accounts without exercising some caution. Apparently the bad guys have hit on the trick of creating "imposter profiles" that seem like the real thing, even prominent people you might know.

ESSENTIAL

Study after study of social networking behaviors show that a large percentage of network members accept random friend requests from strangers. It's fun to meet people on social networks—that's partly why they exist—but most social networking mavens advise against accepting a friend request from someone you don't know, or who hasn't been referred by someone you do.

Another security problem posed by the use of social networks in the office: too much talk about the business. Employees who are cranked up about a project sometimes forget that they shouldn't be sharing the details of their employers' intellectual property with their Facebook pals. They forget that the competition is listening.

CHAPTER 5

Facebook: The Social Network That Ate the World

Facebook (*www.facebook.com*) is the world's most popular social networking service. Its membership was nearing 500 million in 2010, and half of those members visit the site every day. People use Facebook to keep up with friends and family, to reconnect with classmates, and to promote their careers and businesses. Companies use Facebook to network with customers, and nonprofits use it to connect with supporters. It's simple to join Facebook, but navigating its features can be confusing at first. Here's what you need to know to get the most from your Facebook experience.

A Bunch of Harvard Kids Messing Around

Facebook was founded in 2004 by four Harvard University classmates: Mark Zuckerberg, Dustin Moskovitz, Eduardo Saverin, and Chris Hughes. It started as a student-oriented social networking website developed in a college dorm room. Called "Thefacebook," it was initially distributed to Harvard freshmen, but the network grew quickly to include other Boston universities. It was renamed "Facebook" in 2005, and by 2006 was reaching beyond the schools.

A Social Utility

The founders of Facebook like to think of their networking service as a social utility, a new kind of mechanism for connecting people with their friends and "others who work, study, and live around them," according to the company. Basically, it's a website on which Facebook members post personal messages and updates on the events of their lives. Members who are part of their circle can read those posts and respond to them with their own comments. In this way, Facebook members share their thoughts, feelings, opinions, personal milestones, birthday greetings, graduation announcements, trials, and tribulations among friends who are often thousands of miles apart.

Members can also post photos, video clips, and links to other web pages. They can send and receive private messages that don't get posted for others to see. They can join groups with similar interests, play games, and run a growing variety of Facebook-specific applications. And there's even a live chat feature that allows members who are visiting the site at the same time to communicate in real time.

But this social utility has also attracted the attention of an expanding range of users who see Facebook's burgeoning memberships as a potential market for their products and services. Many see it as the ideal medium for targeted advertising to self-identified groups of like-minded people.

Social Impact

The story of Facebook's affect on society at large is still unfolding, but there are examples that suggest it will be profound. When a teenager went missing in San Diego in early 2010, the family set up a Facebook page and called for volunteers to help with the search. Search organizers reported more than 6,000 volunteers came together to search the area surrounding the park where her car was found.

The U.S. Census Bureau has turned to Facebook and other social networks to help spread the word about "being counted" by creating a Census Page. To the question posted on the page, "Can I fill out my form online," the bureau wrote: "Not this time. We are experimenting with Internet response for the future."

And politicians simply can't compete nowadays if they don't have a Facebook page. Former Alaska governor and vice presidential candidate Sarah Palin's Facebook page boasts nearly 1.5 million fans, and her posts regularly make the evening news.

ESSENTIAL

In 2008, MySpace was the leading social network in terms of the number of monthly visits. But a year later, web traffic analysts at Complete.com saw Facebook "surging past" MySpace. TechCrunch, a techie trends website, reported that more than 220 million people visited Facebook in December 2008, while MySpace clocked around 125 million during the same time.

And Facebook is not immune from misuses. Along with genuine relief efforts, fundraising scams for Haitian earthquake victims invaded the site before the company was able to shut them down. And in 2009, the site's managers pulled down a page asking members to vote yes or no on the question, "Should [President] Obama be killed?"

Facebook's Funds

Tech-industry blog Inside Facebook was the first to break the news that the company could bring in more than $1 billion in 2010. But Facebook membership is free, so where does all the money come from?

In a word, advertising. Facebook reportedly makes most of its money selling brand advertising, ads from name-brand vendors whose commercials you might see on TV. In early 2010, the company actually stopped running banner ads in favor of "engagement advertising," which allow users to comment, give a virtual gift, or become a fan of the brand's Facebook page.

FACT

In 2004 Facebook co-founders bought the domain name "facebook .com" for a reported $200,000. By early 2010, industry watchers were expecting the company's revenues to hit the billion-dollar mark. Rival social network Friendster offered to buy the company for $10 million in 2004, and other companies—including Yahoo!—have expressed an interest. But CEO Mark Zuckerberg shows no interest in selling.

But the company also makes money on so-called virtual goods. These include what you might call non-corporeal products, such as e-cards or accessories for online games, such as the enormously popular *Mafia Wars* and *FarmVille* from San Francisco-based game maker Zynga. Members pay for virtual goods through a Facebook online payment service called "Credits."

Facebook Basics

Getting started on Facebook is very easy. The account is free, but you must be at least thirteen years of age to open one, and the site requires you to provide a valid e-mail address. To sign up, point your web browser to the Facebook sign-up page; enter your name, e-mail address, a password, your gender, and your birthday; click "Sign Up," and you're on your way. Facebook requires your date of birth "to encourage authenticity and provide only age-appropriate access to content." The company doesn't say why it needs to know your gender. You can hide this information later, but Facebook still has it. The company promises in its privacy policy not to share your information with advertisers without your consent, but your account's privacy settings are ultimately your responsibility. More on this later.

You might be confronted with a "Security Check" that requires you to interpret some distorted text in a box. Don't take it personally; that's becoming standard operating procedure on many websites.

First Friends

When you first sign up, Facebook asks if you want to search for members you might already know by giving the website temporary access to your e-mail account. Doing this allows Facebook to search through your personal contacts file for people who might also be Facebook members and automatically add them to your friends list. Facebook promises not to store your e-mail password during his process, but they will use the info to generate suggestions for you and your contacts on Facebook.

You can skip this step outright, or use it to generate a list of your contacts who are also on Facebook. Any of these contacts you select will receive an e-mail invitation to join your list of friends. You can also skip them all and go on to the next step.

Your Basic Profile

Step 2 begins the process of developing your basic Facebook profile. You can skip any part of this step and revisit it later, but it makes sense to provide some of the information requested at this point. This is a social network, after all, not a place to lurk anonymously. You'll be asked to fill in things like the names of your high school and/or college, the years you graduated, and the company you work for. Click "Save & Continue." If you have any of those things in common with other members, Facebook will give you a chance to invite those people to join your friends list, too.

Your Facebook profile is where you list the personal details you'd like to share with your group of friends. It's where the network says, "Tell us a little about yourself." You can reveal a lot or a little, and you can add and subtract information any time you like. Some of the profile information is innocuous ("What are your favorite movies?"); and some is pretty darned personal ("Are you looking for a date?")

If there's a rule of thumb here, it might be to start by including things you wouldn't mind telling someone you met at a party. Your marital status, where you got your degree, and the names of some of your favorite bands are the kinds of personal tidbits that might come up in a casual conversation at your next-door neighbor's retirement soirée. And remember: You can edit your profile information any time.

Adding Your Profile Photo

In the third and final sign-up step, you have the opportunity to add your picture to your Facebook page. It's rare for a Facebook member not to include a picture (it's called *Face*book, after all), but you can skip this step if you really want to. Facebook allows you to upload a photo from your computer, or to take one on the spot with your webcam. Facebook profile pictures are easy to change, and members do it all the time. Once you upload your photo, click "Save & Continue," that's it: you're on Facebook.

Your Profile Page

Your Profile page is where you can tinker with your personal information—add info to the questionnaires, switch your picture, change your status. Clicking on "Edit My Profile" gives you access to all the forms used in building your profile. Along with your basic information, you can enrich your profile with interesting personal facts (favorite movies, books, TV shows; hobbies; activities, etc.), as well as job and educational information.

You'll also have an opportunity to write something about yourself, sort of a personal blurb, that will appear under your profile picture. There doesn't appear to be a word limit, but it's best to keep it brief and punchy. Think of it as your personal elevator pitch, and give it some thought.

If you find that you like Facebook and plan to continue participating, it's worth taking a minute to buff up your profile. Give your friends more than just your name, rank, and serial number. And maybe add just a few personal details that might spark a connection with a new friend.

The Wall

At the center of your Profile page is a large central column called "The Wall." This is where you post public notes, photos, and videos, which are known as "status updates." Friends who visit your Profile page can post messages to you on your wall, and you can post messages on theirs. Wall messages include a Comment box, in which other members may write a note about the original post. The resulting conversational strings can be quite long.

Wall posts are meant to be public, and the content of your Wall is streamed to the News Feed (more on this later). Facebook provides features for private interactions, and there are privacy settings that give you some control over who sees what, but you can't keep Wall posts private. Facebook is an open and public social networking service, and the Wall is emblematic of that model.

What's on Your Mind?

Near the top of your Profile page is a large box with the message "What's on your mind?" Facebook calls this the Publisher, and it's where you enter the text of your Wall notes. There's a similar box at the top of your Home page, and both function the same way: they provide the means of sharing updates with your friends.

Below this text box are four icons, which allow you to add photos, videos, event information, and links to other websites to your message. You can also import external blogs and RSS feeds and add a virtual gift from the Facebook Gift Shop.

The Publisher also allows you to designate your message "Friends Only" by clicking the icon of a padlock next to the Share button.

Your Home Page

Your Home page is where you end up when you first log on to Facebook, and it's where most of the action takes place. The layout was recently redesigned with much fanfare to make it more easily navigated, and for the most part, people seem to like the changes.

Your Home page consists of a large central News Feed column, which is where you and your friends' status updates appear. Across the top of the page is a blue toolbar, where you'll access some drop-down menus and a search window. On the left end of the toolbar are menus of Friend Requests, Messages, and Notifications. On the right are links to your Home page, your Profile Settings page, and a drop-down list of account settings. This "Accounts" menu is where you'll find links to Facebook's "Help" pages and the "Logout" command.

ESSENTIAL

Your Home page is only one type of Facebook page. Musicians, artists, performers, politicians, and businesses create Facebook pages to promote their "brand." Facebook members can become fans of a page and receive updates from it in their News Feeds. Keep in mind that Facebook does not currently allow you to hide your fan pages from the people you allow to see the content of your Wall.

To the left of the News Feed window is a list of several types of Facebook content, including the News Feed, the Messages page, your Event lists, and your Photo albums and Video clips. You'll also find a link to your Facebook applications, games, and groups, as well as your current Friends list. At the bottom of this menu panel is a list of friends who are currently online and available for chatting.

On the right side of the page you'll find sponsored links (essentially ads), event and birthday reminders, lists of friend requests, and the Facebook Chat application.

The News Feed

The News Feed window is the first thing you see when you log on to your Facebook account. It displays a stream of status updates from your friends in reverse chronological order, including their notes, responses from other friends, their photos, their friend requests, their status updates, their group memberships, and event RSVPs.

The News Feed page offers two viewing options: "Top News," which displays what Facebook determines to be "the most interesting content that your friends are posting, and "Most Recent," which displays all the actions of your friends in real time.

It is also possible to filter the content that appears on your News Feed page. Click on "Friends" in the left-hand navigation panel to access two options: "Recently Updated," which displays new friend requests and friends that have recently updated their profiles; and "Status Updates," which displays and the latest postings of all your friends. The Status Updates window also allows you to post a message. Click on "Update Status," and a new message window opens.

FACT

In February 2010 Facebook received a patent for its news-feed technology. Entitled "Dynamically providing a news feed about users of a social network," the patent covers Facebook's method for generating news items around its members' activities. The technology limits access to a news item to "a predetermined set of viewers" and establishes "an order to the news items" it displays on the site.

Friend Lists

When you click on "Recently Updated," you'll notice a button in the upper right corner of the News Feed window labeled "Create a List." Lists are incredibly useful on Facebook, especially as your roster of online *compadres* grows. This feature allows you to add a friend to more than one group, say, "Family" and "Christmas," or "Professional" and "Company Softball." And you can apply privacy policies specifically to each list; say, you let your family see your pictures from your latest Halloween party, but you don't want your co-workers to see you dressed up like the Wicked Witch of the West.

Clicking on the "Create a List" button opens a very straightforward dialog box that allows you to organize your friends into groups. Type a list title in the Enter a Name window, select the friends you'd like to include, and click "Create List." The name of your new list now appears in the navigation panel under "Friends."

Direct Messages

Clicking on "Messages" opens a list of messages that have been sent directly to you by your friends, along with some tools for managing them. These messages don't appear on the News Feed, and you can respond to them directly. Just click on a message in the list to open it, and then type your response into the "Reply" box. You can create a new message by clicking on the "New Message" button in the upper right of the page and filling out the message form. You can also attach a photo, a video, or a link to another web page.

ALERT

Facebook describes the "poke" as a fun way for members to interact. Reportedly, some members use it as a kind of online flirting. But the jury is still out on how many members are amused by this virtual nudge. Poking simply causes an icon to appear on a member's Home page. But those icons come in a variety of flavors, thanks to third-party app developers, including naughty pokes, sexy pokes, "voodoo" pokes, kinky pokes, office pokes—there's even an app for "poke wars."

You can click on a message subject and open up the thread, which shows all the messages exchanged on that topic, displayed in reverse chronological order. Clicking on a friend's name takes you to his or her home page. You can also delete selected messages, or mark them as "Read."

Events

"Events" is a Facebook application designed to allow members to organize gatherings, parties, or other social functions with their Facebook friends. Click on "Events" in the left navigation panel to display a list of upcoming events posted by your friends, as well as birthdays and past events. Clicking on the "Create an Event" button on the upper right opens a step-by-step guide to creating an event, posting the details, and inviting friends.

Photos

"Photos" is another Facebook application. This one displays photos posted by your friends, and provides a set of tools for posting and organizing your own pictures.

Collections of pictures called "Photo Albums" are created on your Profile page. You simply open your Profile, click on the Photos tab, and then click "Create a Photo Album." The program walks you through the process of uploading photos from your computer and creating the album. The process allows you to add and delete photos any time, and it prompts you to decide who gets to see them.

If you haven't downloaded the Facebook Photo plug-in, a little piece of software that allows you to upload pictures, you'll be prompted to do so the first time you try to create an album.

Applications and Games

An increasingly important part of the Facebook experience involves software programs designed specifically for the social networking service. Thanks to its growing membership, Facebook has become a popular platform for application developers, who create programs just for Facebook members, including apps for business, education, sports, and utilities, among others.

Clicking on "Applications" displays a list of the applications you currently use, applications your friends are using, and applications that Facebook recommends.

The Games group displays the same type of information as the Applications group, but strictly focused on gaming. You'll see a list of your games, your friends' games, your friends' activities within their games, and games featured by Facebook. Facebook games cover a range of categories, including card games, board games, word games, action and arcade games, role-playing games, and virtual-world games.

Your Settings

Before you plunge too far into the Facebook universe, you should take a moment to make sure you understand your Facebook account settings. Clicking "Account" in the upper right corner of your new Facebook page opens a drop-down menu listing links to several Facebook utility pages. You'll notice "Account Settings," "Privacy Settings," and "Application Settings." This is also where you go to edit your friends list, access your Credit online payment service account, find answers to the most commonly asked questions about the site ("Help"), and log out.

My Account

Clicking on "Account Settings" opens the My Account page. This is where you fine-tune your personal information and tweak certain preferences. Near the top of the page you'll notice seven tabs. Click on "Settings" to edit your real name, your user name, your e-mail address, your password, the list of other web accounts linked to your Facebook account, your security question, some privacy controls, and to deactivate the account.

Under the "Settings" tab, you'll find:

- **Name:** This is the name that people see, and Facebook is adamant that it be your real name. The company actually maintains hidden code in the site designed to ferret out fake names. The truth is, it's not impossible to insert a pseudonym here, but why would you want to? Facebook is about people interacting as themselves, not alter egos.

- **E-mail:** Facebook uses your e-mail address to send various notifications. Any valid e-mail works here.
- **Password:** If you need to change your password—and security experts advise us to change it regularly—here's where you do it.
- **Linked Accounts:** Click here to open a drop-down list of other websites that you might like to connect to your Facebook account. Selecting an account (the current list includes Google, MySpace, Yahoo!, MyOpenID, Verisign, and OpenID) and providing its web address means that when you log onto to that website, you'll automatically be logged on to Facebook.
- **Security Question:** A security question is a now-commonly used device for authenticating your identity. If Facebook ever has doubts about you, you forget your password, or you need to prove who you are, this thing will kick in. If you chose a question you might forget the answer to, ("What was the first concert you attended?"), be sure to stash the answer somewhere.
- **Privacy:** Clicking on "Privacy Settings" takes you to the Privacy Settings page. This is where you establish and manage your privacy settings. More on this later.
- **Deactivate Account:** This one is self-explanatory; however it's worth noting that you can't actually delete your Facebook account. "Deactivation" hides your information from your friends, and your posts, photos, etc. are no longer available. But they're waiting for you should you decide to restart your account. Clicking here brings up a long list of deactivation options, including "This is temporary. I'll be back," and "I don't feel safe on Facebook."

Networks

This is where you can connect your primary Facebook account with other Facebook networks. These are networks of people with common connections to things like schools, cities, companies, and geographic regions. For example, entering "Des Moines" in the Network name box produces a drop-down list that includes Grand View University, Mercy Hospital, Federal Home Bank, and the Des Moines Radio Group.

Notifications

This is where you choose to receive or not receive e-mail and text-message notifications about "actions taken on Facebook about you." If you don't log onto Facebook very often, this can be an important feature that keeps you up-to-date. You can select from a long list of notification options. Keep in mind that each Facebook application has its own setting.

Mobile

This tab opens a page that allows you to activate Facebook Mobile, which sends notifications, friend requests, messages, wall posts, and status updates to your cell phone. Facebook doesn't charge you for the text messages it sends to your cell phone, but your mobile service provider does. Depending on how active you and your friends are on Facebook, you could receive dozens of messages a day. Unless you already pay for unlimited texting, you should make sure *not* to register your phone number here, or select "Send notification to my phone via SMS" on the Notifications page.

Language

If you're reading this, your choice here is probably English, and that's the default setting, but Facebook does provide other language options.

Payments

This tab takes you to a page where you establish your preferred method of payment for virtual gifts, e-cards, gaming accessories, etc. You can set up a credit card, buy Facebook Credits, manage payments, and even change currencies.

Facebook Ads

This page can be a bit confusing just now. The first option, "Ads shown by third party applications," isn't actually active. But Facebook wants you to choose whether you want to allow other apps and ad networks to show your information to your friends, in case it decides to allow this in the future. You can choose not to allow this kind of access, which might be a good idea until Facebook makes up its mind. The other option here, "Show my social actions in Facebook Ads to," is located way down at the bottom of the page. As the company explains it, ads posted on Facebook are sometimes paired with what it calls social actions, such as becoming a fan of a Page or joining a Group. The default setting allows Facebook to share your name and profile photo to advertise products associated with those actions to your friends. Facebook insists that it will never sell your information to advertisers, but this default setting feels like a privacy violation to some people. You opt out by selecting "No one" in the drop-down menu.

Privacy Settings

Facebook is designed to be a social environment, a place where people not only share their lives with existing friends and family members, but meet and interact with new people with similar interests and concerns. However, nobody expects you to walk down Main Street in your birthday suit. There's nothing wrong with putting in a few restrictions that meet your personal preferences and comfort level. The good news and the bad news is, it's up to you to manage just who gets to see what you post on Facebook.

In the spring of 2010, Facebook sparked a controversy by implementing a plan to increase its reach with "social plug-ins." Announced at its annual f8 developer conference, the plug-ins made it easier for websites outside Facebook to share info about Facebook members who visit them. The effect was to make your data more public, including your current city, hometown, education, work, likes, interests, and friends. The pages that you "Like" (which replaced the "Fan" designation) became part of your public profile.

Facebook's plan drew intense criticism from social-media mavens, not to mention its own membership. At one point, three United States senators— Senator Charles Schumer of New York, Senator Michael Bennet of Colorado, and Senator Al Franken of Minnesota—called on Facebook to make it easier for its users to protect their privacy during a press conference on Capitol Hill. Later, the Federal Trade Commission indicated that it would look into the matter. Facebook quickly backed off its original plan, and founder Mark Zuckerberg vowed to make it simpler for members to control their privacy.

The New Privacy Framework

As of this writing, Facebook had begun to roll out a new privacy framework. The settings in this new framework are easier to understand and simpler to manage. You can now opt in to Facebook's "recommended" settings, or customize your settings to share your information with friends, friends of friends, or "everyone." Once you've established your privacy preferences, Facebook says it will recognize them as the default setting when applying privacy settings to any features it introduces in the future.

Clicking on "Account" and then "Privacy Settings" takes you to a page entitled "Choose Your Privacy Settings," which shows your current settings and provides access to tools for customization. This page displays a list of the different types of information you can share on Facebook, including:

- My status, photos, and posts
- Bio and favorite quotations
- Family and relationships
- Photos and videos I'm tagged in
- Religious and political views
- Birthday
- Can comment on posts
- E-mail addresses and IM
- Phone numbers and address

You can chose to share the information in each of these categories only with the friends on your own Facebook friends list, your friends plus the people on *their* friends lists, or everyone who belongs to Facebook or visits the website. Clicking "Everyone" makes every category openly available. Clicking "Friends of Friends" makes the first four categories visible to friends of friends and the rest to friends only. Clicking "Friends Only" makes all categories visible to your friends only.

Clicking on "Customize settings" takes you to a detailed list of the information types you've included in your Facebook profile, and it allows you to decide which of the three privacy levels to apply to each.

Facebook Recommends . . .

Clicking "Recommended" implements the privacy settings that Facebook hopes you'll adopt. It opens up the first three categories—status, photos, posts, your bio, your favorite quotations, and your family and relationships—to everyone. This setting makes the photos and videos in which you have been tagged (identified), your religious and political views, and your birthday visible to your friends and theirs. The final three—who can comment on posts, your e-mail addresses, instant messaging ID, phone numbers, and address, are reserved for friends only.

Application and Websites

The "Choose Your Privacy Settings" page also allows you to control the information that's shared through Facebook games and applications. Click on "Edit your settings" under "Applications and Websites" to gain access to this set of security preferences. Here you can edit who can see your gaming activities and application dashboards, and what information is made available from the websites you and your friends visit.

This is where you can opt out of the controversial "Instant Personalization" feature, which shares personal information about you with your friends when you log on to a partner website (Yelp, Pandora, etc.). When the feature is turned on, which it is by default, if you click a "Like" icon on a web page or make a comment, you authorize Facebook to publish it on your Facebook profile and in your friends' news feeds.

Here, you can also enable the "Public search" feature, which controls whether the information you have chosen to share with "everyone" shows up in search engine searches on your name, both on and off Facebook. This feature is off by default.

Block Lists

"Choose Your Privacy Settings" also gives you access to the nuclear option of Facebook privacy: "Block lists." Block lists allows you to shut out individual Facebook members completely by preventing them from interacting with you or seeing your information on the network. It also allows you to automatically ignore application invitations from specific people.

CHAPTER 6

MySpace:
The Social Network Rock Star

MySpace (*www.myspace.com*) was the first social network to grab the public's attention in a big way, and with more than 100 million members, it's still one of the most popular web destinations on the planet. And it's also one of the richest social media environments in cyberspace. MySpace has distinguished itself with a dazzling array of features and content—some have argued, too dazzling. With so many bells and whistles, it can be a noisy and confusing environment. Here's what you need to know to get around in this lively and colorful network.

Friendster Fans Build a Better Network

MySpace originated as a side project at Los Angeles-based eUniverse, an internet marketing company founded in 1998 by Brad Greenspan, and which later changed its name to Intermix Media. The story goes that employees of eUniverse joined the Friendster network, saw its potential, and set out to do it better. The project involved Chris DeWolfe (later MySpace CEO), Josh Berman, Toan Nguyen, and Tom Anderson; they reportedly finished the first version in about ten days.

MySpace was officially launched in January 2004, and within a month reported its first million registered users. The company claimed 5 million members by November of that year. By the time Rupert Murdoch's News Corporation bought Intermix in July 2005, MySpace was reporting a membership of 20 million. The corporation's MySpace division is now headquartered in Beverly Hills.

Ups and Downs

The history of MySpace is marked by early internal power struggles, financial ups and downs, and a couple of headline-grabbing lawsuits. The founder of Intermix resigned from the company in 2003 under a cloud of accounting problems, but retained a significant ownership position in the publicly traded company and later fought the News Corp deal. Co-founders Chris DeWolfe and Tom Anderson, often credited with the rapid early growth of the MySpace network and much of its dynamic evolution, were apparently asked to step down from their executive positions in 2009, though they both remain on the company's board.

One of social network's most popular features, the on-demand MySpace Music streaming service, was born from a lawsuit. In 2006 Universal Music Group sued for damages from copyright infringement. The record label accused MySpace of complicity in its users' illegal uploading of thousands of music videos. The two settled the dispute by forming a joint venture: MySpace Music. That same year, the family of a fourteen-year-old girl who was allegedly raped by a nineteen-year-old man she met on the network, sued for $30 million. The company subsequently instituted new security features aimed at protecting minors. That lawsuit was dismissed in 2007 when a judge ruled that interactive computer services like MySpace are protected by the Communications Decency Act of 1996.

Innovation and Acquisition

MySpace rode an early wave of interest among young, tech-savvy digital natives, who jumped onto the network and filled it with splashy, custom home pages and a fire hose of shared media. And the company hasn't been shy about acquiring the technology it needs to support the social networking habits of those users. The network acquired photo-video hub Photo-Bucket in 2007, social music discovery service iLike in 2009, and the online music service imeem in 2009.

In 2008 the company launched SlingShot Labs, an "incubator" where it planned to develop new web ventures and nurture new features and technologies for MySpace. In 2010, amid rumors of a SlingShot shutdown, an events feature it developed called SocialPlan was used to upgrade the MySpace Events page.

FACT

In 2010, MySpace cranked up its social gaming strategy. Speaking to attendees at the Game Developer Conference in San Francisco, co-president Mike Jones unveiled a new MySpace Games initiative that he said would showcase online games on the site and draw more developers. MySpace has hosted social games for a long time. The new strategy was meant to refocus the company on the gaming market.

How MySpace Makes Money

MySpace generates most of its revenues from advertising—a lot of advertising. But the network has also explored brand integration into short videos from the likes of Discover, TMZ, and Atomic Wedgie, as well as offering premium content, and it's is even producing original short-form series.

In 2010, in a controversial move, MySpace began offering its users' real-time data, including things like blog posts, locations, photos, reviews, and status updates, to third parties for packaging and resale. Austin, Texas-based InfoChimps was the first to package 24-hour hunks of MySpace's data stream. But MySpace isn't *selling* the data. "MySpace provides developers . . . with free access to publicly available real-time data . . ." MySpace said in a statement. Infochimp added, "By giving developers free access to publically available real-time data . . . MySpace reinforces its commitment to powering the real-time social web and the development of open standards."

A Multimedia Maelstrom

No social network in operation today is as media-packed as MySpace. It swirls with photos and videos, and throbs with music. Its members enhance their home pages almost as they would a full-out web page, filling them with images and sounds and special effects. It is perhaps evidence of its youth-orientation that members talk about "pimping your profile," which is slang for adding fancy features and striking visual and audio elements to a MySpace Profile page. MySpacers are free to pile on a range of dynamic elements, including images, videos, and photo slide shows. They can also take advantage of the power of HTML and CSS. Profile pimping has spawned a cottage industry of third-party MySpace Profile page designers.

Redesign

A common criticism of MySpace in the early days was that the network was too busy, noisy, and chaotic. It underwent a makeover in 2008 to clean things up and calm things down. But it's still the liveliest social network on the web. The Home page was redesigned, the Profile page design features were updated, and MySpace Music was launched. In 2010, the network added a recommendations engine, which generates recommendations for things like music, videos, and games based on a member's search habits.

The Pop-Culture Conversation

MySpace management describes the network as "a global lifestyle portal that reaches millions of people around the world." It has also been called "a platform for discovering culture," which is an apt description if you're talking about pop culture. In 2010, MySpace co-president Jason Hirschhorn acknowledged in an interview with the website Mashable that the network's focus on "the pop culture conversation" makes it especially appealing to fourteen- to thirty-four-year-olds, with "a very sweet spot with the eighteen to twenty-four demographic."

Pop singers and rock bands helped build MySpace's popularity, and they're still a big part of the network's unique identity. But MySpace is known for drawing a wide range of musicians, filmmakers, comedians, photographers, and politicians. And celebrities—don't forget the celebrities. A MySpace feature called MySpace Celebrity is a directory of the profiles of famous members.

A Haven for Starving Musicians

Because of MySpace's skew toward a younger membership, lots of mainstream recording artists use it to promote their music. But the network has also earned a unique reputation as a place for promoting indie bands. Indie artists with MySpace accounts use the network's tools to upload their music videos, interviews, live performances, and include links to their web pages. In 2009, the network began allowing indie bands to stream their music on MySpace Music in exchange for a piece of the ad revenue the service generates. The network allows musicians to post and sell music using MyStore widgets, a feature developed by a company called SNOCAP, owned by Napster creator Shawn Fanning, which was later acquired by a company that MySpace later acquired.

MySpace Basics

MySpace integrates user profiles, blogs, classifieds, forums, galleries of photos, and a range of so-called entertainment content. The result is what the network describes as a "community where users can do everything from plan their weekends to connect up with friends to discover new music."

When MySpacers log onto the network, they can see who else is online and available for a chat. They can reach out to existing friends, or strike up conversations with potential new ones. They can access another member's profile just by clicking on that person's name or photo. They can read and comment on the intra-network blogs they subscribe to, and post to their own. They can play games online with other members, view videos, listen to and share music, and participate in group activities. MySpace video content ranges from user-generated videos to actual programming.

Signing Up

A MySpace membership is free, and signing up is simple. You must be at least fourteen years old and have a valid e-mail address, an Internet connection, and a web browser. From the MySpace home page click on "Sign Up," and then fill out the Sign Up for MySpace form.

As soon as you fill out the form, you'll be sent to Find Your Friends on the MySpace dialog box. (You can start searching for friends here, or skip this step.) This feature taps into your existing e-mail contacts to search for members you might already know. As a security measure, MySpace will ask you to return a message sent to your e-mail address.

Next, MySpace presents you with a chance to add music, videos, and applications to your account. Keep in mind that adding apps gives the third-party makers of those applications access to your display name, public photos, and friends list. You can skip this step and search for them later. Click "Continue," and you're off and running.

Your Basic Profile

The first thing MySpace asks you to do is to upload a profile picture "so that your friends can recognize you." You also have the option of taking a photo with your webcam on the spot. Or you can skip this step and add a photo later. Photos must be less than 5MB in size, but several file formats are supported, including JPEG, GIF, BMP, TIFF, and PNG.

It's easy to upload a photo: just click "Browse" and MySpace allows you to search a folder on your computer for a photo. Once you find one you like, click on the photo, then click "Upload," and MySpace adds it to your profile. You can revisit this option any time to add more photos, but be sure to follow the rules (no nudity, nothing sexually explicit, nothing violent or offensive, and no pictures copyrighted by others).

With the next page you begin creating our basic profile. MySpace asks a series of questions about where you live and where you went to school. These questions are designed to provide a basic background that allows other members of similar background to find you. How much personal information to include in a social networking profile is always a highly individual decision. You can add the information requested, or skip it for now and add it later.

Your Home Page

Your Home page serves as a kind of personal command center. This page is a completely private space visible only to you. From here you can edit your profile, upload photos and videos, deal with your e-mail and blog, search for and interact with friends, find applications, access music features, launch games, adjust your settings, and just generally control your presence in the MySpace network.

Start by clicking the "Edit Profile" link under the Hello greeting. This opens the profile editor, which gives you access to a list of pages where you add information about yourself. The About Me page, for example, asks you to write a little description of yourself and the people you'd like to meet in MySpace. The Interests page asks you to list your favorite music, movies, TV shows, books, and personal heroes. The Basic Info page is where you access your contact information and the photos you've uploaded for your profile. The Headline box is where you write a personal blurb, which gets displayed with your photo.

As you go through this list, keep in mind that you don't have to fill in every blank. MySpace would argue that the more complete your information, the richer your experience on the network will be. There's a Schools page and a Companies page, both of which ask for fairly innocuous information. But the Details page gets pretty personal, asking about your dating interests, your race, your religion, and your sexual orientation, among other things. A good rule of thumb anytime you're considering the personal information options of any social network: Include only the things you're comfortable sharing with the world.

When you're finished, click on "View My Profile" in the menu bar and you'll see the MySpace page you're presenting to the network. Notice that the menu bar also includes "Account Settings," which takes you to a page where you can change your contact information and your password, adjust your privacy level, and decide when and how you're notified of MySpace activity.

MySpace Friends

With all the images, music, and video swirling around the MySpace network, it's easy to forget that its main purpose is social networking. And that means finding old friends and making new ones.

Of course, nothing is stopping you from randomly striking up conversations with strangers on MySpace, and plenty of people do that, but MySpace insists that it doesn't encourage this kind of social networking. The idea here is to meet new people with whom you have friends or interests in common. The absolute safest social networking strategy is this: Network only with people you know in the real world.

Finding Friends

To find people you already know on MySpace, hover your cursor over "Friends" in the Home page menu bar to open the drop-down menu, then click on "Find Friends." This opens a search engine that allows you to search for people by their real names, their display names (which can be different, right Scooter?), or their e-mail addresses. If you've been adding friends to your list, MySpace might include the names of some potential mutual friends under "People You May Know." You can also narrow your search by school and areas of interest.

This page also gives you another chance to let MySpace look at your e-mail address book to check for existing members. "Find People You E-mail" provides links to several e-mail clients, including Gmail, Yahoo! Mail, Hotmail, and Outlook, as well as the Windows Live Messenger and the AOL Instant Messaging service.

To search for new friends, click on "Browse People" in the Find Friends drop-down menu. Here you can search by things like gender, age range, relationship status, body type, lifestyle, sexual orientation, and education.

You can also look for friends on so-called fan sites. If you're a fan, too, these are people with whom you already have something in common. Scroll down to the Comments section and click on a photo of a MySpace member, then click "Add to Friends."

In most cases, the people you reach out to need to be invited. You'll be prompted to issue an invitation when you find them through a search, but you can also click on "Invite" in the Find Friends drop-down menu to send a direct invitation to a MySpace member whose e-mail address you already know. You can also search via your e-mail contacts from this page. This is also where you check on the status of an invitation. MySpace will send you an e-mail each time someone accepts a friend invitation.

Managing Friends

MySpace provides several tools for managing your friend lists. You can, for example, edit the order of your lists of Top Friends, send your friends direct updates, and allow only selected updates from friends to appear in your Stream.

MySpacers can leave comments on each other's Profile pages in the Comments sections. By default, all viewers can read these comments, but you may delete any comment, and you can require that all comments be approved by you before they are posted.

You can also delete people from your list, which removes them, but doesn't keep them from sending you messages and seeing the public parts of your Profile page. If you're really interested in cutting ties, you can block former friends from contacting you through MySpace (except in groups). They'll still be able to see the public areas of your Profile Page. If you kiss and make up later, you can unblock and re-add them to your list.

The Stream

MySpace's Stream is the equivalent of Facebook's News Feed. It displays the status updates of your friends on your Home page in a large central column, in reverse chronological order. It also displays their uploaded photos, videos, music playlists, and event announcements (called Bulletins). The MySpace Stream is highly customizable: you can filter what's displayed by content type (blog postings, shared links, status updates, etc.)

At the top of the Steam column, next to your Profile photo, is a box with the message "What do you want to share?" This is where you enter the text of your status updates. Below this box is a row of icons for attaching photos, videos, and web links to your updates. The photo and video commands allow you to upload a photo or video from your computer, or take one on the spot with your webcam. There's also an icon that opens a stunningly long list of "moods" you can attach to your update—everything from "adventurous" to "weird"—along with a selection of animated smiley faces.

MySpace Groups

Groups are extremely popular on MySpace. In fact, the network supports some 10,000 groups in twenty categories. The network includes, for example, nearly 50,000 groups in the Food, Drink & Wine category, nearly 25,000 in the Places & Travel category, and more than 90,000 groups in the Games category.

To find groups that interest you in the MySpace network, hover your cursor over "More" in the menu bar to open the drop-down menu, and then click on "Groups." This opens the Groups Home page, from where you can select from the existing list of group categories, or type in a keyword. Clicking on "Advanced Search" allows you to narrow your keyword search to a specific category, country, and region.

Once you find a group that interests you, joining is simple: Just click on the group to open its Group page, then click the "Join Group" button, which you'll find on that page.

To start your own group, go to the Groups Home page and click on "Create Group." You'll be prompted to provide a brief description, a group name, and a location. Once you get your group set up, you can add images, audio, and video to jazz up the page. You can, of course, invite people to join, and post bulletins about group activities or events.

If you ever need to remove a member, you simply go to the Groups Home page, click on My Groups, click on your group's photo or name to pull up a current membership roster. Then click "Edit Members," find the member in question, and click "Delete Member."

Customizing Your Profile

Your Profile page is what the rest of the MySpace universe sees. The network allows you to use some third-party tools and straight-up web-page technologies to enhance your Profile page, including HyperText Markup Language (HTML) and Cascading Style Sheets (CSS) code.

HTML is a simple, tag-based language used to create web pages. It controls the font colors, styles, and sizes; the background styles and element alignments; and the borders. The files themselves are plain text, which get translated into colorful text and graphics by the web browser.

Web developers use CSS to control designs and layouts across multiple web pages. It allows them, for example, to control such HTML elements as fonts, backgrounds, alignments, and borders from a single style sheet. Changes that occur on one page show up on others. It makes life a lot easier for MySpacers with multi-page Profiles.

The Profile Editor

The MySpace profile editor is where you go to choose themes, add layouts, and move or hide elements on the page called "modules." The profile editor is only available if you are using the Profile 2.0 design framework.

Clicking on "Customize Profile" in the menu bar takes you to the profile editor and a number of options for enhancing your profile, including galleries of themes and modules. Clicking on "Appearance" displays 143 themes, which are easy-to-apply, pre-designed home-page layouts. Themes range from abstract designs with labels like "gothic," "cherry," "evil," and "girlie," to photo collages of actors, sports stars, and rockers. As MySpace puts it, "you can change your themes as often as you change your clothes."

QUESTION

What are MySpace Moods?
"Moods" on MySpace are the little emoticons that MySpacers use to convey their current emotional states: happy, sad, confused. The networking service added this feature in 2007, and it has become very popular. Third-party companies offer galleries of emoticons for use on MySpace. Changes of MySpace Moods are called "mood swings."

Clicking on "Modules" opens a gallery of Profile page elements. Some of these, such as Activity Stream, are standard; others, such as Companies, Groups, and Interests, are optional. To add a module to your Profile page, click the plus sign within the module box, then click "Publish."

You can also change the Profile page layout by dragging and dropping modules to other locations, or inserting a layout template. You can add your own photos for a background, change the theme colors, and customize the content area.

Profile Privacy

MySpace gives its members a lot of control over their privacy. Click on "Account Settings," and you'll open a page that allows you to decide whether you want to let people know when you're online, to hide or display your birthday, to block individual members from seeing your profile, and to pick who can view your comments. You can also report spamming messages and account abuse.

Spend some time thinking about your privacy settings, and revisit these options regularly. In other words, *manage* your settings; don't just set 'em and forget 'em.

MySpacers must be at least fourteen years old, and the network takes this restriction seriously. The network will delete profiles of underage members who have lied about their age to get in, as well as fourteen- to seventeen-year-olds who represent themselves as eighteen or older.

ALERT

MySpace allows parents to delete their children's profiles if those kids are under thirteen (not allowed on MySpace); under sixteen with a public profile (not allowed); under eighteen but listed as older (also not allowed); if they display "nudity, obscenity, violence, or hate-based images or content," which are not allowed, period; or if they engage in cyber bullying.

And if you ever feel overwhelmed by the MySpace maelstrom and want to step back for a while, you don't have to delete your carefully constructed Profile page and everything you've built into it. MySpace actually allows you to hide your profile, to just sort of disappear from the network with your profile intact. Just go to the Customize Profile page, click on the padlock, and choose "Just me."

Your Blog

A potential key element of your MySpace identity is your blog. Facebook offers something similar with its Notes application, but the MySpace version is a straight-up, intra-network blog.

To create your own MySpace blog, start from your Page, hover your cursor over Profile in the menu bar to open a drop-down menu. Click on "My Blog." Find "Post New Blog" and click on it. You'll open something that looks a lot like an e-mail form. Enter a title for your first blog in the Subject box. You can also pick a category if you like. Now click in the Body window and start typing. Commands along the bottom of this window allow you add photos, videos, and links to other websites. Click on "Preview & Post" to see what you've created before anyone else does. If you're happy, click "Post;" if not click "Edit."

You have control over who sees your blog. The Public setting allows everyone to read it; "Diary" turns your blog into a private, for-your-eyes-only journal; click "Friends" to show your blog only to the people on your friends list; and "Preferred List" allows you to show your blog to a group of people you specify.

To see a long list of MySpace blogs you might like to subscribe to, click "Most Popular Blogs," which takes you to a long list of popular blogs, listed by categories ranging from fashion to food, games to movies.

MySpace Media

Music, videos, games, and even television programming are a big part of the MySpace experience. Music in particular is huge on MySpace, and the network has become the epicenter of a thriving music scene. MySpacers can listen to millions of songs and create both public and private playlists.

You can upload songs you own or buy them from MySpace Music, and add them to your Profiles and play them on a pop-up music player module the network provides. You can create and publish playlists and share them with friends. You can promote the music and artists you like through the iLike Sidebar, a plug-in for iTunes and Windows Media Player. You can even track concert schedules and buy tickets.

MySpace Music

Clicking on "Music" in the menu bar takes you to the MySpace Music page. This is the MySpace digital music service, which features a catalog of music and videos that are available for download or streaming to your Home page. You can buy concert tickets here, merchandise, and engage in "other music-related commerce." The site also includes links to artist pages; you can even add the artists to your friends list.

Creating a playlist is easy: Click on the plus sign next to a song, and you'll open a dialog box for adding that song to your playlist. You can add it to an existing list, or create a new one on the spot. You also have the option to make that list private.

MySpace allows you to create "an infinite number" of playlists, each of which can hold up to 100 songs, at no charge. Once you create a playlist, click on "Music" in the menu bar to open the MySpace Music page, then click "My Music" to access your playlists.

You can search for music by artist, album, or genre, and access artists' Profile pages. Read the artists' biographies, listen to their songs and watch their videos, as well as download them to your profile page. You can also post comments and in some cases become "friends" with the band.

MySpace Videos

MySpace users can record and upload their own videos to the network, and they do so at the startling rate of about 80,000-plus videos every twenty-four hours, according to the company. To upload a video, click "Video" in the menu bar. This takes you to the video section of the MySpace Music site. You'll notice just below the main menu bar two commands shown in red: "Upload" and "Record." Click "Upload" and you'll be able to browse your computer for video files. The videos must be under 500 MB.

Simply select the file and click "Upload Video." As the file loads, add a title, a description, a category, and tags if you wish. You have to check the box that says you agree to the terms and conditions under which MySpace allows the upload. Clicking on "Show optional settings" gives you options for making the video private or public, and for choosing who you want to share it with. Now the video goes into your My Videos folder.

If you want to record a video, you must have a webcam installed. You just click on "Record a Video," and follow the prompts. MySpace allows you up to twenty minutes of recording time directly from the website.

TV on MySpace

Along with a gigantic catalog of music videos, the MySpace Video page lists actual commercial content, including television programs, which you can watch without paying a fee. This so-called licensed content is primarily short-form video from the likes of TMZ, Atomic Wedgie, and clips from the Discovery Channel and the E! Cable Channel. But thanks to partnerships with YouTube and Hulu, MySpace is also featuring clips from such prime time shows as *Bones*, *MadTV*, and *30 Rock*.

CHAPTER 7

Friendster: The Social Network That Started It All

Before there was Facebook or MySpace, there was Friendster (*www.friendster.com*). Launched two years before the former and four years before the latter, Friendster is arguably the first of the modern social networks. Although its light faded in the United States, Friendster is still dazzlingly popular in Southeast Asia, and some web watchers believe the service is poised for an American comeback. If you're interested in trying out the service that got the social-networking ball rolling, here's what you need to know to make the most of your Friendster experience.

The First Web 2.0 Social Network

Facebook and MySpace command the current social networking spotlight in the United States, but they weren't always the favorite sons of the social web. Before they were a gleam in their creators' eyes, there was Friendster. Despite a reputation in America as a failed enterprise, it's still one of the world's most popular social networking services, and it was arguably the first of the modern breed.

A Circle of Friends

Friendster was the brainchild of former Netscape software engineer Jonathan Abrams, who founded the network initially as a dating site. The story goes that he developed the site to create an online network that wasn't as "creepy" as existing dating sites, one that more closely resembled the way people met in the real world. His model was what is known as *degrees of separation*, then popularized by the movie *Six Degrees of Separation*. The idea is that no one on the planet is more than six people away from anyone else. Essentially, Abrams set out to develop a network made of friends and friends of friends. He soon dropped the dating focus, and the site evolved into a modern social network.

FACT

Friendster is a blend of "friend" and "Napster." Today Napster is an online music service that sells MP3s, but back then it was an online social network for sharing music files. (The original Napster was shut down for violating copyright.)

Abrams launched Friendster in 2002, reportedly from a server in his living room, and during its first few months of operation, signed up an estimated three million users. It also grabbed early buzz—*deafening* buzz—and lots of press. It was the subject of articles in *Time*, *Vanity Fair*, and *Esquire*. Abrams even appeared as a guest on the late-night talk show *Jimmy Kimmel Live*.

Patented Pioneer

Friendster received one of the first social networking patents, for its "system, method, and apparatus for connecting users in an online computer system." That patent was awarded by the U.S. Patent Office in 2006. By mid-2010, Friendster, Inc. had received five social networking patents, covering many of the key components of social networking, including establishing connections, sharing and distributing content, managing connections over time, assessing compatibility between users, and sharing information with third party databases.

Friendster also pioneered several features that are standard social networking capabilities today, including comment boards, testimonial boards, shared photos, and blogs connected to users' accounts. And the social network often gets credit for originating the idea of forming social groups around bands, which would later become MySpace's meat and potatoes.

ESSENTIAL

As pioneering blogger and social software expert Tom Coates has defined it, social media support, extend, or derive added value from human social behavior. The groups of individuals gathered in this environment have been called "smart mobs." Author James Surowiecki has described this kind of collective intelligence as "the wisdom of crowds."

How It Makes Money

Friendster has been generating its revenue through advertising and sponsorships for many years. It's acquisition in late 2009 by MOL Global (more on this later) opened up new revenue streams. A new payment platform provided by MOL allowed the network to begin selling virtual gifts, goods, and games—something Facebook and MySpace already have in place.

Rise and Fall . . . and Rise

About a year after its debut, Friendster showed up on Google's radar, and the search engine giant tried to buy it, reportedly for $30 million. But Abrams decided not to sell his Silicon Valley startup, according to reports at the time, on advice from several well-respected local venture capitalists. Friendster's subsequent slide from U.S. popularity made that decision seem like a bad one to a lot of industry watchers.

In 2006, in an article entitled "Wallflower at the Web Party," *New York Times* reporter Gary Rivlin described Friendster as "a company that is shorthand for potential unmet." And that about sums up the company's rep in the United States today. It was a groundbreaker, and a first mover, but it has been so overshadowed by MySpace and Facebook that few seem to remember how popular Friendster once was in this country.

Plenty of people have speculated on the cause of Friendster's fall. It was shortsighted management, slow page delivery, bad advice from investors, buggy technology, or failure to keep up with popular features. Or all of it. The answer is probably in there somewhere.

However, what too often gets lost in the cautionary tale of Friendster's fall is that its failure to maintain a market lead in this country was *not* the end of the story. If its published membership numbers are to be believed, Friendster now has more users than MySpace. Its founders didn't become billionaires, but the network is still going strong.

Southeast Asia's Favorite

Facebook and MySpace grabbed the lion's share of the U.S. social networking market after 2004, but Friendster continued to rack up respectable membership numbers in other parts of the world. The social network claimed a membership of 110 million in early 2010, which puts it way behind Facebook (nearly 500 million), but neck-and-neck with MySpace (100 million), and well ahead of LinkedIn (60 million).

In 2010, William Shatner, best known for his portrayal of Captain Kirk in the Star Trek television series and movies, launched a sci-fi-themed social network. Called MyOuterSpace, the splashy network targets sci-fi fans who'd like to pursue careers as writers, game designers, animators, or actors specializing in science fiction, horror, and/or fantasy. Members become citizens of "planets" and submit resumes to projects called "starships."

According to the web traffic watchers at Alexa.com, the United States currently accounts for less than 10 percent of Friendster's visitors. The social networking site draws most of its traffic from Southeast Asia. Almost a third of its visitors live in the Philippines according to Alexa; about 15 percent live in Indonesia; India and Malaysia account for about 5 percent each; nearly 4 percent live in South Korea; nearly 3 percent live in Japan; and China and Singapore each account for just over 2 percent.

Acquisition

In October 2009, Friendster announced a partnership with MOL Global, a Malaysian online payments company, whose software would run a new feature, the Friendster Wallet. This new feature allowed members to purchase services and products on Friendster using stored account balances of Friendster Coins. The Wallet also supports a variety of payment methods including prepaid cards, mobile payments, online payments, and credit card payments.

This was a key addition to the network's capabilities. As Friendster explained at the time: "Since most youth consumers in Asia do not possess credit cards, the availability of alternate payment methods is essential for Friendster's core user base to spend and transact within the community."

Few were surprised when, two months later, this partnership turned into a merger, and MOL Global announced that it would be acquiring Friendster. The operations of the online payment company and the social network would be combined to create "Asia's largest end-to-end content, distribution, and commerce network," the companies said.

Makeover

Just before the merger announcement, Friendster unveiled a full-scale makeover. The old-school social network was suddenly sporting a new layout, a new color scheme, a new slogan, and a new logo. The word at the time was that Friendster was trying to attract a younger crowd, aiming for sixteen- to twenty-four-year-olds. And the ad campaign reflected this strategy: "Nobody wants to hang out some place plain and boring!" declared a narrator over shots of attractive, hip Asian youths crowding around a laptop.

Lots of web watchers suggested that the new Friendster layout resembled Facebook, which was hardly a revelation; many social networks are starting to look like Facebook. But the design is cleaner and simpler, emphasizing the most popular features. In the new Friendster, every user's logged-in home page includes a redesigned network activity Stream and Shoutout publishing box, which together make it easier to keep track of what other members are doing, what content is being shared, and what new photos have been uploaded, among other things. Each user also has a new Shoutout history page, called the Shoutout Stream, where Shoutouts are aggregated. Friendster members and their friends can check the Shoutout Stream to view the ones they missed when they were originally posted.

The new Friendster puts a lot of emphasis on customization features. Every user can select a home and profile page color scheme. There's also a Friendster skins directory, from which you can choose among forty layout themes and templates. And you can upload your own images, designs, and colors. Friendster also simplified the site's other pages, including the Friends, Messages, Comments, Photo Browsing, and Photo Uploading pages.

Friendster's Newest Features

The new Friendster Wallet was an important part of the social network's makeover. Based on MOL's MOLeTopUp online micropayment system for content and services, it supports the two other big feature additions: The Friendster Gift Shop and Friendster Games.

The Friendster Gift Shop is another feature with a cultural framework. As Ben Dunn, Friendster's vice president and global head of brand experience, explained it: "As public displays of affection are an important part of the culture in Southeast Asia, Friendster is in the perfect position to make gift giving even more visible and easier for our millions of users."

FACT

In 2010, Friendster formed a strategic partnership with the Southeast Asian branch of Yahoo! to integrate product features from that Internet-services company with the social network. The deal put a Friendster app on the Yahoo! website, promotional placements for Yahoo! products on Friendster, enhanced search results for Friendster user profiles and Friendster Fan Profiles within Yahoo! Search, and the ability of Friendsters to link their accounts on the social network with their Yahoo! accounts.

Network members can go to the gift shop to "send personal gestures of kindness, celebrate significant accomplishments, and recognize friends and family on special days, like birthdays, or just for fun." The gift shop opened with an inventory of virtual gifts in a number of categories, including birthday, collectible, greeting, premium, romance, seasonal, and "thank you," among others.

Gaming has emerged as an import component of social networking, and Friendster has jumped on that bandwagon with Friendster Games. It's an in-network gaming destination with all the features you've come to expect from Facebook and MySpace. Some Friendster games are available for free through the Fun menu item on the navigation bar; others you have to purchase with your Friendster Wallet. Among the site's most popular games are *Mario's Adventure*, *Naughty Classroom*, and *The Farmer*, which is similar to Facebook's *FarmVille*.

Friendster Basics

Getting started on Friendster is easy. Membership is free, but you must be at least fifteen years old to join, and the site requires you to provide a valid e-mail address. To sign up, point your web browser to the Friendster Home page, enter your e-mail address, and click "Join Now." You'll have to respond to a confirming e-mail as Friendster verifies your e-mail.

Verifying your e-mail takes you to the Create Your Account page, where you enter your name, create a password, and provide some personal information. Click "Register" and you're in. You'll have the usual opportunities to add photos and other components to your user profile, to allow the network to trawl your contacts for other members, and you can also publish your updates to a Yahoo! account.

Your Friendster Profile

Friendster allows you to customize your profile in a number of ways. Click on "Profile" on the green navigation bar to open your Profile page. Then click on "Edit Profile" to open a page that gives you access to all your personal information options. Click on the "Main" tab and you'll see your basic information list (names, birthday, gender) along with some status items (single, married, interested in dating men, just looking around, etc.), your city and country, your occupation, your favorite TV shows, and your education, among others. Fill out this page with as much information or a little as you'd like. Only your name, birthday, gender, and country are required.

Click on the "College" tab and you'll see a form for including up to three colleges in your profile. The School tab allows you to display three other schools.

Click on the "Custom" tab and you'll have access to Friendster's new skins directory. You can select one of these pre-designed backgrounds, or design your own using CSS and the HTML. You can also add music and videos to your profile. Just paste the URL for the file you'd like to add, and the media content will appear in your Media Box.

The profile page includes a newly redesigned About Me section at the top next to a larger version of your Home page photo. You'll also find a Treasure Chest illustration that displays the number of gifts you have received, and links you directly to the Gift Shop. And there's the familiar list of your shoutouts and comments.

Once you set up your profile, you'll see the changes reflected in your Home page. This is home base for Friendsters. It was redesigned during the makeover, and now supports a number of customization options. You can give your Home page and your top navigation bar a color. Your notifications for new Friend Requests, Comments, and Messages are displayed in a navigation panel on the left side of the page. And your friends' upcoming birthdays and the latest bulletins from your network are shown on the right. The right-hand panel also features two ad windows.

Your Friendster Friends

Friendster provides a number of options for adding friends to your network. You can send an invitation via e-mail by clicking on "Friends" in the navigation bar to open your Friends page. In the My Friends menu box on the left, click on "Invite Friends" and you'll open an e-mail form page. Friendster supports several online e-mail services, so you can invite friends from, say, your Yahoo! or Hotmail address books. If you don't use any of these services, you can enter the e-mail address manually by clicking on "Enter e-mail addresses manually." If your friend accepts your invitation, she will be added to your network.

You can also perform what's called a "user search," which sends the Friendster search engine out to look up existing Friendster members. You can search by name or e-mail address. If you find the person you're looking for, you add him as a friend, which sends him a notice of your invitation on the network. If he accepts, he's on your list. The easiest way to invite someone to join your network is by clicking on the Add Person as Your Friend link on his profile page.

Your Activity Stream and Shoutouts

The Friendster Activity Stream is the equivalent of Facebook's News Feed, and MySpace's Stream. It displays the messages, status updates, and announcements of your friends and all the events happening within your Friendster network. It shows the latest messages from your friends, as well as the photos they upload, the new apps they install, the comments they receive, the gifts they get, and the new friends they add. You can add comments to each of these items, and add the same friends and apps they have added.

Friendster status updates are called "Shoutouts." You post a Shoutout on Friendster by typing in the box near the top of your Home page "Tell your friends what you're doing now . . . ." It's just like Facebook's "What's on your mind?" (Though nobody's saying who invented what here.) Friendster calls this box "the Publisher."

Clicking "View All" on your Home page takes you to the Shoutout Stream, which displays all your Shoutouts and comments to your Shoutouts. Friendster now allows your friends to comment on your Shoutouts, and you can comment back. Friendster provides features that allow you to receive e-mail notifications when friends comment on your Shoutouts, and when someone comments on Shoutouts you have already commented on.

Additional Features

The Friendster makeover added several new features to the site, but it also gave this lean social networking service a chance to refine and update some existing features, including Groups, its photo-sharing tools, its applications and games catalog, and its blogs and forums.

Friendster Groups

Friendster Groups are collections of network members organized around a common interest or cause. The site hosts thousands of groups covering a truly broad range of topic areas including Health & Fitness, Cities & Neighborhoods, Food, Drink & Wine, Gay, Lesbian & Bi, Sports & Recreation, and Pets & Animals. You can browse the groups by category, or search them by keyword. And anyone can join public groups, but private groups can restrict access. You might be able to join, but you have to ask to be invited by the group's creator.

You have to be a Friendster member for at least seven days to create a group. After that, you just hover your cursor over the Fun tab in the navigation bar, and then select "Groups" in the drop-down menu. Then fill out the form on the Create Groups page.

Friendster Photos

Friendster upgraded its photo-sharing features during the makeover. The network now allows its members to upload 1,000 photos per day. Photo comments are more prominent "so sharing thoughts with friends around photos is easier." There's also a new photo module on the Profile page, larger photo albums on the Photo Albums page, a photo-album-sharing option, and a faster and improved photo-uploader program.

The social networking service also supports not only photo sharing, but also photo-album sharing, both with Friendster friends, and with friends and family not on the network. You just go to your photo albums, choose the album you want to share, and click the "Share" link under the album cover. You then enter the e-mail address or addresses of the people you want to share the album with, and click "Share."

QUESTION

What is SMO?
If you're into web marketing, you've heard of Search Engine Optimization (SEO). The advent of social media marketing has generated another web marketing term: Social Media Optimization (SMO).

Friendster has also added a new option that allows you to receive an e-mail notice whenever your name is tagged on your friends' photos. It is highly recommended that you avail yourself of this option.

Friendster Apps

Friendster uses "apps" and "widgets" as synonyms, but whatever you call them, they're the same kind of third-party software programs you might find in Facebook's Applications repository. They can be games, photo slide-shows, and media players, among other things.

You add applications to your profile by hovering your cursor over the Fun tab in the navigation bar. This activates a drop-down menu. Click "Apps" in that menu and you'll open a software repository of hundreds of applications. You'll find everything from SocialHub, a video upload tool, to the *War2* massively multiple online role-playing game. Apps are listed by Most Popular, New Releases, Alphabetical, and My Apps.

Blogs and Forums

Friendsters can publish their own blogs on the network, and read the blog postings of other members. They use blogs to publish their running thoughts on life, as journals of life experience, as running commentary on specific subjects, as vehicles for offering information to others, and even as family newsletters.

Starting your own blog on the network is easy. Just hover your cursor over the Fun tab in the navigation, and then select "Blogs" in the drop-down menu. Now just type in a name or descriptive title in the box and click "Create a blog." Friendster actually gives you a unique URL in the form of MyBlog.blog.friendster.com. This means that anyone on the web could see it, depending on the settings you chose. This is a very cool extra feature that provides a safe home base for anyone who's thought about blogging.

Friendster also hosts forums and discussion boards that cover a wide range of topics. Anyone can read Friendster forum posts, but only users with verified e-mail addresses can create their own topics, post messages, and reply to messages posted by other Friendster users.

Privacy Settings

Friendster is, of course, a social environment where people not only share their lives with existing friends and family members, but meet and interact with new people. But here, as on every social network you join, you must tend your privacy settings.

Friendster is a relatively lean social network, and its privacy settings are correspondingly basic. You can decide whether to accept friend requests automatically, whether to display your last name on your profile page, whether you want to view other profiles anonymously, who you'll allow to view your full profile (just friends, or friends of friends, too), who can send you messages (just friends, or friends of friends, too), and whether to show your birthday to your friends.

It's not a sophisticated set of options, and not nearly as confusing as Facebook's options once were. So it's a good news-bad news situation. It also means that you have no excuse not to look over these settings from time to time. Be open. Be friendly. And be careful.

CHAPTER 8

LinkedIn: The Social Network for Professionals

People were building and maintaining professional relationships long before there was such a thing as web-based social networking. But anyone who isn't online today taking advantage of the efficiencies and sheer scope of these services is simply going to be left in the dust by the competition. LinkedIn (*www.linkedin.com*) is the oldest and largest social network developed specifically for business and professional networking. It's a user-friendly service, but it's not without its quirks. Here's what you need to get started and make the most of this powerful networking tool.

"Relationships Matter"

LinkedIn is the world's leading social networking service for businesspeople and professionals. A LinkedIn membership is free, as are memberships in most of the leading social networks, but unlike Facebook and MySpace, LinkedIn is focused on career and business connections. LinkedIn's motto, "relationships matter," refers strictly to relationships in a work context.

This isn't the network you join to post your vacation photos, re-connect with your high school sweetheart, or share the latest release from Vampire Weekend. This is the network you join to promote your career, find a sales lead, connect with business partners, supplement a job search, offer job opportunities, and just generally nurture your relationships with professional colleagues, customers, clients, and enterprise associates. One of the great strengths of the LinkedIn network is its focus on professional connections, and all its networking features are geared to that purpose.

The Most Connected Man in Silicon Valley

LinkedIn was founded by in 2002 by Reid Hoffman, Allen Blue, Jean-Luc Vaillant, and Konstantin Guericke. Hoffman is the most high-profile name in that group. A former executive at PayPal (before it was sold to eBay) and the company's founding CEO, Hoffman is a well-known high-tech entrepreneur who has been called "the most connected man in Silicon Valley." He has said that LinkedIn grew out of his own early interest in technologies that enable and enhance social connections.

Hoffman's interest in social media in general is wide-ranging. He has been involved as an investor in or advisor of more than sixty startup companies, including such social media superstars as Facebook, Zynga, Flickr, and Digg, among others. His first company, SocialNet, was mostly about online dating, but it included some features that more closely resembled the offerings of modern social networks.

A Slow Start

LinkedIn didn't blast off like MySpace, and it doesn't yet command the vast membership numbers of Facebook, but this specialized social network experienced a significant growth spurt in 2008 that got a lot of attention from web watchers. Some industry wags even called 2008 "The Year of LinkedIn."

By the first quarter of 2009, the network was claiming more than 36 million users. A year later LinkedIn membership was passing the 60 million mark. According to the company, LinkedIn now adds a new member every second, and industry prognosticators are expecting it to go public any minute.

In 2010 LinkedIn announced that it would be establishing its international headquarters in Dublin, Ireland. "Being based in Dublin gives us access to a highly skilled workforce and enables us to coordinate our business growth across Europe and beyond to deliver the best possible service to our members," Kevin Ayres, LinkedIn's managing director in Europe, said in the statement at the time.

The "Freemium" Model

LinkedIn's business strategy is sometimes called the "freemium" model. It combines the free membership and bundle of networking tools with subscription-based premium services. The company also makes money on advertising.

In 2008, LinkedIn launched an application developer network and released an API, which lets third-party software makers connect their apps with LinkedIn profiles and networks. The company also provides a set of widgets designed to allow app developers to add the most used LinkedIn features to their offerings with a few lines of JavaScript.

LinkedIn's premium services (which can be accessed by clicking "Upgrade Your Account" at the bottom right of your Home page) are bundled into three account levels: Business, Business Plus, and Pro. Each provides some level of access to InMail, deeper and more saved searches, access to the Profile Organizer, a Who's Viewed My Profile feature, a Premium Badge, and the Open Link Network.

A Platform for a Professional Presence

LinkedIn is a career and business-oriented social networking service that was created specifically for professional and occupational networking. Members build profiles that are essentially professional biographies in which they throw a spotlight on their expertise, credentials, and accomplishments. One of the great strengths of the LinkedIn network is its focus on professional connections, and all its networking features are geared to that purpose.

The network is occasionally mischaracterized as a professional matchmaking service, but that label misses the mark by a mile. It's also sometimes compared to services such as Plaxo, which is a great online address book with social networking capabilities that's well worth taking for a test drive, if you don't already use it. But it's much more accurate to describe LinkedIn as a platform for a professional presence.

As LinkedIn puts it, this is "an interconnected network of experienced professionals from around the world . . . . You can find, be introduced to, and collaborate with qualified professionals that you need to work with to accomplish your goals."

Who's Using It and How?

According to LinkedIn, the average member of this network is a college-educated forty-three-year-old making upwards of $100,000 a year. Members use the network primarily to manage their professional connections and nurture their professional relationships. It's also a vehicle for presenting a professional face to the world—it gives you a kind of control console for the professional information that is published about you.

LinkedIn members use the tools the network provides to assemble their existing contacts in a web-based platform that is much more powerful and feature-rich than the average e-mail account. Those tools also allow members to expand their networks, to discover and establish new connections with prospective customers and colleagues. They also use the network to share professional expertise, to ask questions, and offer answers.

LinkedIn allows you ask for help from potentially millions of specialists and authorities in your field who have actually volunteered to respond. And those experts use LinkedIn so that they can expand their own reputations and reach—to, as they say, increase their visibility. And many members use LinkedIn to research clients before sales calls.

Job/Candidate Search

In its March 2010 issue, *Fortune* magazine reported that consulting firm Accenture planned to hire 50,000 people that year. The company's head of global recruiting, John Campagnino, told the magazine that he planned to make as many as 40 percent of those hires through social media.

ESSENTIAL

Don't forget to include your picture in your profile. Virtually every marketing strategist out there flogging tips and tricks for improving your LinkedIn results insists on it. Why? People don't do business with the faceless, and employers don't hire them, either.

There's no doubt that employers are using social networks to publish and circulate job postings, and job seekers use those networks to respond to them. LinkedIn provides several job features, which you can access directly from your home page, including tools for posting job openings, searching for positions, and managing your job/candidate search.

LinkedIn enhanced its job search capabilities in early 2010 with a new feature called Real-Time Profile Matches. This feature uses a proprietary technology to search the network's membership for likely candidates for job postings. The search is launched as soon as the job is posted, and it returns up to twenty-four pre-qualified matches, displayed for the job poster in business-card format. The job poster can then reach out directly to the members.

The idea is to make it faster and easier for users of the service to find the right job opportunities, and for potential employers to find the right job candidates. If you want to make sure that you are included in the search, you must have a complete, up-to-date profile. In particular, the Experience, Skills, and Summary sections must be filled out, and you need to include a Professional Headline. Then, use the Status Update feature to indicate that you're looking for a job and are available.

As of this writing, the new feature was available on the network as a "beta," which is a version that's just about ready for prime time, but might still have a few kinks to straighten out. Although the beta was offered as a free service, access to the final version would most likely require a fee.

Separating the Personal and the Professional

One clear advantage of the LinkedIn network is that it provides a distinct separation between your personal networking and your professional networking. LinkedIn co-founder Reid Hoffman has said that he believes most people who use social networking will belong to at least two, and maybe more, networks. Facebook and MySpace have their advantages for business, but the lines in those environments are blurred. LinkedIn keeps things sharp, and distinctly uncluttered in a purposeful space for pros to network.

LinkedIn is about managing and improving ongoing professional connections. It's about evaluating potential employees, reconnoitering companies and customers, and tracking the careers of colleagues. It's about increasing your exposure to opportunities and potential alliances. It's about keeping up with events in your industry. It's about advancing your career.

The LinkedIn Facelift

In November 2009, LinkedIn began tinkering with a redesign of its website. The result was a much cleaner, more Facebook-like Home page. A global navigation bar at the top of the page takes you to your profile, your contacts list, your groups, job listings, your inbox, and other features. The center of the page is taken up with a column of members' status updates. Other features and a bit of advertising take up a column on the right.

My Connections

One of the most elegant interface changes implemented by LinkedIn can be seen in the way it now allows you to access your contact information. Hover your cursor over "Contacts" to activate a drop-down menu, and click "My Connections." You'll open a page that provides a column of mini-profiles of your connections that include a picture and their current positions. It's a nice view for scrolling quickly through your contact list to see if anyone has changed jobs.

QUESTION

What is the OpenLink Network?
If you pay for the Business Plus or Pro premium accounts, you have access to the OpenLink Network. This network within a network provides an additional level of access to LinkedIn members interested in meeting new people. Essentially, it allows unlimited direct contacts, via OpenLink messages, to anyone else with the service.

Clicking on a mini-profile opens an expanded view of that contact that shows the number of his connections and new contacts, e-mail address, and tags. Clicking the e-mail opens your e-mail so you can send your contact a message that way; clicking on "Send a Message" takes you to an in-mail message form. Clicking on "Edit tags" allows you to not only select or deselect from the standard tag group (classmates, colleagues, friends, group members, and partners), but add a custom tag. You also have access here to your contact's contacts.

A menu on the left tells you how many contacts you have by company, location, industry, recent activity, and even tags. You can see how many people in your contact list you've indentified as colleagues, for example, or how many work for IBM, are located in your city, or work in public relations. You can also see how many of your contacts are new, and how many of your contacts have new contacts. From here you can also import contacts, organize profiles into folders, add notes to contact information, and track important profiles in a dedicated workspace.

Status Updates

The Home page also includes a Status Update window that's very similar to what you see on Facebook. This optional feature allows you to post a status update, which LinkedIn says is driven by the question, "What are you working on?" (On Facebook, it's the answer to the question, "What's on your mind?")

You can choose how many people see your status updates. LinkedIn allows you to make your status visible to your connections, your network, or everyone who visits your public profile. If you allow your connections to see your updates, they are posted on their home pages under Network Activity. Those connections may then comment on your status.

Twitter Link

LinkedIn is now integrated with the Twitter microblogging service—which means you can send a tweet from your Home page. You link the two accounts from the Edit Profile page. Just click on "Add Twitter account" and follow the prompts. Once you've linked the two accounts, a Twitter icon will appear next to the status update box. Now you simply enter your 140-character message and click the icon, and it will appear in the twitterstream. The link between the two accounts also allows you to update your LinkedIn status through Twitter.

LinkedIn Basics

It's easy to get started on LinkedIn. You simply point your browser to the Linked In website, type in your name, e-mail address, and a password into the boxes under "Join LinkedIn Today," and then click "Join Now." You'll be asked a few questions that'll give you a sense of the focus of the network: Are you employed, a business owner, a student, or someone looking for work? At which company do you work, at which school are you a student, or in which industry are you seeking employment? What's the name of the company you work for or own, or the school you attend? You'll also be asked to enter a country and a zip code.

Now you'll have an opportunity to import your contacts from your e-mail accounts. Providing access to your e-mail client (Gmail, Hotmail, Outlook, etc.) allows the network to see if anyone you know is already a member. You can skip this step and come back to it later. You'll also have to confirm your e-mail address. LinkedIn sends you a message and a link, to which you must respond to continue the sign up process. Once you do, you're in. LinkedIn has a premium e-mail service, InMail, that allows Linked In members to send a limited number of private messages directly to other members, whether they are connected or not.

Account Types

LinkedIn provides its users with a free account that's bursting with features, but if you're willing to spend some money, you can get even more. Here's a rundown of the features of the different account types. (The monthly fees listed here are, of course, subject to change.)

The Standard Personal Account

This one is free. It allows you to have five introductions open at a time, permits you to receive an unlimited number of InMail messages (though you can't send any), save three searches with weekly alerts, and view 100 results per search.

The Business Account

For about $25 a month, you get to send up to three InMails per month (unused credits carry over up to nine), save five searches with weekly alerts, have fifteen introductions open at a time, view 300 results per search, use the Profile Organizer feature, have access to the OpenLink Network and unlimited messaging within it, exploit unlimited reference searches, and "access additional search refinements."

The Business Plus Account

For about $50 a month, you get to send ten InMails per month (with up to thirty unused credits rolling over), seven saved searches with weekly alerts, twenty-five introductions open at a time, view 500 results per search, use the Profile Organizer and twenty-five folders, have access to the Open-Link Network and unlimited messaging within it, exploit unlimited reference searches, and "access additional search refinements."

The Pro Plan

For about $500 a month, you get to send fifty InMails per month (up to 150 rollovers), ten saved searches, forty open intros, view 700 results per search, use the Profile Organizer and twenty-five folders, have access to the OpenLink Network and unlimited messaging within it, exploit unlimited reference searches, and "access additional search refinements."

Your Profile

No one on LinkedIn is there to look up your favorite movies or music, but they are very interested in your professional qualifications, your job history, and recommendations from employers, colleagues, and customers. In fact, those three things constitute your basic LinkedIn profile.

Remember that your LinkedIn profile is a summary of your professional accomplishments, not your resume. These are slightly different animals. A resume targets a specific job; your LinkedIn profile is what the network calls "your public face." This is what anyone who logs onto LinkedIn and searches for your name will see (though the network does allow you to hide parts of it from non-members).

ALERT

Your profile is most effective when it's highly professional. Don't include anything you wouldn't want the people you work with to see. And all the experts recommend strongly that you don't lie; a lot of people are going to see this, and your chances of getting caught—and embarrassed—are quite high.

To begin building your basic profile, hover your cursor over "Profile" in the menu bar and click on "Edit Profile" in the drop-down menu. This opens a page that gives you access to all of the elements of your profile. (Clicking on the "View My Profile" tab shows you what the rest of your network sees.) You've already entered your name, company, and current position, which appear at the top of your profile page. LinkedIn calls this your "snapshot," and likens it to a "next-generation business card."

Along with your snapshot, your LinkedIn profile elements can be edited from this page. "Current" displays the same job information in your snapshot, but you can add another current position, if that's appropriate, or edit the one you signed on with. "Past" is where you list the jobs you've held before your current position. "Education" is where you list the schools you've attended and degrees you've earned. "Recommend" is where you start stacking up the positive blurbs from colleagues, clients, and former employers. "Connection" is another link to your contact list. "Websites" is where you provide your company URLs. You'll also see a link to the new Twitter feature.

Filling out everything on this page, carefully and completely, is going to provide you with the strongest basic profile. If you're not willing to provide your job history, your educational background, and to publish recommendations, there's really no point in being on the network.

That said, it is up to you how much information you share. You might not choose to publish, for example, your phone number, physical address, IM account, birthday, and marital status. If you provide your e-mail address, anyone on your network can reach you.

Your "Headline" is a line of text under your name on your Profile page. LinkedIn calls it your "Professional Headline," which sounds sort of overblown, but actually underscores its genuine importance. This is the first thing people who look at your profile will see, so it's got to be sharp and specific. You create it initially when you fill in your current position during sign up, but you shouldn't be afraid to tweak it later.

Your Network

One of the easiest ways to begin building your LinkedIn network is by using your existing contact list as the foundation. LinkedIn provides several ways to import your contacts from a range of e-mail programs, both from the web (Gmail, Hotmail) and from your desktop (Outlook). No one is automatically added to your LinkedIn contact list, which is called "My Connections." On this network, members have to agree to join. In fact, they have to accept an invitation.

Here's how that works: You hover your cursor over "Contacts" and then click on "Add Connections." This takes you to a form for entering e-mail addresses. Add the e-mail address of the person you'd like to invite, click "Send Invitations," and you're done. That person will get an e-mail that says "I'd like to add you to my professional network on LinkedIn." If they want to join, they click "accept." You'll get an e-mail notice of their decision, one way or the other. If the person you invited is not already on LinkedIn, he or she must join to accept.

All the people on your LinkedIn connections list are known as "first degree" connections. These are the people you know and trust. The contacts on *their* lists are your "second-degree" connections—they're two people away. A third-degree connection is three people away, and so on. (Their profile summaries are marked "2nd" and "3rd" depending on their relationship to you.) If you'd like to add a second-degree connection to your own list, you'll need to ask for an introduction from a mutual contact.

Here's how that works: Find the LinkedIn profile of the person you'd like to meet. Hover your cursor over the profile, and if they're available, a "Get introduced" link will appear on the right. Click on that link and you'll be sent to a form for requesting the introduction. (This only works with second- or third-degree connections.)

LinkedIn members are free to introduce anyone on their contact lists to each other, but they're not required to. An introduction expires after six months, and the number of introductions you're allowed depends on your service level.

Recommendations

LinkedIn advises its members to send Invitations only to people they know and trust—people you work with, you've been to school with, or hired. One reason you really do want to populate your connections list with people who know you is that you want them to *recommend* you.

The Recommendations list is a key component of a complete LinkedIn profile. These things are exactly what they sound like: comments written by other members, in which they sing your praises. The recommendations you receive are visible to members within your network, but also, to Fortune 500 companies that use the LinkedIn Recruiter corporate tool. According to LinkedIn, members with recommendations from co-workers, colleagues, customers, clients, business partners, and former employers "are three times more likely to receive relevant offers and inquiries through searches on LinkedIn."

LinkedIn members can access recommendation options by clicking on "Recommendations" in the Profile drop-down menu. This opens a tabbed page that lists the recommendations you've received and sent. Click on the "Request Recommendations" tab to ask for a thumbs up from the people in your connections list; click the "Sent Recommendations" tab to see a list of the recommendations you have provided. At the bottom of the Received Recommendations page is a place to send recommendations of your own.

LinkedIn has an outstanding Help feature that includes detailed explanations of just about everything you need to know, and many video demonstrations of exactly what to do. Be sure to check out a help entry entitled "10 Ways to Use LinkedIn by Guy Kawasaki." Mr. Kawasaki is the managing director of VC firm Garage Technology Ventures, a former Fellow at Apple Computer, the author of nine books, and an all-around smart guy when it comes to social networking.

CHAPTER 9

Photo Sharing:
A Picture Beats 140 Characters

The web is exploding with images, and an awful lot of them are getting there through social media. Thanks to a relatively new generation of online services, billions of user-generated photos are now live on the web. About two dozen websites specialize in image hosting and/or photo sharing, and more are showing up every day. Most of these services are fairly accessible, but the range of tools and technologies can be confusing. Here's what you need to know to pick the photo-sharing service that's right for you.

What Is Photo Sharing?

"Photo sharing" is what social media mavens call it when you upload your digital photographs to a website equipped with tools for storing, organizing, and displaying them. You share your photos with others by giving them access to your displays. Those others might be your immediate family, fellow users of the website, or the whole world.

The websites are run by image-hosting services that offer their users a number of ways to share their photos, from online albums to slide shows. Memberships in most photo-sharing sites are open to the public, and most offer at least some level of free membership. And many support communities as vibrant as any social network.

Most photo-sharing and image-hosting services are designed with the needs of average shutterbugs in mind, but a few are aimed at professional photographers and others with an interest in selling the images they create. These sites offer fee-based features for marketing and selling a member's images, and some offer revenue-sharing deals. But the top photo-sharing sites prohibit this kind of commercial activity.

QUESTION

What's the difference between "photo sharing" and "image hosting?"
The terms are often used interchangeably, but there's a difference. Photo sharing is about the tools and services that allow you to publish your photos on the web so that your friends and family can see them. Image hosting is about the website where your photos are stored, backed up, and sometimes displayed. Communities have evolved around image-hosting services with photo-sharing capabilities.

Photo Finishers

The current crop of photo-sharing websites evolved from online photo-finishing services that began appearing in the late 1990s. Websites like Ofoto, Shutterfly, and Snapfish came on the scene within a few months of each other to offer customers a new way to order prints of their favorite digital photographs. You simply upload the files to the websites, and the photo finishers created the prints and sent them to you in the mail. Some of these websites also offer film-processing services, and Ofoto even had an online frame shop.

Photo finishing is still one of the services offered at many of today's image hosting sites, and for some, the photo-sharing component seems to be little more than a means of generating print-buying customers. But the most popular photo-sharing sites are all about managing and displaying digital images on the web.

Online Archives

The early print-oriented services established a key component of photo sharing as we know it today: online file storage. Image-hosting sites provide users with space on their servers, not just to tweak and display their pix, but to store their photo files. Some services provide users with specialized desktop software through which they upload and manage their files; some are entirely web-based. But all provide offsite storage and centralized access to your photographs.

In theory at least, your uploaded photos live on secure, backed-up, professionally administered servers forever. No need to grab the family photo albums when the dam breaks or your *flambé* experiment gets away from you in the kitchen. They're all on the web, organized in one spot, and you can get to them from any web browser.

That said, you should *never* rely solely on any photo-sharing or image-hosting site to store your photos. Uploading directly from your camera, when that capability is supported, is fine, but be sure to keep copies on your computer, and back them up.

Pixels for Pay

Some photo-sharing sites are wholly subscription-based, while others offer enhanced services for a fee. And lots of them make money from advertising. But these services also benefit from additional revenue streams unique to their social media niche, including photo finishing; sales of photo-related merchandise, such as picture frames; and such subscription-only capabilities as turning photos into photo books, greeting cards, posters, and calendars.

In recent years, the social networks have been cutting into those revenue streams by snagging some of the photo-upload action—make that *a lot* of the action. In terms of sheer numbers of images uploaded, Facebook has pulled ahead of everybody. At one point, according to comScore, users of the world's leading social network were uploading photos to the website at the rate of 3 billion per month; in 2010 about 65 percent of online photo sharing was actually taking place on Facebook.

Blurring the Lines

Recently, there's been a lot of integration among social media services. Blogger, for example, allows its users to link their blog postings to photos stored on the Flickr image-hosting service. Slides created on the Webshots photo-sharing site can be uploaded to MySpace and LiveJournal. And the market leader, Photobucket, which is owned by Fox Interactive (which owns MySpace) allows users to view and share their public photo albums on Facebook.

And even if the lines between the social media services weren't blurring in this way, the social networks have a long way to go to match the capabilities of the photo-focused sites. Many users don't realize, for example, that the images they upload to their favorite social networks are often stored at lower resolutions, which reduces the photo quality. And if they fail to save copies of those files on their computers, that quality is gone forever. Photo-sharing sites typically maintain file sizes large enough to produce nice, big prints.

The Photoblog

All this intermingling of social media types, plus the advent of the camera phone, has produced an interesting hybrid called a "photoblog." As the name fairly shouts, a "photoblog" is an image-oriented weblog. This combination of blogging and photo sharing includes at least some text, but the emphasis is definitely on the images, which are displayed in the reverse-chronological order of a standard blog.

Photoblogs are hosted on some traditional blogging sites, such as Blogger, on some photo-sharing sites, such as Flickr, and on websites that specialize in this blogging format, such as Fotolog. And some tech-savvy photobloggers prefer to host their picture-posts on their own servers.

Some industry analysts have identified a sub-category of photoblogging called mobile blogging or "moblogging." Essentially, moblogging is the act of uploading photos from your camera phone to a photoblog. But so many of the blogging services and the photo-sharing services now support cell phones as photo sources that the category is becoming obsolete.

Photo-Sharing Basics

The features and options available on photo-sharing services vary, but some of the basics apply to just about all of them. Each one provides a way for you to upload your digital photos to the website. They all provide a place for you to store and organize them. They offer tools for editing, arranging, and displaying your photos. Most provide a way for others to leave comments and tags. And they all support privacy settings that allow you to control who sees your pictures.

If you created the photo, you own the copyright unless you sell it to someone else. Even online. No one can use the photos you own—except in news reporting and other "fair use" circumstances—without your permission.

Uploading Your Photos

Virtually all photo-sharing sites allow you to upload your pictures directly from the website. On Flickr, for example, you can simply click on "Choose photos and videos" to open folders on your desktop computer. Find and click on the image, and you're back on the website. Click on "Upload Photos and Videos," and you're done. Webshots, Photobucket, and many others provide a similar capability.

Some services also provide an optional desktop application to manage your uploads. The Flickr desktop application is called Uploadr; the service says that it's for "heftier uploading needs or offline photo management." The Webshots Uploader provides a manager for your entire photo collection.

A growing number of photo-sharing sites also support uploads directly from mobile phones. The SnapFish Picture Mover program, for example, can upload photos directly from a camera or memory card each time they are connected to your desktop computer. Some allow you to upload from programs developed by third-party providers. And some services even allow you to send photos to the website via e-mail.

Editing Your Photos

All photo-sharing services provide a basic toolbox of photo-editing tools. Red-eye reduction, lighting adjustments, color tuning, cropping options, and a range of special effects are available. You'll find editing commands you might already know from your desktop software, such as "rotate," "resize," "sharpen," and "add text." Look also for "one-click fixes," which provide automatic corrections to a photograph.

Those photo-sharing toolboxes can also contain customizable effects, font galleries, customizable frames, and so-called seasonal shapes (hearts for Valentine's Day, stars for Christmas, etc.)

Managing and Displaying Your Photos

In general, photo-sharing sites allow you to organize your photos into groups and subgroups using descriptive headings, and with keywords called "tags." Photobucket and many others use the "album" metaphor for organizing your pix. Flickr allows you to create "geotags" for your photos as well, using Yahoo! Maps; users can drag their photos over a map and drop them on a site to provide geographic context. Photo-sharing services generally provide some or all of three presentation formats: photo albums, scrapbooks, and slideshows.

"Slideshows" are just what you think they are: sequential displays of your photos. They can be automatic, or require the viewer to click through. They can be designed as standard strip-style slideshows, or employ a range of special effects provided by the service.

Sharing Your Photos

You get to decide who sees your photos and how they are viewed. Most sites allow you to designate whether a photo or group of photos is public or private. Private photos can be seen only by you; public photos can be seen by anyone.

You can, however, give your friends and family access to specific collections of your photos. Typically, you tag those pix "friends and family."

Most photo sharing sites prefer that your folks join up—and it is simpler to designate a fellow member as someone who can see your photos—but not all require them to; friends who aren't in the club can usually view your pix with some kind of "guest pass" or temporary password.

The Services

Image-oriented social media sites come in a range of shapes and sizes and offer an assortment of tools, features, and options. If you had to pick the top three services today, you probably couldn't go wrong with Flickr, Webshots, and Photobucket. But the list of photo-sharing sites and image-hosting services is long and ever evolving. Ofoto, once the premier online photo sharing and finishing website, was acquired by Kodak and renamed, while Flickr kept its name when it was acquired by Yahoo! Some sites, like Webshots and Photobucket, have a high profile, while others, like Multiply, command a small but ardent following. HP now owns Snapfish.

Photobucket

If the sheer number of images stored is any indication, Photobucket (*www.photobucket.com*) is the world's most popular photo-sharing service. The website claims to host around 7 billion images. Launched in 2003 (after Webshots and before Flickr), Photobucket is sometimes recognized as the first big photo-sharing service.

Owned by Fox Interactive Media, Photobucket allows users to upload both photos and videos. It offers a fee account with one gigabyte (1GB) of still-photo storage and five minutes of video. A "pro" account, for which you pay a fee, gives you 10GB of storage and ten minutes of video. And users can upload photos from their cell phones.

You can organize your photos into private, public, and selectively seen albums. And you can add titles and tags to your photos. Other Photobucket members can comment freely on your public photos, and even offer a rating. The service is integrated with MySpace, Facebook, and Blogger, among other social media services, which means that you can display the photos you upload to Photobucket on those sites.

Photobucket offers photo-finishing services, and users can purchase pho-tobooks, posters, T-shirts, mugs, and mousepads adorned with their photos.

Flickr

Another popular image hosting and photo sharing service, Flickr (*www.flickr.com*) claims to host more than 4 billion images. The service debuted in 2004, the offspring of a set of tools originally developed for a massively multiplayer online role-playing game (MMORPG) called *Game Neverending* (which it outlived). Yahoo! bought the service in 2005.

Flickr is an image-hosting and photo-sharing service with a large mem-bership and a strong community component. In fact, its website looks a lot like a social network. Members create customizable profiles, develop friend lists, and start and join groups. And there's a "photostream" feature that resembles the status update stream seen in many social networks.

Flickr allows users to upload both photos and videos. The free account allows members to upload 20 MB of images per month and to create three photosets. The photostream views are limited to the 200 most recent images. The "pro" account limits monthly uploads to 2 GB, and allows unlimited storage, bandwidth, and photosets, and provides permanent archiving of high–resolution images.

Flickr allows users to organize their photos into online albums called "photosets," and they can be presented as slideshows. The service also sells prints in a range of sizes, as well as photo books, cards, calendars, collages, and "photo canvases" through a partnership with SnapFish.

Webshots

Launched in 1999 as an online community, Webshots (*www.webshots.com*) is one of the oldest photo sharing services on the web. In 2010, Web-shots was claiming 23 million visitors per month. The service offers a free account, which allows members to upload a thousand personal photo-graphs. A premium membership includes storage for 5,000 personal pictures, as well as unlimited downloads from the site's gallery of 520 million profes-sional photos (reportedly the largest on the web). With the premium service, members can actually license their own photos to the Webshots gallery.

Webshots provides users with a free desktop application for managing uploads and organizing your photos on your local hard drive. The desktop app also manages batch uploads. And the service supports photo uploads from mobile phones.

Uploaded photos can be organized in both private and public albums. You can buy prints from the site, as well as customized greeting cards, mugs, calendars, and mouse pads. Webshots does not allow you to upload video files. And unlike other community-oriented photo-sharing services, it doesn't support viewer comments.

QUESTION

What's a gallery?
A gallery is a collection of publicly available photographs posted on a photo-sharing website. They're often organized around a theme, such as architecture or the Olympics. Members of online photo-sharing communities build and "curate" galleries, which are usually available for all to see.

Other Photo-Sharing Services

This roundup of photo-sharing services is by no means comprehensive, but it includes some of the other big names, some up-and-comers, and some niche players. It's meant only to give you a feel for what else is out there. If your tech-savvy friends recommend a service not on this list, by all means, check it out. And keep your eyes peeled for new features in established services and new websites to take for a test drive.

- **Kodak Gallery:** (*www.kodakgallery.com*) This online photo-sharing site from the iconic old-school photo-film provider was originally launched in 1999 as Ofoto, but that company was acquired by Kodak in 2001, and the service was renamed. It's sort of a mainstream photo-finishing service with a social component.
- **Fotki:** (*www.fotki.com*) This is a photo-sharing service with a social network that was founded in 1998 by a married couple who wanted to share their photos with friends and family around the world. They later

developed a commercial version, which launched in 2003. This site has a bit of an international audience. It also includes blogging capabilities.

- **SmugMug:** (*www.smugmug.com*) This is one of the leading fee-based image hosting services. The emphasis is in high-quality photos. It offers three membership levels. Members can upload an unlimited number of photos. It provides extensive backup and lots of galleries. It also includes features aimed at professional photographers, and allows video clips.

- **Snapfish:** (*www.snapfish.com*) This service combines online photo-sharing and photo-printing services. Now owned by Hewlett-Packard, the service was launched in 2000, and claims about 70 million members. Membership is free, and storage is unlimited, but there's a per-image fee for downloads of high-resolution files. It supports video uploads with a subscription.

- **Shutterfly:** (*www.shutterfly.com*) Founded in 1999, this photo-sharing service calls itself a "social expression and personal publishing" service. Shutterfly provides free online storage for members for life. ("We never delete photos!") It supports a community of nearly 3 million members. Its photo sharing iPhone app, released in 2009, grabbed some headlines. It also allows uploads from e-mail.

- **Multiply:** (*www.multiply.com*) This is a media-sharing site with a big emphasis on community. There's a strong family orientation. The site supports photos and videos, and promises to store your media "permanently and in full resolution."

- **Picasa Web Albums:** (*www.picasaweb.google.com*) Google acquired the Picasa photo organizer in 2004, and then came out with this photo-sharing component. The organizer is free, and so is membership in the Web Albums. But you do have to download the Picasa desktop software to use it. Users can store 1GB of photos for free, and the service supports videos. The site offers geotagging, standard editing tools, and photo-sharing options.

- **deviantART:** (*www.deviantart.com*) Photos aren't the only images being shared online. This service specializes in showcasing the artwork of its 11 million members. Some of it is photographic, but you'll also find paintings, illustrations, digital art, Flash-based art, and "skins" for applications. You'll also find some literature and stock photos. It's user-generated content at a whole new level.

CHAPTER 10

Video Sharing: Not Your Father's Home Movies

The practice of sharing digital photos with friends and family over the Internet has enriched the social web immensely, but it was user-generated video that really got this party started. Homemade videos are all over the Internet these days. You can find everything from helpful how-tos to simple home movies, citizen journalism to personal exhibitionism, wacky send-ups to sophisticated mashups. Uploading video clips is pretty simple, but the world of user-generated video gets more complicated every day. Here's what you need to know to get started, both as a consumer and contributor.

Video and the Social Web

The Internet today is buzzing with video content from mainstream media, but it's throbbing with user-generated clips. It's the social web as infinite cineplex. You can thank the birth of the video-enabled camera phone for a lot of this non-mainstream content. But people create web-suitable video with camcorders, digital cameras with video capabilities, and even webcams. The technical barrier to entry here is very low. You've also got to give credit to the advent of broadband Internet access; there would be no surge in online video if we were all still using slow-as-molasses dial-up modems.

Online video clips have become incredibly popular. Digital marketing intelligence experts at comScore found that 33.2 billion online videos were viewed in December 2009. It's hard to nail down which clips were user-generated and which were mainstream media content. But comScore did find that a big chunk of those viewers went to two social media sites: YouTube drew 134.4 million viewers, who watched more than 13 billion videos, and MySpace drew 44.9 million viewers, who watched 423.3 million videos.

Video sharing is also the area of the social web where social media and mainstream media collide. A great many average joes post their homemade videos to YouTube, for example, but the site also features video content from commercial sources. In 2009 the site became a destination for "thousands of television episodes and hundreds of movies," which visitors can watch, and members can comment on, "favorite," and share.

Also, user-generated video isn't just about community or sharing. It's also about promoting yourself, your products, or your project. Musicians and comedians post videos online to get their careers going. Performers and filmmakers post videos to promote their shows. Teachers give away free lessons online to encourage you to pay for more. And businesspeople post videos to market their companies.

Video-Hosting Services

Photo-sharing sites and social networks both provide their members with some video-sharing features, but the lion's share of user-generated video ends up on websites created specifically to provide homes for this type of content. These video-hosting services are a lot like photo-sharing sites, but their focus on video makes them different in a significant way. Because of the nature of user-generated video—that video clips are presentations, demonstrations, performances, or records of events usually meant for an audience—these websites function more deliberately as distribution platforms.

By and large, the content of these sites is open to the public, and you don't have to be a member to view it. But if you want to upload clips of your own, you have to sign up. Most of the hosting services are free, paid for by advertising, but some offer paid memberships that include additional storage and services for the video makers. Memberships also typically make you a part of a community that offers many of the same features as social networks, including personal profiles, contact lists, blogs, and groups.

ESSENTIAL

The second most popular website for viewing videos in 2009 was the Facebook social network, according to Nielsen. It ranked just behind YouTube, and just ahead of Hulu.

YouTube is the best known of these hosting services/communities, but there are probably a dozen or more video-hosting sites that post user-generated clips. They range from specialty sites such as TroopTube, which hosts video for military families, to more general-interest sites, such as Vimeo and Revver.

Uploading Videos

Uploading procedures vary, but many sites provide some type of uploader software that you download to your desktop computer and use to send your clips to the website. You typically plug your camcorder, camera, or phone into an Internet-connected desktop or laptop and transfer or copy the video file to that device first (this is called downloading), and then you upload it to the website from there. But increasingly, the web hosters are making it possible to upload your clips directly from your mobile phone or Internet-connected camera.

The big advantage of downloading your videos to your desktop first is that you can spruce them up, add special effects, music, and titles with video-editing software. You can buy special programs for this purpose, but many modern desktops come with at least a basic video-editing program. But you'll often find tools on the site for customizing your videos once they've been uploaded.

Some sites offer video album options similar to what you'd find on a photo-sharing site, with comparable privacy controls. And increasingly, these sites provide options for posting your videos to other social media sites, such as Facebook, Twitter, and Digg.

File Size and Format

File sizes and formats represent a unique issue you'll have to deal with when you're uploading video clips. Video-hosting sites post their policies and restrictions, but it's mostly about the size of your file; they seem to bend over backward to accommodate a wide range of formats. They also offer lots of help and advice for a very wide range of formats, and for compressing big files.

"Video compression" is the process of reducing the number of bits required to store and transmit a video file. MPEG-2 coding system can compress digital video by as much as thirty times without lowering the quality of the picture—at least that you'd notice. Compressed videos are easier to upload.

QUESTION

What's viral video?
"Viral video" is a term that refers to online videos that really take off, essentially by word of mouth, but enabled by e-mail and the web. You might remember the Star Wars Kid with the light saber, or the clips of Charlie biting his older brother's finger.

The common file formats of the clips created on modern camcorders and other devices are widely supported by video hosters. Among the most common file types are .AVI and .MPG files. For file types not supported, there's software out there for converting older recordings to modern, web-ready formats.

Virtually all of the hosting sites put restrictions on the size and duration of the clips you can upload. No three-hour epics, please.

Once your files are uploaded, assuming you hope to attract viewers, you'll want to make them as easy to find as possible. The video-hosting sites will often provide features for categorizing and describing your videos with "tags."

Inappropriate Content

And there's always some kind of policy about "inappropriate content," though those policies vary. Sexually explicit videos, copyright-infringing content, hate speech, and harassment are typically prohibited. Nudity and vulgarity that don't cross the policy line are often segregated as "adult content."

Who determines which content is "adult" also varies with the site. Some pre-screen and flag that content based on their policies; some, in a truly literal interpretation of the term "community standards," publish first and allow the members of the video-hosting community to decide.

YouTube: Broadcasting Yourself

It's hard to imagine there ever was a world without YouTube (*www.youtube.com*). The video-sharing site is just a few years old, but it has already woven itself into the fabric of our media-centric society. Rare is the newscast that doesn't show a YouTube clip or two. The late-night talk shows love them. And there are even a handful of mainstream cable shows whose content is derived almost exclusively from them.

YouTube was founded in 2005 by Chad Hurley, Steve Chen, and Jawed Karim, three former employees of the PayPal online payment service. (For those of you keeping track, that makes three social media companies founded by former PayPal people: YouTube, Yelp, and LinkedIn.)

By mid 2006, YouTube was reporting that videos were being uploaded to the site at the rate of 65,000 *per day*. In July of that year, *USA Today* reported that 2.6 billion videos had been watched on YouTube during the previous month, and the company was claiming 100 million video views per day. In 2008, web watchers at comScore ranked YouTube as the top "U.S. video property," with 3.4 billion videos viewed in January. The company's Video Metrix service found that YouTube accounted for one-third of the 9.8 billion online videos viewed by U.S. web surfers that month.

By then, Internet search-giant Google had already snapped up the nova-hot video-sharing service. Less than two years after it was founded, YouTube sold for a reported $1.65 billion. Today, the service operates as a Google subsidiary.

The web info experts at Alexa.com rank YouTube among the top three most visited websites today, behind only Google proper and Facebook. In 2009, comScore's Video Metrix service found that 120.5 million viewers had watched nearly 10 billion videos on YouTube.com in August alone. YouTube, itself, claims that fifteen hours of video are uploaded to the site every minute.

Signing Up

You don't have to be a registered member to watch YouTube videos. The content is open to any visitor to the site. But you do have to join if you want to upload anything. YouTube members are free to upload an unlimited number of videos to the site.

Signing up for a YouTube account couldn't be simpler. Just point your browser to the YouTube website, click on "Create Account," fill out the form (user name, age, zip code, gender), and accept the Terms of Service (which you should read). Completing this form takes you to a page that allows you to sign up using an existing Google account. If you have Gmail, you just sign in using your existing password and user name. If you don't, you create one in the form provided.

ALERT

In 2008, the UK Telegraph reported that YouTube had consumed as much Internet capacity in 2007 as the entire network consumed in 2000. People were actually talking about the potential of user-generated video taking down the entire Internet.

Once you've signed up, you'll have a chance to customize your account. Click on your name in the upper right-hand corner to open a drop down menu. Click "Account" and you'll open a My Account page. The menu bar on the left displays a number of options. Edit your profile on the Profile Setup page. Here you can add a picture, a personal description, a link to your own website, and fill out lists of personal details, location, career, education, and interests—all the standard social networking stuff.

Customizing Your Home Page

"Customize Homepage" provides you with a number of modules for displaying YouTube-chosen "Spotlight Videos," the latest video from the channels to which you subscribe (more on this later), videos that the site recommends based on your activities, subscriptions, and recent activity, top videos being watched right now, the most popular videos, "Videos Near You," and others. Click these boxes if you want these items displayed for you on your home page.

"Playback Setup" provides options for video playback, including "I have a slow connection. Never play higher-quality videos" and "Always choose the best option for me based on my player size." The "Captions" option allows you to choose whether you'd like to see captions in videos generated by speech recognition programs. "Annotations" allow you to display or hide annotations (more on these later).

"E-mail" options allow you to enter a new e-mail address. "Manage Account" allows you to change your password and delete your account, and it shows you account status items, such as the standing of your account in relation to community standards and how many third-party sites are authorized to access your account.

In 2006 CNN Money.com reported that Universal Tube and Rollerform Equipment Corp. of Toledo, Ohio, which sells used machinery for making tubes, was seeing millions of visits to its website, utube.com—68 million hits in August of that year—by people looking for YouTube. The traffic jammed the site and kept Universal Tube's customers away. The owner sued YouTube for the trouble, and eventually changed the website's name to utubeonline.com.

There's also a Mobile Setup page, where you'll find an e-mail address that you enter into your smart phone's contact list, and which you use to upload videos directly to YouTube. You'll find a couple of videos there explaining how to play YouTube videos on your phone, and how to create them with your phone.

YouTube Channels

The YouTube platform has a lot in common with other social media sites, but one thing that sets it apart is the concept of "channels." A YouTube channel is the page that displays the information you've decided to share with the public from your account, including your profile, your favorite videos, your subscriptions, etc. When you manage the details of your account, you're setting up your channel.

Clicking on the "Activity Sharing" link, for example, takes you to a page where you can tinker with the visibility of your "activity feed," which includes things you might be doing on YouTube, such as favoriting, rating, or uploading a video. You can decide to show your activities to the world, or keep them private. You can also choose to share or hide specific activities. And now there is an option that allows you to post your activities on YouTube automatically to your Twitter and Facebook accounts, and to an RSS feed reader.

This is what people see when they subscribe to your channel. To see your channel, click on your name in the upper right of the YouTube page. To see another member's channel, click on that person's username wherever you find it and you'll be directed to her channel page.

Whatever else you decide to do, be sure to take a moment to consider your privacy settings. You have the option of deciding who sees what, and you should make a conscious choice here. You can decide to allow only friends to send messages or share videos with you; to let others see your "channel" on YouTube if they have your e-mail address; to allow your account info to be used to provide advertisers with "relevant advertising" based on your YouTube interests and activities; and to share or hide "interesting statistics" about each of your videos with your viewers.

Watching YouTube Videos

You can watch YouTube videos whether or not you're a registered user. All you need is a web browser with the free Adobe Flash Player plug-in. (Apple famously doesn't support Flash on its iPhones, but these devices can display YouTube videos. In 2007, YouTube began "transcoding" its Flash videos to Apple's preferred video format, H.264.)

The browser can be on your desktop computer, your laptop, your tablet PC, or, depending on your carrier and the model, your smart phone. Just point your browser to the YouTube site, click on a thumbnail image of the video that interests you, and it plays automatically. (You'll also need some speakers if you want to hear the audio, but most of these devices have them built in.)

The site's newly designed video page displays the video in the main window, with little thumbnail graphics and links to related or similar clips in a column on the right. You'll find a description of the video, including tags, ratings from other viewers, options for sharing the video, traffic statistics, comments and responses about the video, among other features. There's also an ad window that cycles paid advertising on the right.

Finding Videos

You can find videos on YouTube by clicking on the Browse link at the top of the main page. From here, you can search for videos in a couple of ways. You can type a keyword into the Search box. You can click on a category in the list in the navigation column on the left. Or you can click on one of the thumbnail graphics for the Spotlight videos currently featured. Once you've called up a video, you'll still have access to the Search box, and you can click on any of the thumbnails that come up beside the main display window. The Search box is available on nearly every page on the YouTube site.

You can also take advantage of additional search capabilities by clicking "Search Options" in the upper left of search results pages. This gives you access to a number of search filters, which allow you to narrow your search in several ways. For example, limit your keyword search results based on result type, upload date, view count, categories, and the length of the video.

If you find a video that you like and you want to keep up with that channel, you can subscribe to it. Just click on "Subscribe" when you're watching a clip, and the latest videos from that channel will be posted directly to your home page from now on. You have to be a registered user to get this feature.

Uploading Your Own Videos

Uploading your videos to YouTube can be accomplished in a couple of ways. The service provides a program that you can download to your desktop computer for multiple files, or you can just click on "Upload" at the top of the screen to open the Video File Upload page. YouTube displays the file limitations on this page. They must be high-definition videos, up to 2GB, and no longer than 10 minutes.

If you want to save yourself some hassle, check first that the video you want to upload is in one of the file formats supported by YouTube. You can tell what the file format is by checking the file's *extension*—that's the part of the file name that comes after the "dot" near the end. The list of files You-Tube supports includes, as of this writing: Windows Media Video (WMV), 3GP (cell phones), AVI (windows), MOV (mac), MP4 (ipod/psp), MPEG, FLV (Adobe Flash), and MKV (H.264). These are all listed on the YouTube website.

ALERT

After a few lawsuits, YouTube has gotten serious about copyrighted materials appearing on the website. As the service states: "Anytime YouTube becomes aware that a video or any part of a video on our site infringes the copyrights of a third party, we will take it down from the site as required by law." Your safest bet: Don't upload any TV shows, music videos, concerts, or commercials unless they consist entirely of content you created yourself, or you have written permission to use them.

When you click "Upload," you'll have the option of uploading a video from your desktop computer, or recording a video with your webcam directly to YouTube. (You'd be surprised how many people do this.) You'll probably want to edit the file before you upload it, but YouTube provides editing tools if you decide you want to tweak it later.

Click on the "Upload Video" button to access your desktop computer files. Find the file you want to upload and double click it. That starts the upload process. You'll be able to watch the uploading progress from the Video File Upload page. Once the video is copied to the website, you'll see a frame-by-frame preview, which allows you to trim the clip. You'll also see a URL, which is the address of your video on the YouTube website.

While the video uploads—it could take several minutes—you can fill out your video information and privacy settings. You'll also have the option of embedding a link to the video in your own website, or link it to Facebook or Twitter. Be sure to click the "Save Changes" button.

YouTube allows you to upload ten videos in a single uploading session.

Annotations, Comments, and Promotions

A big part of the YouTube experience is the interactivity it provides. For example, users can comment on a video in the "Respond to this video" box displayed below the video window. Previous comments are listed below that box in reverse chronological order, as you might see in a blog. Hovering over those comments activates some option icons that let you vote thumbs up or down on the comment, and to reply directly to the commenter. You can also flag the comment if it looks like spam and the YouTube people will take a look at it.

In one of those weird media crossover moments, the TiVo video recording service began allowing its set-top boxes to play YouTube videos in 2008. In 2009, YouTube launched "YouTube for TV," which was a version of the website customized for set-top boxes.

The annotations feature allows you to make your videos highly interactive by creating links within the video. YouTube provides an annotations editor that allows you to add speech bubbles, which contain text and can be programmed to pop up in your videos; notes, which are simple pop-up text boxes; spotlights, which highlight areas in a video—as YouTube explains it, "when the user moves the mouse over these areas the text you enter will appear;" video pauses, which halt the video for a period you specify; and others.

Typically, the people who publish videos to the YouTube site are looking for an audience. YouTube offers a fee-based service for publicizing and promoting your videos and your channel. It's called YouTube Promoted Videos, and it's connected to Google's AdWords. YouTube describes the service as "an advertising solution that allows YouTube users, partners, and advertisers to promote their video content within the YouTube website."

YouTube also gives its members free access to some great performance statistics about their videos with YouTube Insight. This is a reporting tool that tracks how popular your videos are, how often people view them, what types of people view them, which countries are generating the most traffic, and other statistics.

Other Places to Find User-Generated Video

YouTube is the largest platform for user-generated video on the web, but it's certainly not the only one. If this type of social media interests you, you'll definitely want to check out some of the other video hosting sites.

Following are just three of the sites you might want to visit. They were included to show the range and depth of these services. Their order here is *not* a ranking.

Vimeo

Launched in 2004, Vimeo (*http://vimeo.com*) actually predates YouTube and the user-generated-video tsunami. The service supports all kinds of videos, but nothing commercial, nothing pornographic, and no games. This is a true, user-generated-video site that prides itself on sticking to that guideline. As the website puts it: "Vimeo is a place for people to showcase their own work and receive feedback on what they have accomplished."

As of early 2010, Vimeo claimed to have more than 3.4 million members and an average of more than 20,000 new videos uploaded daily. In 2007, the company began supporting High Definition (HD) videos. The site's membership has created nearly 79,000 channels in a range of categories, from music to nature, experimental video to comedy clips, documentaries to web series.

The service also prides itself on its support for many different file formats, including HD. Non-members can view videos, but you must register to upload any files. Members get a free Desktop Uploader as part of the free basic-membership package, which also provides 500 MB of storage every week. A fee-based membership package includes additional storage and features.

Members also get a profile, features for sharing videos, social networking capabilities within the Vimeo community, tools for creating video albums, and a bunch of privacy controls (always welcome). And members can post videos on other social media sites, including Facebook, Twitter, MySpace, Flickr, and Digg.

Revver

Launched in 2005, Revver (*www.revver.com*) was one of the first user-generated video-hosting services to offer revenue sharing with its contributors. Video clips get paired with targeted ads, and the site splits the ad revenue fifty-fifty with the creators of those clips. The service is famous for hosting early user-generated video stars like LonleyGirl15 and Ask a Ninja.

Revver bills itself as a "viral video network," which underscores the site's emphasis on promoting its videos to make money for their creators. As the service puts it: "To get your videos seen by as many people as possible, we've been hard at work building our network of syndication partners. This means partnering with lots of websites and web services platforms to get your videos in front of as many eyeballs as possible."

But there's also a community feel to the service. Users create profiles, set up contact lists, and other social networking features. Registration is free, but this is a video-distribution platform that really wants you to get involved with revenue sharing. Not a bad idea, unless it's not your thing.

Non-members can search the site by category and view videos for free, but you have to be registered to upload files. Clips are ranked by "Most Watched," "Highest Rated," and "Most Responses" per month, week, and "all time."

Revver is also a publishing platform, which means that, in addition to hosting videos, it provides tools for others to develop websites that display videos in the same way. These "Revverized" websites are built by third-party web developers. The tools Revver provides allow these developers to build the identical functionality of the Revver site into their own sites.

Blip.TV

Founded in 2005 (apparently a big year for video hosting sites), Blip. TV (*www.blip.tv*) is a free videoblogging, podcasting, and video-sharing service that hosts thousands of grassroots videos. The service claims to provide services to more than 50,000 independently produced, original web shows, developed by more than 44,000 creators.

In February 2010, the site hit 85 million video views, and announced that 85 percent of its videos were "monetized," meaning they made money. Blip.TV makes its money by selling advertising with a fifty-fifty revenue share with the makers of the videos it distributes.

This is a video hosting site with an emphasis on independent web shows, with actors and scripts and episodes—not just clips of your cat on a skateboard. (Which is, of course, hilarious, just not what they do here.) This service thinks of itself as a next-generation TV network, and says that its mission "is to make independent web shows sustainable." In other words, profitable. Blip.TV is what is known as a "prosumer" video service, which means its members make 'em and watch 'em.

Blip.TV membership is free, and the service provides you with a ton of support. It supports lots of file formats, too. Blip.TV members get access to an especially useful tool for independent web-content producers: a dashboard that becomes a central location for their shows. From the dashboard they manage their episodes, distribution, players, community, statistics, and advertising revenue.

Complicating this little corner of the social web, Blip.TV distributes its content to other video hosting sites, including YouTube and Vimeo, but also iTunes, AOL Video, and MSN Video, among others. It also crosses the social media line and distributes to *television* (Verizon FiOS Video on Demand, TiVo, Sony Bravia, Roku, and others).

Some of Blip.TV's better known shows include the popular videoblog "Rocketboom," "The Joke Project," the "Wallstrip" average-guy stock market show, and "Alive in Baghdad," which collects interviews and videos of Americans and Iraqi correspondents on the ground in that city, and "Goodnight Burbank," a sendup of local television news.

CHAPTER 11

Social Bookmarking: Sharing Your Favorite Links

The World Wide Web has become a dense forest of information and images. Finding and keeping track of the useful, the valuable, and the interesting in that wilderness, even with the help of increasingly sophisticated search engines and feature-rich web browsers, isn't easy. But you're not alone out there, and the ever-innovative denizens of Web 2.0 have evolved a technique that allows you and your fellow travelers to mark your trails and drop a few bread crumbs along the way. It's called social bookmarking, and here's how it works.

What Is Social Bookmarking?

If you've done any web surfing at all, you've probably bookmarked a page or two in your browser. If you're using Internet Explorer, the native Windows browser, your bookmarks are called "Favorites." The Safari browser that comes bundled with a Mac (though it can run on a Windows machine, too) calls them "My Favorites." The open source Firefox browser actually calls them "Bookmarks."

Bookmarking is nothing more than the act of saving the address of a web page so that you can easily return to it later. That address is called a Universal Resource Locator, or *URL*. Whenever you see *http://* or *www.* followed by a string of words and forward slashes, you're undoubtedly looking at a URL. When you bookmark a web page in your browser, you're simply telling it to stash that URL for future reference. Your favorites list is essentially a group of those URLs presented as clickable links. And it's all stored locally, which means that they're in a folder on your computer that your browser accesses.

"Social bookmarking" adds a communal dimension to this basic, and usually solo, activity by moving everything to shared web spaces. Instead of saving your favorites with your browser and storing them on your computer, you save them to a special-purpose website that allows you to organize and share them with friends, family, and total strangers.

ESSENTIAL

Bookmarking itself is nothing new. It's been around since the first web browser, Mosaic, was released back in 1993. What we know now as Favorites were once called "Hotlists." Tim Berners-Lee, the computer scientist most often credited with inventing the World Wide Web, also gets credit for the Bookmark.

Storing your favorites online on a social bookmarking site offers some distinct advantages over storing them locally. For one thing, bookmarks that have an online home are highly portable. Because they're stored and organized on the web, you can access them from any computer with an Internet connection. Essentially, you can take them with you to share with friends, access them from a hotel room when you're on the road, or to work with them at school. You can also add new bookmarks from any computer connected to the web.

But perhaps more importantly, social bookmarking gives you access to the favorites of other users. This access can be enormously valuable. Although search engines like Google and Bing are indispensible tools that seem to be getting better every day, they have the entire World Wide Web to deal with—that's about 50 million websites. It's not uncommon to get search results that list thousands of web pages. A social bookmarking service acts as a kind of human-driven pre-search engine. Members of the community have already done the needle-in-a-haystack work and sorted out the sites that best suit their needs, the sites they feel are *worth* bookmarking and sharing.

The Human Layer

If the only thing the bookmark-sharing sites did was host a place on the web where people could store, organize, and share their favorites, they'd be providing a truly useful service. But people do more on these sites than stash URLs. They describe the sites they're bookmarking, comment on their content, and tag them with telling search terms. Other users effectively rate those bookmarks by adding them to their own collections or leaving them out. All of which introduces a distinctly human layer to this process.

People have culled the bookmarks collected on these sites from the web. You might say they've been handpicked. Users of social bookmarking services get to take advantage of the expertise and interests their friends and family, and potentially thousands of people they've never met. You could also call these services peer-to-peer search engines, because they allow you to search for subjects by user-generated keywords and find results recommended by the community.

Which is not to say that technology is completely absent from the bookmark-sharing equation. These services often add their two cents with automated tools designed to rank a website based on the number of times users have bookmarked it, for example. Popular bookmarks rise to the top, and unpopular ones drift to the bottom. And a good search engine is essential. Users search the combined favorites of hundreds of people by keywords, user names, and popularity.

Tagging

Bookmark-sharing sites have also been largely responsible for popularizing a very human form of information organization called "tagging." A tag is nothing more than a keyword you attach to a piece of web content, such as an online article, a blog posting, a digital photo, a video clip, or a website. Techies call this kind of thing "metadata," or data that describes other data. You can think of a tag as a one-word label: "business," "sports," "butterflies," "funny," or "recipe," for example. A piece of content can have more than one tag, say, "sports" and "rugby," which gives people more than one way to find it.

Tagging creates an informal, user-generated system of classification that works beautifully to organize bookmarks. It creates what social media mavens call "folksonomies," which differ dramatically from "taxonomies." Taxonomies are hierarchical classification systems, like a company's organizational tree, or the scientific groupings of animals, or the file-and-folder system on your computer. Folksonomies are non-hierarchical systems that rely on an informal structure.

A striking example can be seen in something called a "tag cloud," which is essentially a swarm of words on a page. (Talk about non-hierarchical!) The more important, popular, and/or relevant tags are displayed in large text, often in striking colors, usually near the center of the swarm. The less important, popular, and/or relevant tags are displayed in smaller text and muted colors in more peripheral positions on the page. The big, bright words appear nearer, while the smaller, duller words seem to recede. It's a highly visual way of presenting information, and gives you an immediate sense of relationships of the items being organized.

A bookmark sharing service called Delicious.com (*http://delicious .com*) was among the first to embrace tagging. Today, tagging is widely used by social media services of all kinds. Microblogs, such as Twitter, use something called a *hashtag*, which allows users to turn any word in the short messages into a tag by adding a hash mark (*#*) in front of it. In fact, the form has spread beyond social media, and now "text clouds" and "data clouds" are almost commonplace.

"The Tastiest Bookmarks on the Web"

The original social bookmarking service was del.icio.us, which was founded in 2003 by Joshua Schachter, and acquired by Yahoo! two years later. In a 2004 interview with engineer and author Michael Lopps on his Rands in Repose blog, Schachter explained the origins of the name: "I'd registered the domain when .us opened the registry, and a quick test showed me the six letter suffixes that let me generate the most words. In early discussions, a friend referred to finding good links as 'eating cherries' and the metaphor stuck, I guess."

That awkward and oh-so geeky construction was changed to Delicious. com when a redesigned version of the site (popularly known as Delicious 2.0) was launched in 2008. A year later, Delicious claimed to have reached 9.5 million users and more than 180 million bookmarks.

Simple and Sweet

Delicious offers its users a simply designed website with no flashy graphics, but lots of practical features. Anyone can visit the site and explore hotlists, tags, and the most popular bookmarks being saved by its registered members. The bookmarks are displayed in a column on the main page as thumbnail images of the websites next to hyperlinked headlines. Clicking on the headline or the thumbnail opens the page directly. The number of people who have bookmarked each page is posted there, too, which indicates their popularity in specific numbers.

The "Fresh Bookmarks" tab takes you to a list of the bookmarks most recently added to the website. The "Hotlist" tab takes you to a list of the most popular bookmarks—the ones with the highest numbers of people adding them to their favorites lists. And "Explore Tags" takes you to a page that organizes bookmarks by the keywords the site's users have assigned to them. As a registered member, you can search other users' bookmarks and tags, build a network with members with shared interests, and subscribe to specific tags.

The Delicious Button

Delicious is free to join, and sign up is easy. Click on "Join Now," and follow the steps. If you have a Yahoo! account, you can use your existing user name and password. You'll be asked to create a Delicious account with its own URL, and you'll have an opportunity to add a Delicious button to your favorite web browser, or if you use Firefox or Internet Explorer, to install an add-on.

QUESTION

What is a bookmarklet?
A "bookmarklet" is a small application or applet, usually written in JavaScript and designed to allow you to send bookmarks directly to a social bookmarking service with a single click of the mouse. They typically appear as buttons on your browser's link bar.

Choosing the Delicious button actually installs two buttons on your browser's toolbar: "My Delicious," which takes you directly to the bookmarks you've saved on the Delicious.com website, and "Save to Delicious," which allows you to add a new bookmark. All the major web browsers are supported.

Installing the add-ons for Firefox or Internet Explorer puts an additional set of tools for creating, managing, and searching bookmarks on your browser. (You get the buttons, too.) Among other things, the add-ons synchronize the changes you make to your bookmarks with your browser and on your Bookmarks page on the Delicious website.

Saving a Bookmark

You save a bookmark on Delicious by clicking on the "Save to Delicious" button. This takes you to the "Save a new bookmark" page, where you'll be asked to provide tags (some options are suggested), a title, and some descriptive notes. The URL and Title fields should be automatically filled in, but the Notes box will need some attention. This is where you enter your description of the site, the reason you bookmarked it, and why you think other members of Delicious might want to bookmark it, too.

The Send field allows you to send the bookmark directly to the people in your Delicious network. Their names appear in a list, and you just click on the ones you want to receive the bookmark. Delicious also allows you to share your bookmarks on Twitter.

You can also mark the URL as private, which means that only you can see it. Public bookmarks are available to all members. As of mid 2010, Delicious had yet to develop a feature that allows its users to share bookmarks only within specified networks.

Social Networking Features

Delicious provides its members with several social networking features through Yahoo! For example, users create a profile, but it's done through Yahoo! A Delicious/Yahoo! profile includes the usual personal information—name, city, birthday, photo. Users can post personal status updates in the "What are you doing now?" window. There are privacy settings, profile editing features, and a contact list. To get out of the Profile Page and back to Delicious.com, click the "Back" button or the "My Delicious" button if you installed it.

Other Bookmark-Sharing Services

In mid-2010, Delicious.com was still the market leader among social bookmarking services, both in terms of membership numbers and total bookmarks. But it's by no means alone out there in Web 2.0 land. Social bookmarking services come in a range of shapes and sizes. Here's a short list of a few others you might want to investigate.

Simpy

Launched in 2004, Simpy (*www.simpy.com*) is a free, no-frills social bookmarking service that offers a bookmarklet and browser extension for Firefox, which supports one-click bookmarking. Simpy does the indexing, but users save, tag, and search their own bookmarks and other users' links and tags.

And Simpy loves tags, which its members use "to create virtual, dynamic folders on the fly." The site features a large tag cloud.

Groups are supported on Simpy, and even encouraged. But privacy is respected. You can keep your bookmarks to yourself if you want to, or share them with groups you create or join, or share them with the entire membership.

Simpy supports full-text searches of bookmarked pages, which means that the search digs into the content of the pages, not just the metadata. And users can attach searchable notes to their bookmarks. Users can also upload their existing favorites from a long list of browsers, including Firefox, Mozilla, Netscape, Internet Explorer, Safari, Opera, Galeon, and Konqueror. The site is synced with Delicious.

There's a strong social component to this site. Simpy wants you to know that you can find like-minded users on the site. Simpy users can subscribe to each other via Watchlists, which allow you to watch "over the shoulders" of other Simpy users as they save links.

Faves

Formerly known as Blue Dot until it was relaunched in 2007, Faves (*www.faves.com*) is a bright and lively bookmark-sharing site with a big social component. Membership is free, and users set up profiles with viewer preferences and adjustable privacy settings. There's also an e-mail feature, which helps users to build friends lists.

The site emphasizes opinion sharing almost as much as bookmark sharing. A member bookmark is called a "fave," but it isn't complete without comments on the web page from the users and other members, and tags. Users vote on bookmarks by clicking on up or down arrows in little "Vote" boxes displayed next to each posted Fave.

Faving is supported with browser buttons, which you download from the site. Member bookmarks are displayed with thumbnails based on a user-chosen image from the web page.

Faves connects its members though a unique Topic Network. Users select topics of interest from a list that includes Cars, Food, Movies, Technology, Shopping, Travel, Sports, and News, among others. Once you select your topics, your home page displays the latest and most popular bookmarks under that topic heading. Users can add and remove topics anytime. The Most Active Topic Groups are also displayed on the home page.

BlinkList

Social bookmarking service BlinkList (*www.blinklist.com*) claimed 450,000 users in mid 2010. The service is free, and the website is simple and straightforward. The interface has been described as iTunes-like, and the site itself claims that it will sort your web pages like iTunes.

Social networking doesn't seem to be emphasized on this bookmark-sharing site. User profiles are very basic. But you can add friends to your profile. The site also supports private groups, and allows users to follow the bookmarking activities of friends.

BlinkList describes its search engine as "lightning fast," vowing that it will allow you to find any of your links in 0.18 seconds or less. And you can use it to search public bookmarks.

Users can also add a "Blink" button to their web-browser toolbars for one-click bookmarking. Rather than taking you to the website, clicking the "Blink" button opens a small form locally, which users fill out with the tags, a description, and a rating of the website. You can also send the URL to a friend from this form. One particularly nice feature: highlighting a section of text on the website before clicking the button causes that text to appear in the notes field.

And unlike most social bookmarking sites, it allows its users to save a copy of a web page locally, on their computer. The site also provides some nice video tutorials.

QUESTION

What is the most socially connected country?
If the researchers at the Nielsen Company are right, it's Brazil. In 2010, they found that 86 percent of the web users in that South American nation spent an average of five hours a month visiting a social networks.

Muti

The Muti (*www.muti.co.za*) social bookmarking site is "dedicated to content of interest to Africans or those interested in Africa." South African Ian Gilfillan is credited on the site with originating the idea. He wrote in a blog posting that he conceived of a "South African reddit."

Registration is free, and signup is easy. The site's bookmarks are displayed without thumbnails as straightforward hyperlinked headlines, each flanked by a voting button. You must be a registered member to vote. Users can comment on bookmarks, vote on them, and add tags. The site introduced tagging in 2007, and now a tag cloud called "Hot Tags" is prominently displayed.

Muti uses what it calls "co-operative tagging," by which it means that any registered user may tag any item. You do not have to be the submitter of that item nor do you have to save a copy of that item to tag it. All tags by all members are shown below each item.

The site allows non-members to browse its public bookmarks, which are grouped under four "views." The Hot view is the default. Bookmarks are displayed on this page according to their vote counts. Top vote getters lead. The site explains that the Hot view is dynamic and changes over time. "Once an item stops getting votes, it will start to drift down in its ranking . . . ."

The New view lists submissions in the reverse order in which they were submitted, with the newest at the top. The Top view organizes bookmarks based on a combined score of their total votes and the number of times they have been viewed. And the Most Viewed view displays bookmarks based on number of viewings, which reflects their popularity among readers.

Linkroll

Linkroll (*www.linkroll.com*) bills itself as a "link blogging" service, which is a little confusing. But the site is very accessible and straightforward. Membership is free, but unlike some bookmark-sharing sites that allow you to decide who sees your links, all bookmarks stored on Linkroll are public.

The site's bookmarks are displayed on the main page as hyperlinked headlines with summaries, tags, and a link to a list of the poster's other bookmarks. The bookmarks are accessible to non-members, but you must register to post links and to access the site's advanced subscribe and ignore features. All your bookmarks on the site are sortable and searchable by category and date.

The site provides users with bookmarklets for one-click bookmarking; the buttons are installed by a simple drag-and-drop over the browser toolbar. Bookmarked web pages must be categorized and commented on. Users can subscribe to categories, and to links by user, "so you can track what links your friends are bookmarking."

A notable feature of this site: "Pretty much everything is available as an RSS feed." In 2010, the site added a new feature that allows members to create "personal podcast channels," which are essentially links to media files in their Linkroll posts.

CHAPTER 12

The Social News: All the News You Think Is Fit

The web has become a platform for the publication of a staggering amount of news. Traditional media outlets now offer much of their print content on their websites. A new generation of online magazines publishes exclusively on the web. And the blogosphere is ever expanding. The prospect of sifting that burgeoning pile for the stories you'd really like to read with nothing but a web browser can be daunting. Fortunately, the social media world has found a way for you and your fellow searchers to help each other find the good stuff. Here's how.

Recommending the News

Can you think of a newspaper or magazine that doesn't have a website today? Even tiny-circulation local publications maintain at least a nominal web presence. The major publishers offer a wealth of rich online content, both free and subscription-based. It's a great thing, truly. We live in an age of unprecedented access to news and information. But there is such a thing as too much choice.

That's where the social news sites come in. They represent a uniquely social-media-oriented answer to the question, "What should I be reading on the web?"

What is Social News?

The term "social news" gets thrown around a lot, both in and out of social media circles, and definitions vary. "News aggregator" is a commonly used synonym, but social news differs in a significant way. Aggregator sites collect headlines and links to news stories, but social news sites provide a platform for the news consumers to *recommend* news stories, articles, images, blogs, and videos. And not just recommend that content, but *rate* it. A social news community member submits a story for consideration by the entire registered membership, and whether it stays on the website, and how prominently it's featured there, is largely up to that user community. In other words, the "value" of the content submitted to a social news site is determined collectively, usually through some kind of voting system.

Social news sites can focus on specific topic areas, such as politics, entertainment, or technology, or they can cover topics of general interest. Most social news sites require you to register before you can submit a story that you'd like to recommend or to vote on others, but the links to the stories themselves are usually displayed on a main page that's accessible to all visitors. Many of these websites also allow (and even encourage) users to comment on the stories they submit, adding yet another layer of user-generated content to the web. Most of the mainstream-media sites, from the *Washington Post* to CNN.com, now feature a selection of icons or buttons (sometimes called "badges") that readers can click to recommend an article to their favorite social news communities.

Slashdotted and the Digg Effect

The social news sites have spawned a unique phenomenon, originally known as the Slashdot Effect or "being slashdotted," but lately more widely referred to as the Digg Effect. Slashdot is the venerable social news site focused on science and technology stories; Digg is the popular general-interest social news site. Both have been responsible for huge spikes in web traffic to the sites featuring the stories their users recommend. This is no big deal if you're the *Washington Post*, but if something you wrote on your personal blog captures the attention of the masses, your home server or even a shared-hosting service could be overwhelmed by your sudden popularity.

The immediate result of the Digg Effect is that thousands of users who want to read the recommended story can't get to the site on which it was published. Big media sites are prepared for this surge of interest, but it tends to fry the little guys. Fortunately for the little guys, the Digg Effect tends to be specific to a particular story, and for the most part, it's temporary. The big guys, of course, love this side effect, and sometimes seek to prolong it or turn it into an overall increase in traffic to their websites.

Gaming the Systems

It has been argued that social news sites are inherently prone to abuses. Critics have charged that some social news sites leave too much control in the hands of users, which results in unfair rankings and poor-quality recommendations. But the critics have also charged that some social news sites exercise too much control, which results in skewed recommendations that don't reflect the true feelings of their communities. Charges have also been leveled that companies have paid to have stories submitted to some social news sites, though submission alone doesn't guarantee status. Another concern is that the popularity of a news story, feature article, or blog among social news community members doesn't have anything to do with its accuracy. The potential consequence here is that misinformation can get magnified. Media watchers also worry that social news sites can be used by small groups with personal or political axes to grind to promote stories that support their cause or point of view.

Virtually all the social news sites have developed strategies and algorithms—even varying levels of human intervention—to prevent these kinds of abuses, whether intentional or otherwise, and they continue to refine their technologies to prevent users from gaming their systems.

Digg

The web's most popular social news community at the start of 2010 was Digg (*http://digg.com*). The site claims to support more than 40 million users, and the web traffic watchers at Alexa.com have ranked the Digg website among the world's 100 busiest. It was launched in 2004, reportedly as an experiment by its founders. That experiment took off, and now the Digg icon appears on just about every media website worthy of the name.

Digg is a general-interest social news site. The content recommended by its members covers a range of topics, including politics, entertainment, technology, and general news. Members can recommend different types of content, including text-based news items and blogs, but also images and videos.

"Democratizing Digital Media"

The Digg community calls what the site does "democratizing digital media," which means that community members "participate in determining all site content by discovering, selecting, sharing, and discussing the news and videos that appeal to you."

FACT

To make sure that even readers on the go can give a thumbs up or down to articles they pull up on their smart phones, Digg launched its first iPhone app in March 2010. iPhone users can digg or bury stories and add comments directly from the browser launched by the phone. The Digg iPhone app quickly shot to the top of the App Store "news" category. A few weeks later, Digg launched a similar application for the Android phone.

Anyone can read the stories collected on the Digg website, but you must be a registered member to recommend a story and participate in the voting. Signing up for membership is easy: You have to provide the usual username and password and your e-mail address, and a few personal details. Digg sends you a verifying e-mail; you respond, and you're in.

Digg is a community, so you'll be asked to build a profile. It's not as extensive as, say, a Facebook profile, and it's completely optional. You can also create a friends list of your e-mail contacts, just as you can on most social networking sites. And there are privacy settings that allow you to restrict who sees your personal details.

Finding Content

The news, images, and videos submitted to Digg are not published on the website, but links to those items are, along with user descriptions and comments. The most popular items appear in a list on the home page. Items that are new appear on the Upcoming Stories page.

Click on an item's title and Digg opens the page on which it was published. Digg adds the DiggBar across the top to provide you with the tools for voting, commenting, reading comments, finding related content, sharing, and linking to other social media.

Items are also organized into a number of groups and categories, including Technology, World & Business, Science, Gaming, Lifestyle, Entertainment, Sports, and Offbeat. You can also search for items classified as News, Videos, and Images.

Submitting

Once you've signed up, you'll be able to recommend news, images, videos, and other web content. When you click on the icon of the little guy with a shovel next to a *Wall Street Journal* story, you'll open a Digg form for submitting a link. The form comes prefilled with the story's title and, if one was available, a summary from the media site. If a description wasn't available, you can add your own using up to 248 characters. You also have to choose a topic heading from a drop-down list, and type in a security word. When you click "Submit," Digg asks you to sign in; once you do, your story is sent to the Upcoming Stories list.

Dugg and Buried

Digg community members vote on the stories they like by clicking on digg buttons, which display a little thumbs-up icon. Each posted link displays that button, along with the number of diggs that story has received. Diggers can also give an item a thumbs-down by clicking on "Bury." Items that receive more Diggs get promoted, and the items with the most Diggs appear on the Popular page. Items that receive few Diggs or a lot of buries eventually slip off the site completely.

You can also click on "Who Dug This" to find out who else gave the item a thumbs up, "comments" to read other members' thoughts on the item and to post your own, and "share" to e-mail the link to a friend, or to send it to Facebook or Twitter.

According to the Digg Help page, "The promotion or burying of stories is managed by an algorithm developed by Digg, and there is no specific threshold of Diggs or buries required to promote or bury a story. Instead, our algorithm takes several factors into consideration, including (but not limited to) the number and diversity of Diggs, buries, the time the story was submitted, and the topic."

Slashdot

The granddaddy of social news communities is Slashdot (*http://slashdot .org*), which has been around since 1997. Long before anyone was talking about Web 2.0 or social networking, Slashdot's founders were getting their feet wet with recommendations and comments on technology- and science-related web content.

QUESTION

Why is it called "Slashdot?"
The name may sound like the website for a teenage horror film, but it's actually what the founder reportedly called "an obnoxious parody of a URL" meant to confuse. A URL, or universal resource locator, is a web address that is typically full of slashes and "dots." So if you read it out loud, the Slashdot URL would be "h-t-t-p-colon-slash-slash-slashdot-dot-org."

Slashdot actually started out as a blog, evolved into more of a news aggregation site, and then added social features and capabilities. Its founder,

Rob Malda, was a computer science student posting under the *nom de blog* "Cmdr Taco." He still uses that handle in his Slashdot blog.

Today, Slashdot claims to serve up approximately 40 million pages and attract 5 million unique visitors per month. It's also linked to Facebook and Twitter.

"News for Nerds"

Owned by Geeknet Inc., the site bills itself as "News for Nerds," and that's a fair description in the friendliest sense of those words. The site features user-submitted summaries of stories on a range of technology topics—everything from Linux and open-source software to book reviews, general science and technology, to Apple products. Each summary includes a link to the original source of the story.

The top story summaries are displayed on the home page, and they're collected under Upcoming, Recent, and Popular categories. The home page also features links to subsections that include original Slashdot content. Clicking on "Ask Slashdot," for example, takes you to a page of advice offered by Slashdot community members on things like jobs, computer hardware, software glitches, and "philosophical problems." Clicking on "Book Reviews" takes you to a section where you can read—and write—original reviews of mostly (but not necessarily, as the website puts it) tech books.

The Conversation

Unlike other social news sites, Slashdot allows non-members to submit story recommendations. But if you want to do more than hand over the article's web address (URL), you'll have to create an account and log on. Once you log on, you'll be able to write what the site calls a "Journal Entry," which is a short summary of the story.

That journal entry isn't usually a neutral summary, but the first of the reader comments that accompany these story postings. These conversational threads are the heart of the Slashdot community.

It's important to note that, although Slashdot readers tend to post stories about technology and related topics, they are not restricted to those areas. Articles on political subjects, for example, have been the source of some lively threaded discussions on the site.

Slashdot commenters get rated on a scale that's based on the moderation of their comments. A commenter's rating is her "Karma." The Slashdot karmic scale rates commenters as Terrible, Bad, Neutral, Positive, Good, or Excellent. Essentially, Karma is used to determine who moderates and who doesn't on Slashdot.

The Moderation System

Unlike other social news sites that put the fate of submitted stories almost entirely into the hands of members of the community, Slashdot relies on something of an editorial vetting process. Users submit stories, but the editors have to approve them.

Also, the comments that accompany those stories are managed by what the site founders call a moderation system. According to Rob Malda, moderators are the cream of Slashdot contributors, chosen by the system for their high-quality posting and commenting. Any Slashdot reader is eligible to become a moderator, depending on factors that include length and regularity of readership, the reader's "Karma," and willingness to participate, among others. Every thirty minutes the system tallies the number of comments posted and hands out "tokens" to a "proportionate number of eligible users," Malda explains in the site's FAQ page. Get enough tokens, and you're a moderator. The tokens bestow additional "points of influence," which moderators use to temper user comments. Moderators rate user comments by adding or subtracting points based on their assessment of whether the comment is perceived as normal, off-topic, funny, insightful, redundant, or interesting, among other descriptors.

Slashdot editors have unlimited "mod points." The site has been criticized for this practice, but Malda sees it this way: "You can argue that allowing admins unlimited moderation is somehow inherently unfair, but one of the goals of Slashdot is to produce readable content for a variety of readers with a variety of reading habits. I believe this process improves discussions for the vast majority of Slashdot Readers, so it will stay this way."

Mixx

Mixx (*www.mixx.com*) is a relative newcomer to the world of social media, and compared to Digg, its user base is small. But this general-interest social news site has earned praise for its simplicity, the speed with which it breaks new stories, and features that allow users to customize their experience.

The Mixx website was launched in 2007 by McLean, Virginia-based Recommended Reading, Inc. The CEO and founder, Chris McGill, was the former head of strategy at *USA Today* and one-time general manager of Yahoo! News. Within months of the site's launch, the company announced "content partnerships" with *USA Today*, Reuters, The Weather Channel, the *Los Angeles Times*, and CNN.

Today, this general-interest social news site allows members to submit stories, photos, and videos from the web in a wide range of categories, and to vote and comment on them. Topics covered include business, entertainment, sports, health, and technology, among others.

Mixx members can also create tweets for the Twitter microblog about the stories they submit directly from the Mixx website. And Mixx is linked to Facebook.

"You Find It; We'll Mixx It"

The most popular stories submitted by Mixx members are displayed on the website's main page, along with the top photos and top websites. Anyone can browse these lists and click on links that take you to the original source material. A navigation bar near the top of the page takes you to lists of other popular stories, photos, and videos, as well as links to content from CNN, *USA Today*, and stories flagged as "Breaking News."

Links in the navigation bar take you to top news stories, organized in categories, such as National, World, Politics, and even Obituaries. The navigation bar includes links to similar collections under Business, Entertainment, Sports, Life, Health, Tech, Science, Fun, and Community (which takes you to a listing of Mixx communities and groups).

Mixx content can be sorted by level of popularity, the age of the posting (how recently it appeared), and by number of accompanying comments.

Submitting a Link

Mixx users can submit links to the website by clicking a Submit a Link button and filling in the site's URL. But many websites now display the Mixx icon, and registered members can click on that icon to summon a page similar to the forms used by Digg and Slashdot. If you click on the Mixx icon on a website, this form comes prefilled with the story's title and description. You can add a "tag" or keyword to the submission, and you can add it to a public category (News, Health, Business, etc.) You can also designate the content as Mature.

You can also add your own comment here. It's not required, but it gets the conversation started.

Once you click "Submit," Mixx gives you a chance to add or edit your comment, change the categories you chose, or back out altogether and delete the submission. You have fifteen minutes to make the changes, and the site displays a countdown timer.

"Your Blend of the Web"

Anyone can browse the content submitted to Mixx, but you have to register to vote and comment on it. Registered members set up YourMixx pages, which allow them to establish preferred content categories. Submitting a photo during signup allows Mixx to create an avatar, which accompanies your comments. Once you've signed up, "YourMixx" is added to the navigation bar.

Mixx members are invited to create profiles and generate groups of friends, but neither is required. The "YourMixx" page displays content based on your preferences. Clicking on the "Front Page" button takes you to a list of popular stories "as voted by people like you." There's also access to an e-mail feature, access to editing tools for your Profile and status updates, a Friends list, a page that displays conversations you're following, and a Share History page that catalogs the items you've shared on the site.

Once you're all signed up, Mixx gives you access to the Up arrow that you'll see next to each story. Clicking the arrow adds your thumbs-up vote for that article.

Mixxing it Up in Groups

Mixx members can also share text, photos, and video within groups. A Mixx group can include your friends, family, co-workers, or simply other like-minded members. A group can be private, which means that it's totally invisible to other Mixx members, or it can be public, which means that all Mixx members can see the content. Depending on the type of public group, others can't participate without an invitation, can request an invite, or can freely join.

Mixx groups can be of virtually any size, and members contribute by submitting, voting, and commenting on stories, videos, and photos. And groups have two levels of membership: "owners" and "members." Members can view content in the group, comment, and vote on it; owners can do all that, plus they can invite others to join and ask existing members to leave.

Reddit

Reddit (*www.reddit.com*) is also a relatively young social news site, but one that has earned a respectable following. It was launched in 2005 by a pair of twenty-two-year-olds (Steve Huffman and Alexis Ohanian), and the service was acquired in 2006 by magazine publisher Condé Nast. In 2008, Reddit became an open-source project, which means that the computer code behind the social news site was made available to any software developer who might want to download it and submit improvements and changes.

No Frills Social News

Reddit is something of a no-frills social news site. The design is very simple and almost graphics-free, which makes it unusual in the often flashy, image-packed world of social media. Even the Pics page displays only a column of thumbnail images stacked next to hyperlinked headlines. (You have to click on the thumbnail or the headline to open the source of the image.)

The top news items are displayed on the main page as simple hyperlinked headlines. A tiny navigation bar running across the top of the main page provides links to stories and images grouped by topics. And a set of tabs provide links to different layers of each topic page.

QUESTION

How do you pronounce "Reddit?"
The story goes that Reddit was named by co-founder Alexis Ohanian, who came up with it while browsing the University of Virginia's Alderman Library. You pronounce it as you would "read it," in the question "Have you read it?"

Reddit Registration

To vote or comment on stories and images posted to the Reddit website, you have to become a member, but signing up is very simple. You click on "Register" to create the usual user account with a verifiable e-mail address, username, and password. Once you've established an account, you can submit stories, comment, and vote. Voting on a story and/or an image is simply a matter of clicking the up or down arrows next to a story. The number of up-votes is displayed right there between the two arrows.

Scores are determined by a simple equation: the number of up-votes minus the number of down-votes. Reddit doesn't display the scores of new submissions immediately. In an effort to "mitigate the bandwagon effect" the system refrains from reporting vote counts for a few hours. In the end, the high vote getters "bubble up" to the main page, but they don't necessarily stay there long. The Reddit community is all about constantly refreshing content.

More Karma and Moderators

Reddit also uses the "Karma" concept to rank its users. A user's Karma is displayed next to her username as a number. That number, Reddit says, "reflects how much good the user has done for the Reddit community." The main way to accumulate Karma points on Reddit is to submit lots of popular links to stories and images.

Reddit also uses moderators, which it describes as regular Reddit members with "a few humble duties within a particular community," and "no special powers outside of the communities they moderate." A moderator's duties include, among other things, establishing the limitations of a community, such as deciding whether its members need to be over eighteen; designating a link or comment as an official community submission; removing objectionable links and/or comments from the community (Reddit cites spam and porn as examples); and banning spammers and "other abusive users" from submitting to the community.

Subreddits

The Reddit maintainers like to describe the overall community as a collection of sub-communities, which it calls "subreddits." These subreddits focus on specific topics, such as science, music, sports, gadgets, and various cities. When you register as a member, Reddit signs you up for the most popular subreddits, but you are free to join any that interest you. (Reddit calls this "subscribing.")

Subscribing to a community changes how the main page looks to you when you log on to the website. You can still get to any story or image you want, but Reddit tries to refine its understanding of your preferences by factoring in your community memberships, to provide you with a more customized experience of the website.

Reddit members can browse the website's list of communities, which are arranged in order of popularity. But you can also use the Reddit search page and type in a keyword. And because Reddit is an open source project, a number of unofficial websites designed to organize subreddits are available on the web, including the Subreddit Finder and the Subreddit Directory.

And Many More . . .

The list of social news sites is long, and getting longer. In addition to the sites highlighted in this chapter, you might want to check out some of the social news sites listed here. Some of these are niche sites focused on a particular topic. Treehugger, for example, focuses on environmental issues. IndianPad attracts primarily Indian-American users.

- Fark (*www.fark.com*)
- Propeller (*www.propeller.com*)
- StumbleUpon (*www.stumbleupon.com*)
- Treehugger (*www.treehugger.com*)
- Autospies (*www.autospies.com*)
- Tip'd (*http://tipd.com*)
- Shoutwire (*http://shoutwire.com*)
- Newsvine (*www.newsvine.com*)
- IndianPad (*www.indianpad.com*)
- Plime (*www.plime.com*)
- Care2 (*www.care2.com/news*)
- Kirsty (*www.kirtsy.com*)
- Nowpublic (*www.nowpublic.com*)
- Tweako (*http://tweako.com*)

CHAPTER 13

Opinion and Reviews: Would You Recommend This Plumber?

There's certainly no shortage of everyman opinions in this world, but on the web, they're more organized. In fact, there are online communities dedicated to collecting and publishing the opinions, recommendations, and reviews of average Joes and Janes on everything from hotels to laundry detergent. These communities generally welcome anyone willing to offer a thoughtful thumbs up or down, which adds a layer of user-generated content that is still evolving and often controversial. Here's what you need to know to get the most from these websites, and, if you're so inclined, add your two cents.

Consumer-Generated Media

Social media mavens think of the burgeoning body of web-based opinions and reviews written by end users as a sub-category of user-generated content known as "consumer-generated media." These are not traditional expert opinions or professional reviews. This isn't Consumer Reports or America's Test Kitchen. This is social media content generated by actual consumers sharing real experiences with products and services they've bought or tried themselves.

Some of these opinionated consumers might have a high-level of familiarity or knowledge of a particular product type or service area—moms who've bought a number of baby strollers, for example, or frequent flyers. But they're not professional evaluators; they're *fellow customers*.

And that's what makes these websites so appealing. The reviews and opinions are, generally speaking, from people just like you who already bought the DVD player you're considering, read the book you heard about, or hired the mechanic whose name you spotted on Craig's List. Professional evaluations of products and services are great—no one expects these communities to replace them—but there's just nothing like getting the lowdown from a peer who's been there.

Communities versus Features

Of course, consumer opinions and reviews make up a big part of the content generated on social networks. Recommending stuff is one of the things we do when we interact with friends, family, and co-workers. Lots of people start their shopping homework on their social networks by asking other members for recommendations.

And a growing number of commercial vendors include review/opinion features on their websites nowadays. Amazon.com is one of the most famous examples; eBay is another. The resulting content adds to the volume of social media. But allowing consumers to hold forth on your commercial website is not the same thing as a community.

The value (at least for now) of the stand-alone consumer-review communities is in their ability to provide readily accessible platforms for man-on-the-street sources of opinions on products and services. You can definitely ask your Facebook buddies what they think of the new summer blockbuster, because a bunch of them will have seen it. But what if you want to get the 411 on a particular riding mower or vacation cruise package? The consumer opinion sites essentially expand your network for this one purpose.

Reputation

If you've ever shopped on eBay, you know how important a vendor's reputation is to that person. They practically beg you to give them a good rating after you buy. Why? A bad rating can cost the vendor real money.

That's an example of the power of online *reputation*, and it's the foundation of consumer-generated content. Reputation, in the geekiest technical sense of that word, is part of your online identity. It's the part that is defined by others. It's not really that different from the real-world version, but on the web everything seems to get magnified. Academics talk about the web's "reputation culture," and the opinion sites typically maintain some kind of "reputation system."

Anonymity is generally not allowed in these communities, and some require you to create a profile, just as you would for any social network. Nastiness and ranting are typically discouraged, and the reviews themselves can be rated by other community members and readers. Ratings are typically based on how helpful readers found a review to be. Popular reviewers move up the hierarchy within a community, and their views get prominent placement on the website. And that status is usually subject to continued favorable responses from readers.

Remuneration

Some of these opinion/review communities offer to compensate their reviewers with actual cash. Epinions is best known for this practice, but other communities do it. The UK's Ciao community boasts on its website "Earn money with reviews." They pay up to £3 for a review. The Epinions model gets a lot of press, but most of these communities don't pay their reviewers.

Controversy

Sharing the wealth for writing helpful reviews is one thing; paying reviewers to post favorable opinions is another. Amazon.com's review system has come under attack from critics who charge that companies were paying fake customers and even their own employees to write rave reviews.

(Amazon has always maintained that the majority of its customer reviews are legitimate, and that it's always working to improve its system.)

ALERT

Don't forget that the Federal Trade Commission ruled last year that online product recommendations by reviewers with "material connections" with the products being reviewed have to disclose those connections. If you don't, you could get fined.

In 2010, Yelp was hit with three class-action lawsuits accusing its salespeople of pressuring reviewed companies to advertise by threatening to manipulate reviews. Yelp vigorously denied the claims, arguing that its automated algorithm would prevent that sort of thing. Yelp has also come under criticism for its practice of allowing businesses that advertise on the site to move their favorite review to the top of the list, regardless of when it had been originally posted.

The Communities

Consumer-based opinion and review communities can focus on a single product category, or cover virtually anything you might want to buy or rent. They can draw from the experiences of customers living in a particular area, or dip into the vast, worldwide pool of consumers. Each community provides its own set of rating tools, and enforces its own set of rules.

The list of consumer opinion and review communities isn't that long, but it's probably longer than you think. No doubt you've heard of Yelp and Epinions, and if you travel a lot, TripAdvisor might be on your radar. But how about MouthShut.com?

The following roundup of consumer-based opinion and review communities is not meant to be a comprehensive list. You'll find some big names, some niche players, and some relative unknowns. But it should give you a good sense of what's available in Web 2.0 land for opinionated consumers and the shoppers who love them.

Epinions.com

You know what they say about opinions: like a certain body part, everybody has one. But as far as the folks at Epinions are concerned, that's not necessarily a bad thing. In fact, if enough people respect your opinion, you might even get paid for it.

Founded in 1999, Epinions (*www.epinions.com*) is an extremely popular general-interest consumer website currently owned by Shopping.com (which is owned by eBay). The Mountain View, California-based service considers itself to be a platform for shared user experiences. More than thirty categories of reviewed products and services are listed on the site, which include millions of items. The site makes money through advertising, content subscriptions, and licensing of the service's technologies. Users who conduct product research on the site will often find links to price lists and online retailers.

Membership Services

Membership is free, though it's hard to know how big the community is; for some reason, Epinions doesn't publish the number of registered members. Review writers must be members, but the reviews themselves can be read by anyone with a web browser. Epinions claims not to manufacture or sell any of the products listed on the site.

Members can write reviews on any topic, and Epinions wants its reviewers to be "brutally honest . . . even if it means saying negative things." They can write a product review, which is "intended to give the reader detailed information about one specific product," or an "essay," which is more of a bit of general advice on a type of product. Express Reviews are twenty to 199 words long; Regular reviews are 200 words or more.

Readers rate the reviews themselves by clicking on ratings buttons displayed beneath each review: Very Helpful (VH), Helpful (H), Somewhat Helpful (SH), and Not Helpful (NH).

Epinions reviewers can also earn a piece of Epinions's "Income Share pool," which is a portion of the community's income that gets divvied up among reviewers based on how often their reviews were "used in making a decision" on a reader's purchase.

A "Web of Trust"

A key Epinions concept is something called a "Web of Trust," which includes all the reviewers who get your highest rating. These are the people you have decided provide the most reliable and valuable reviews. According to Epinions, building this trusted group helps the Epinions.com system predict how helpful other reviews will be to you.

Web of Trust is also a safe-surfing tool for your web browser. Popularly known as WOT, it's a free browser add-on designed to warn you about potentially risky websites before you open them. WOT works on Internet Explorer, Firefox, and Google Chrome browsers.

Trusted reviews are displayed near the top of all your searches. You can add members to your Web of Trust with a mouse click. Adding people to your trusted network improves their standing as reviewers. You can also decide to "distrust" them if their reviews become unreliable.

Highly trusted Epinions reviewers might become "Advisors," which Epinions describes as "active members of the Epinions community who help shoppers find the best content on Epinions by rating . . . reviews in their category." The reviews of Advisors carry more weight in the community; they play a more important role in determining which reviews are seen by new visitors, and have the opportunity to offer feedback on new developments in the community.

Yelp

Yelp (*www.yelp.com*) is the best-known consumer-review-based community, not to mention the most controversial. Founded in 2004, the site claims to draw more than 26 million users per month. The site indexes more than 15 million small businesses, including companies that have not yet been reviewed by Yelp users, and has published more than 9 million reviews.

The Yelp community was founded in San Francisco by two former Pay-Pal software engineers, Jeremy Stoppelman and Russel Simmons. It focuses on reviews of local businesses throughout the United States, Canada, the UK, and Ireland. The service makes its money from sales of local advertising. Business owners can set up free accounts on the site to post offers, photos, and messages to their customers. Paid content is labeled "Sponsored

Results," but advertisers who like a review can "promote" it by displaying at the top of their Yelp page.

Yelp Membership

Individual membership in the community is also free, and the site incorporates many social networking features and forms in its website. Members, who are called "Yelpers," must create a profile, for example, that includes a picture, an e-mail address, and some personal particulars. In fact, the Profile Home page acts very much like the home page of any social network, linking you to the reviews you have written; groups of reviews you liked called "Lists," including headings such as My Neighborhood, Top Restaurants, Born to Shop, and The Places I Go Out; a list of compliments you receive on your reviews; and a Friends list, among others. You can add more photos to your profile page if you want to, and there's a community chat feature, called "Yelp Talk."

Yelp describes itself as "an online urban city guide that helps people find cool places to eat, shop, drink, relax, and play," all of which is based on "the informed opinions of a vibrant and active community of locals in the know." In addition to reviews, you can use Yelp to find events, special offers, lists, and to talk with other Yelpers.

Reviews on Yelp cover local services and destinations, including restaurants, bars, salons, retail businesses, doctors, dentists, tennis pros, parks, museums, and many more. You must be a member to write a review, and members can rank them as Useful, Funny, or Cool. Yelp also has a feature that allows the local business owners to post a public comment on a review. And the reviewers can then respond to that business owner in an e-mail.

Top reviews can earn the designation "Yelp Elite," which is similar to Epinions's Advisor status.

Yelp Myths and Applications

Yelp insists that some of its practices are misunderstood, and has gone so far as to post a Myths about Yelp page to set the record straight. To address the charge that its salespeople manipulate reviews, for example, the service claims that, even though it trusts its sales staff, it has taken steps to "avoid even an appearance of impropriety." (You'll find the list of refuted myths here: *www.yelp.com/myths*)

Yelp is also a very mobile-savvy community. Yelp apps are available for the iPhone, the BlackBerry, the Palm Pre, and the Android smart phones.

TripAdvisor

Founded in 2000, TripAdvisor (*www.tripadvisor.com*) calls itself "the most popular and largest travel community in the world" and claims more than 32 million unique monthly visitors to its websites. The community specializes in publishing consumer reviews of travel destinations, and has published more than 30 million of them. The site also offers a pretty wide range of travel planning and assistance features.

TripAdvisor Membership

Membership in the TripAdvisor community is free, and members provide most of the content. The site is going for a relaxed, neighborhood-coffee-shop feel—just a bunch of road warriors, hanging out, comparing notes, and sharing bits of wisdom. But there's no member home page to speak of.

Although the site lists airfares, hotel rates, restaurants, and vacation rentals, it's not a reservation or booking service. The site publishes a travel newsletter, which you can get via e-mail, and best and worst lists on the website that were compiled from member reviews—Best Destinations, for example, and Dirtiest Hotels.

The site doesn't require members to do more than register, and it guides you through the reviewing process. Clicking on "Write a Review" takes you to a series of prompts, asking what you'd like to review (hotel, attraction, restaurant, city/town) and which one (you have to know the name and location). Once you've picked your target, just click "Write Review," and you'll have access to a form with a place for identifying the purpose of your trip (business or leisure) the date of the trip, a window in which to write the review itself, and a long list of check boxes for things like "Quiet" if you're reviewing a hotel, and "Dining options" if it's a restaurant. There are also places to check "thumbs up" or "thumbs down," and a rating.

Travel Forums

The website also features travel forums, where members can ask questions of other members, and an extensive range of travel planning tools, including:

- Flight Search with Fees Estimator, which provides a large inventory of flights with the best deals available. The Fees Estimator is a unique travel tool designed to calculate and compare the entire cost of a domestic flight, including ticket price, fees for checked luggage, and in-flight food service and entertainment. A feature called "SeatGuru" displays the airline's seating maps with user reviews, real-time seat availability charts, and "TripTip!" alerts that sound when business-class or first-class tickets are available for a price close to the coach fare.
- Top Values Index, which is designed to sort out the most popular hotels with the best room rates.
- Listings of more than half a million restaurants around the world, with more than two million ratings and reviews, sortable by location, price, cuisine, and "recommended for."
- Gas Tank Getaways, which help travelers to plan road trips. It finds vacation destination options that are "a tank of gas or less away from home."
- The Traveler Network, which helps members to sort and prioritize the most relevant reviews from among the 30 million-plus published by the community.

Angie's List

You have to be a paid member to see the reviews assembled on Angie's List (*www.angieslist.com*), but you don't have be a member to post them, and they're all consumer-generated. They have been since the service's co-founder, Angie Hicks, put together her first list of local consumer reviews in 1995 by going door-to-door and recruiting her neighbors in Columbus, Ohio. The first list had about a thousand members, but it grew and the community eventually moved to the web. The service now claims more than a million members.

Angie's List still focuses on the same kinds of local services: doctors, roofers, plumbers, auto mechanics, air duct cleaners—all the kinds of services you'd expect a home owner to need. But there are also categories that you might not expect, like Artwork/Murals, Computer Repair, Limousine Service, Pooper Scoopers, and Prosthetics & Orthotics Retailers.

The site prefers "comment" and/or "report" to "review." Those comments form the basis for a company report card, graded A–F. Angie's does the grading, but insists that it's all based on the member comments. The service says that member comments and reports are never edited, but it does use "proprietary technology and human review" to make sure that they meet the website's guidelines before they're posted. Any comments that don't pass muster go back to the member with questions and clarification before posting. This is also how they screen out the companies and service providers who are "self-reporting," and blitz reviews of the same company.

MouthShut.com

It's headquartered in India, but this consumer-generated review website also has a U.S. following. Founded in 2000 as a peer-to-peer network, MouthShut.com (*www.mouthshut.com*) was India's first "Person-to-Person Information Exchange."

The emphasis in this community is firmly on sharing reviews and opinions among fellow shoppers. Membership is free, and you don't have to have roots in India to join. But there is an ethnic identity to this community. As the website puts it, "Culturally, we prefer to consult amongst each other before making decisions." Venture Beat Profiles describe Mouthshut.com as "an online community where the world's most vocal and influential consumers come together to write and read reviews and compare hundreds of thousands of products and services."

Mouthshut.com publishes millions of consumer reviews on hundreds of thousands of products and services. The site covers a truly wide range of reviewable categories: Automobiles, Books, Computers, Education, Electronics, Employers, Entertainment, Fashion, Food & Drinks, Health & Beauty, Household, Internet, Kids, Malls & Stores, Media, Personal Finance, Sports, and Travel.

Since 2008, MouthShut.com has provided its members with integrated social networking tools, which allow them to publish "diary posts," which are basically status updates, send gifts to other members, send bulk messages, and add unlimited photos to their profiles. Mouthshut's hottest reviewers can earn "Star Writer" status, which is similar to Epinions's Advisor and Yelp's Yelp Elite.

CHAPTER 14

Wikis: Getting Everyone on the Same Page

Need proof that social media is about more than just over-the-backyard-fence yakking and sharing your vacation photos? Consider the wiki. You've no doubt heard of Wikipedia, but you might not know that the famous online encyclopedia is just one example of a unique type of social media that more and more people are using to collaborate online. Virtually any organization, company, department, or group—even families—can use a wiki to exchange ideas and information via the web. Here's what you need to know to get started with this fascinating collaborative software.

What's a Wiki?

A wiki (pronounced "wickie") is a website designed to allow visitors to freely add, edit, remove, comment on, and just generally change the content stored there. It's basically a type of content management system, or CMS, operated by a crowd. The content is typically a set of documents or web pages that has been collectively written and edited by anyone allowed access to the site.

Users access wikis through their web browsers. The wiki sites can be set up on servers connected to the public Internet or on private company networks called *intranets*. Wikis can be open and public, allowing anyone with an Internet connection and a web browser to join in, or private and limited to specified groups.

Although it's true that some wikis welcome all comers, most provide access to relatively small groups or membership-based communities. But anyone within the group can edit *any* page with complete freedom.

Wiki pages are edited in "real time," which means that the changes you make appear on the document as you're making them. But users write and edit wiki documents *asynchronously*, which means that all the participants don't have to be there at the same time.

Some Famous (and Not Yet Famous) Wikis

Once you start looking around for them, wikis will start popping up all over the web. There are thousands of them, and you'll wonder how you missed them! You'll find reference wikis; wikis on movies, TV, and books; food and drink wikis; and wikis with a political bent.

Wikipedia (*www.wikipedia.org*), of course, is the most famous wiki, but there are thousands of them up and running today on the web, on individual desktops, and behind corporate firewalls. You might have heard of the Wiktionary (*www.wiktionary.org*), for example, which is a free, Wikipedia-style online dictionary. WikiAnswers (*www.wiki.answers.com*) is a community-generated "social knowledge" question-and-answer platform. There's LingWiki (*http://lingwiki.com*), which is used by language experts. And Wikidweb (*www.wikidweb.com*) is an online directory of wikis.

But all wikis aren't just about replacing the dusty reference books stacked up on your refrigerator. There's the Marvel Database (*http://marvel .wikia.com*), a wiki devoted to Marvel comics and the Marvel Universe. The

CookbookWiki (*http://recipes.wikia.com*) is filled with recipes and user-generated and edited articles about food. And there's the *Criminal Minds* (*http://criminalmindswiki.wetpaint.com*) fan wiki, for example, that's full of user-generated-and-edited articles about the popular TV show.

Wikis are popping up on health related subjects, too. The Diabetes Wikia (*http://diabetes.wikia.com*), for example, features articles about diabetic treatments and products, as well as "stories of personal triumph." The QuitSmoking wiki (*http://quitsmoking.wikia.com/wiki/Quit_Smoking*) is a place where former smokers and smokers who are trying to quit share their experiences, advice, and opinions on topics ranging from nicotine withdrawal to the benefits of quitting, and cancer to asthma. And WikiDoc (*www.wikidoc.org*) bills itself as "the original medical wiki/encyclopedia."

ALERT

Don't confuse Wikimedia, the foundation behind Wikipedia, with MediaWiki, the wiki engine developed for the foundation and used to run Wikipedia. First released in 2002, MediaWiki is one of the top wiki engines and runs most of the wiki hosting sites. The name was a play on "Wikimedia," and many people find it to be annoyingly confusing.

Political wikis are also starting to show up on the web. Conservapedia (*www.conservapedia.com*) for example, which, as the name implies, assembles collections of articles and images with a conservative point of view. WikiRoots (*http://grassroots.wikia.com*) is a grassroots political-action wiki. And the Opinion Wiki (*http://opinion.wikia.com*) site assembles a range of political opinion articles.

WikiWiki!

The first wiki came online, believe it or not, in 1995, and it's still up and running today! Its creator, software engineer Ward Cunningham, originally described it as "the simplest online database that could possibly work." He created it to host a collaborative discussion of software programming patterns. The site still lives on the server of the Portland Pattern Repository.

Cunningham is also credited with coining the term "wiki." The story goes that he was inspired by the name of the speedy Wiki Wiki Shuttle bus system at the Honolulu International Airport. He called his first wiki Wiki-WikiWeb ("wikiwiki" means "real quick"). It's a techie site focused on software development, and today includes tens of thousands of pages. You can check it out here: *http://c2.com/cgi-bin/wiki*.

Cunningham is clear about what he sees as the chief benefits of wikis. On his WikiWikiWeb, he writes: "Allowing everyday users to create and edit any page in a website is exciting in that it encourages democratic use of the web and promotes content composition by nontechnical users."

Patrick Mueller is most often credited with striking out with the first wiki "clone." A *clone* is another version of a software program that is very similar or heavily inspired by the original. Mueller is a software engineer best known for his contributions to the open source WebKit browser engine project.

Shared Authorship

Wikis are designed to get everyone on the same page (literally). The wiki style of content management is what social media mavens call a shared-authorship model, which means that users can add new content and revise existing content without asking permission to do so. Documents on a wiki can be edited very fast, because you don't need the help of a programmer or any programming skills, and you don't have to get anyone's approval.

Fans of this open style of content editing claim that it results in the whole becoming greater than the sum of its parts. In other words, collaboratively edited and maintained documents are inherently richer because they draw on collective wisdom

In his foreword to *The Wiki Way: Quick Collaboration on the Web* (Cunningham and Bo Leuf, Addison-Wesley Professional, 2001), probably the first book ever written on wikis, programming guru Ron Jeffries wrote about a conversation he had with Cunningham, in which he was asked, "What would you get if you had a website where anyone could edit or add anything?" Jeffries wrote: "Boredom, I guessed, or chaos. Boy, was I wrong. You get hundreds, thousands of pages full of information, ideas, conversations, learning, and teaching. You get linkages among ideas, conversations among people. You get a tool for business, a tool for people. You get copies and replicas all over the world. You get . . . the wiki."

Critics argue that this model generates documents that are essentially un-authoritative, potentially biased, and often just plain wrong. Worse, user-editable websites are inherently vulnerable to users who want to insert intentionally offensive, misleading, or inflammatory content. This practice, called "trolling," is a form of sabotage that wikis have managed with varying degrees of success.

There's also the phenomenon popularly referred to as "edit wars," in which one individual or faction edits a piece of content on a wiki, and an opponent re-edits that content back to its original form. WikiMedia, the organization behind Wikipedia, insists that this term is misleading, and feels that "reversion wars," is more accurate. These content disputes get the most press when they happen on Wikipedia, but even behind-the-firewall corporate wikis are not immune to this kind of conflict.

But the pro-wiki crowd maintains that the very collaborative nature of a wiki provides the fix; misinformation may creep in, users may misbehave, and contributors may argue, but someone in the crowd of editors always finds the problem and corrects it. The good guys, they say, always outnumber the bad guys.

Wiki Engines

The software that runs a wiki is called a "wiki engine." This is the application that provides the editing and collaboration features, as well as the look and feel of the wiki. Most wiki engines are open-source software, which isn't surprising given the open nature of the wiki model. ("Open source," remember, means that the computer code behind the wiki engine is available to any software developer who might want to download it and submit improvements and changes.)

The most-used wiki engine is probably MediaWiki, which was used to build and run Wikipedia. But there are likely hundreds of them out there. Most are free—including MediaWiki—but a growing number also offer additional features, capabilities, and support for a fee.

QUESTION

What's Wikitext?
Wikitext is a lightweight markup language, sort of a simplified version of HTML that's used to render web pages. Wikitext is used to write pages on a wiki site.

When people say "wiki," they sometimes mean the websites, and sometimes the software packages used to build and run them, which can be confusing. It might be useful to think of the combination of a wiki website, a wiki engine, and any supporting software as a collaboration platform called a *wiki*. But in strict terms, the *wiki* is the *website*, and the *wiki engine* is the *software*.

All wiki engines allow users to create and edit web pages collaboratively from their web browsers, but the editing tools and collaboration features provided vary from engine to engine. However, a basic list of capabilities would almost certainly include the following:

WYSIWYG Editing

There was a time when you had to know something called *wikitext* or HTML to edit documents in a wiki. But nowadays, any wikis you're likely to work with provide what-you-see-is-what-you-get, or WYSIWYG editing. (It's pronounced "wizzy-wig.") You just click into edit mode, and the way the page looks while you're editing it is exactly the way it will display on the web. It's just like using a word processor. You can format text, insert images, add files, and link to other pages with familiar commands and toolbars.

Version Control

Most wikis provide a way to keep track of and save earlier versions of a page, so they can be recovered in case of errors or abuse, and compared to more recent versions. This audit trail allows every change to be tracked. Many also provide tools for managing and monitoring the activities of participants, with records of who changed what and when.

Invitation System

Wikis are all about user-generated and edited content, and they're built to support that kind of multi-user participation. If it's a company wiki, the participants are probably part of a team. If it's a more public wiki, it might provide an e-mail system for inviting participants. Some include bulk account setup features for adding groups. And some support mailing lists.

Access Control

Contrary to popular belief, most wikis don't allow just anybody to walk in. Wiki engines and wiki hosting services usually provide some kind of user access control features. These tools control who gets in, what they can see, and what they can do, automatically. Essentially, you can create rules that you can apply to individual users or groups of users.

Hyperlinks

Wikis are collections of web pages, so it's only natural to include tools for creating links among those pages. But modern wiki engines also allow you to link to information and resources on other websites, and even other wikis.

Uploading Capabilities

The ability to upload text documents to a wiki has become a standard feature, and wikis are still mainly about user-edited text. But the range of file types supported by wiki engines is growing. Some allow you to upload images, audio files, and even video clips and add them to your wiki page. Some even come with image managers.

Social Networking

The proliferation of social networks has prompted some wiki-engine providers to add social networking tools, as well as connections to such social networks as Facebook and LinkedIn. Links to the Twitter microblog are also increasingly common. You'll also find community forums and even blogging features.

Personal Wikis

A personal wiki is . . . well . . . personal. It's your wiki, set up for your personal use. You can use it by yourself, to browse, edit, search, and link together your own collection of pages. Or you can share the space with others. People use these types of wikis as personal information managers and planners. They use them to generate to-do lists, keep journals, organize research notes, plan projects, store passwords, and engage in "mind-mapping," which is a kind of stream-of-consciousness style of note keeping.

Some personal wikis are built with wiki engines that run on your desktop or laptop computer. These are also called "standalone" or "desktop" wikis. Some wiki engines allow users to set up personal wikis online. Some people just set up traditional wikis, make sure they're password-protected, and then don't invite anyone else to the party. Online personal wikis have the advantage of providing access from any computer with an Internet connection and a web browser, as well as many smart phones. Many of the wiki-hosting services support personal wikis, including some of those highlighted in the next section.

Getting Started Down on the Wiki Farm

The easiest way to get started with a wiki is to join an existing, public site. And the easiest way to do that is through a wiki-hosting service, popularly known as a wiki farm. Wiki farms provide space on the web for multiple wikis. They host them on their own servers and manage all the geeky stuff. All you have to do is sign up.

Wikia

Wikia (*www.wikia.com*), for example, is a free wiki-hosting service aimed at communities. The service was founded in 2004 by Jimmy Wales, co-creator of Wikipedia, and Angela Beesley Starling, Wikimedia Foundation advisory board member and long-time Wikipedia volunteer editor. According to Starling, the service was hosting more than 80,000 wikis in 188 different languages by 2010. Many of the world's largest community-created wikis are hosted by Wikia, including as Wookieepedia (the *Star Wars* wiki), WoWWiki (the *World of Warcraft* wiki), and LyricWiki, a wiki that publishes the lyrics to more than a million songs.

The Wikia website is colorful and lively, featuring lots of graphics and slide shows. It connects visitors to a range of public-facing wikis under the broad categories of entertainment, gaming, lifestyle, and others, each of which is subdivided into many more. Clicking on "entertainment" in the navigation bar, for example, opens a drop-down list that includes movies, television, music, anime, and others. Clicking on a list item opens a page of links to public wikis on that theme. Clicking a link takes you to a sign-up page. (Wikia also seems to handle the sign up.) Once you sign up, you're signing up for Wikia, which gives you access to all the public sites they host.

PBworks

Formerly known as PBwiki, this hosting service (*http://pbworks.com*) was founded in 2005 by David Weekly, Ramit Sethi, and Nathan Schmidt. Weekly pioneered the idea of making wikis much easier to use for non-techies by providing a hosting service. The "PB" in the title stands for "peanut butter." The story goes that the founders believed setting up a wiki should be as easy as making a peanut butter sandwich.

This wiki-hosting service is a bit more sober than Wikia. There's a pronounced focus on the business and legal communities. The service bills itself as a provider of an online workspace for team collaboration. But it also hosts educational and personal wikis. By mid 2010, the service claims to be hosting more than 1 million wikis and nearly 7 million of user content.

PBworks provides its services on a "freemium" basis. (You'll recall that the freemium model combines a basic free membership with subscription-based premium services.)

The service lets you sign up for a personal wiki for free. The membership includes a number of useful features, including collaborative editing, history and audit trails, e-mail messaging, access controls, templates, and security. If you want page- and folder-level access controls, hideable and lockable pages, and some customizable features, you'll have to pay a subscription fee.

Wikispaces

Launched in 2005, Wikispaces (*www.wikispaces.com*) is run by a San Francisco-based company called Tangient. It's not a flashy hosting service, but it offers a simple, usable interface that's proved very appealing to non-technical wikinauts. In 2010, the company claimed to have registered nearly 5 million members and more than 1.6 million wikis. The website boasts of having "products designed for the smallest classroom and the world's largest corporations and institutions."

This one isn't a free service, but it offers many useful and accessible tools for individuals, groups, businesses, and schools that want to set up their own wikis. In 2008, the service made headlines for giving 100,000 free wikis to K–12 teachers.

Wikidot

Wikidot (*www.wikidot.com*) bills itself as the world's third-largest wiki farm, and claims half a million users running 120,000 sites and serving about 40 million unique visitors per year. Launched in 2006, this service combines wiki hosting with blogging and social networking features. Wikidot was developed in Poland by Michal Frackowiak, and maintains headquarters there (though it's incorporated in Delaware).

Another freemium hoster, Wikidot offers free accounts, with premium upgrades available for a monthly fee. It provides its users with a number of tools and features, including the ability to mix forums, wiki pages, templates, modules, custom themes, add-in packages, and reusable site templates, as the company puts it, "to create almost any collaborative web project imaginable."

EditThis.Info

If you'd like to get your feet wet with a no-frills wiki farm, you could do a lot worse than EditThis.Info (*http://editthis.info/wiki*). The site looks a lot like Wikipedia—sparse and uncluttered. Registered members get unlimited pages, an unlimited number of users, wiki spam protection, and RSS feeds. The service is free, and you can have your wiki up and running in just a few seconds. The site emphasizes that it's a community of wikinauts, the members of which share knowledge on their own wikis, and with each other.

EditThis.Info provides an upload feature that supports graphics and audio files, as well as text files. It includes tagging features. A version-control feature saves every edit and an audit trail allows users to track every change made. And detailed statistics are available on the number of users, articles, visits, and page requests, among other things, for the wiki you create.

The Business Case

In the corporate world, wikis have been gaining popularity as flexible, easy-to-implement collaboration tools. They're inexpensive, if not free, relatively simple to set up, and very easy to access from a web browser. Because all the wiki-ing takes place in the individual users' web browsers, wikis present virtually no learning curve. And private wikis set up on the corporate intranet work just the same as public wikis that live on the web.

The success of Wikipedia with its 75,000 contributors notwithstanding, corporate wikis appear to be the most effective when the number of users is small, and the content is specific to the group.

No More E-mail Ping Pong

Instead of exchanging e-mails and attachments, corporate wiki users can work together on private web pages in near real time. Wikis serve as unusually dynamic communications environments that can help corporate teams to remain agile and competitive.

A corporate wiki provides a highly flexible platform for internal collaboration and document management, but because it's online, it provides that same platform to team members who are scattered in different locations. These "distributed" teams can use a wiki as a central location for managing meeting notes, team agendas, and company calendars. The content stored on a wiki can be updated with no real lag time and little to no administrative intervention. And they're browser-based, so distribution is automatic. Because they're browser-based, wikis can also be used to centralize a range of corporate data types—everything from PowerPoint presentations to PDF files.

Corporate Communities

Just as public-facing wikis can be used to create unique communities on the web, corporate wikis can serve as platforms for internal, special-interest "communities" with limited accessibility within an organization. Companies are using internal wiki communities as ongoing collaborative spaces, typically devoted to particular products or product areas. IT organizations (the company computer guys) are also using wikis to develop and maintain the documentation for their in-house software and systems.

A corporate wiki is most often implemented behind the firewall. Unless you're managing an open-source-software project, there's little reason to publish the work-in-progress documentation of a company's activities on the web. Also, limited-access wikis are simply less likely to be misused.

Corporate Chaos?

At first blush, wikis might seem to be unlikely business tools. All this openness and anyone-can-edit-the-documents stuff can feel chaotic. But even the public-facing, come-one-come-all Wikipedia has systems in place for source and version management. The structure of a wiki is essentially organic; once it's set up, a wiki is controlled by its users, not by administrators. But corporate wikis are not free-for-alls.

Savvy corporate wiki managers define their wiki use policies carefully. Some basic guidelines—what might be thought of as *wiki etiquette*—are required around things like deleting and modifying the contributions of others. The last thing you want is for team members to keep their own copies of earlier versions, which would negate the benefits of wiki-style interactions. The wiki gets everyone on the same page, but the company still has to make sure that everyone is speaking the same language.

Enterprise-Friendly Wiki Features

Since the business world discovered wikis, demand has been growing for wiki engines designed specifically for the needs of companies. This sub-genre of wiki software adds some distinctly enterprise-friendly features to the usual wiki toolbox, including, among others:

- Workspaces, which allow companies to organize their wiki-editable information by groups, teams, projects, and/or product categories.
- Permission tools, which are corporate-oriented access-control tools for setting read/edit permission for individual pages or entire Workspaces.
- Notification systems, which allow companies to use e-mail and RSS feeds to let supervisors and others know when a document or page on the wiki has been modified.
- Corporate identity features that allow the company to design their wikis to reflect the look of other company websites and intranet resources.
- Custom permissions tools, which take the access controls to a finer-tuned level.
- Encryption, advanced security, and backup features, to protect the company's data.
- Threaded discussion displays, which post messages (questions, comments, suggestions) among team members alongside the documents they're working on.

CHAPTER 15

Wikipedia: All the World's User-Generated Knowledge

It is without a doubt the most conspicuous example of user-generated content on the World Wide Web: Wikipedia (*www.wikipedia.org*), the free, open source, online, collaborative, multilingual, and controversial encyclopedia, written and edited by its users, misunderstood and mistrusted by many. Love it or hate it (there seems to be no middle ground), this ginormous, web-based reference source has had an impact that would be tough to overstate. Here's what you need to know to understand how Wikipedia works, and if you are so inclined, join the ever-expanding ranks of contributors to this unique publication.

What Is Wikipedia?

The name "Wikipedia" is a combination of "wiki" and "encyclopedia," which should give you an idea of what they're going for on this website. Wikipedia is, first and foremost, a wiki. A "wiki" is a collaborative website that allows visitors to freely add, edit, and/or remove its content, including text documents, images, video clips, and links to other websites. ("Wiki" is Hawaiian for "quick.")

Wikipedia is the world's largest wiki. The English language version is made up of more than 3.2 million articles and nearly 20 million web pages. And that doesn't include the pages written in more than 270 other languages.

It's also the world's largest general reference website. Its founders have called it "an encyclopedia for everyone." But unlike traditional encyclopedias, it's also a source for information on current events, even something of a source for news, because the articles are so frequently updated.

ESSENTIAL

Wikification refers to the process of turning a page of text or a web page into a Wikipedia page using the wikitext markup language. It also refers to the process of adding lots of hyperlinks to a Wikipedia page.

Anyone can read the articles posted on Wikipedia. You don't even have to join up or sign in. And it's an extremely popular resource these days. According to the web traffic watchers at Alexa.com, Wikipedia is the world's sixth busiest website (just behind Google, Facebook, YouTube, Yahoo!, and Microsoft's Live.com). If you spend any time on Google, you'll notice that many searches turn up at least one Wikipedia citation.

Most people get to Wikipedia from their desktop or laptop web browsers, but the techies behind the site have been struggling to provide mobile access since 2004. Finally, in 2009, Wikipedia became available through true smart-phone apps for the iPhone, Android phones, and the Palm Pre.

The Wikipedia project was officially launched in 2001, and the first version was published in English. It was founded by Internet entrepreneurs Jimmy Wales and Larry Sanger. Sanger, a philosopher whose work focuses on the theory of knowledge, was editor of another web-based encyclopedia project, Nupedia, which Wales had founded. Nupedia, which shut down after about three years, wasn't a wiki, but it's usually seen as the forerunner of Wikipedia.

All the World's Knowledge

Wikipedia defines itself as a user-contributed online encyclopedia, and it's made up of thousands of entries along the lines of what you might find in, say, the Encyclopedia Britannica. Wikipedia entries can include photos, charts and graphs, maps, and often tons of footnotes.

The entries in Wikipedia are called "articles," and each article has its own web page on the website. The articles in Wikipedia cover the usual territory of traditional encyclopedias—history, geography, art, science and technology, politics, etc.—but also current pop culture topics, such as the latest movies and television shows and popular music.

FACT

There's a Wikipedia written in Klingon. Technically, it's now just a wiki, but it started out as one of the many versions of Wikipedia translated into languages other than English. It lasted on the site from 2004 to 2005, but the story goes that it proved to be so controversial that the founders gave it the axe (or bat'leth). But this unique wiki is still going strong on the Wikia hosting service. It can be found at: *http://klingon.wikia.com*.

All encyclopedias provide little biographies of historical figures, but Wikipedia ups the "compendium of knowledge" ante in its articles on living people from all walks of life. These articles are essentially little biographies of business executives, pop culture figures, sports stars, and fictional characters from movies, literature, comic books, and computer games.

There's also a massive list of articles in the English edition on American cities, towns, and *villages*. Teeny, tiny hamlets are included in this list. Elgin, Iowa, for example, with a population of 676, has a page; so does Anvik, Alaska, population 104.

Wikipedia articles tend to start out as brief starter pieces called "stubs," which are approximately 500-word summaries of the topic. But because they are perpetually available to editors and contributors, Wikipedia articles are bound to grow. Over time, many have become lengthy, in-depth pieces.

Wikipedia Commons

Wikipedia maintains a repository of nearly 6.5 million freely usable media files called the Wikimedia Commons. The repository contains public-domain and freely licensed media content, including images, audio files, and video clips. The project was launched in 2004, and within two years the repository had reportedly accumulated 1 million media files.

As a wiki project, volunteers do all the contributing and editing, and Wikipedia welcomes contributions. As Wikipedia puts it, "Everyone is allowed to copy, use and modify any files here freely as long as they follow the terms specified by the author; this often means crediting the source and author(s) appropriately and releasing copies/improvements under the same freedom to others."

ESSENTIAL

Wikipedia has sparked a veritable grassfire of related services. Wikirage, for example, tracks which pages in Wikipedia are receiving the most edits over different periods of time. It also tracks things like popular people in the news, the latest fads, and the hottest video games, Internet memes, and trends. (*www.wikirage.com*)

You do have to be a registered member of the Wikipedia community to upload files to the Wikimedia Commons repository. But you don't have to be a member to edit pages.

The Wikimedia Foundation

Wikipedia is owned by the non-profit Wikimedia Foundation, which is headquartered in San Francisco. The original Wikipedia project ran as part of Wales's web portal company, Bomis, along with the Nupedia project. Wales established the foundation in 2003 and sort of combined the two.

The Wikimedia Foundation declares that it is "dedicated to bringing free content to the world." And it's not stopping at Wikipedia to accomplish that goal. The list of other foundation projects includes, among others: Wiktionary (an online dictionary developed as a wiki), Wikiquote (a quotations reference wiki), Wikibooks (a wiki for generating free textbook content), Wikisource (an online library of free reference books), Wikimedia Commons (an online repository of media files), Wikispecies (a wiki project aiming to catalog all species for scientists), Wikinews (a free news source wiki), Wikiversity (a wiki for learning communities), and the Wikimedia Incubator (a wiki testing platform). However, Wikipedia states: "Although the Wikimedia Foundation owns the site, it is largely uninvolved in writing and daily operations."

FACT

Wikimedia Foundation board member Michael Snow publishes a Wikipedia community newspaper called The Wikipedia Signpost (*http://en.wikipedia.org/wiki/Wikipedia_Signpost*), which covers news and events of special interest to Wikipedians, and major events other Wikimedia Foundation projects.

In early 2010, the Wikimedia Foundation announced plans to give Wikipedia a makeover. The plan includes a redesign of the interface aimed at making the site easier to navigate, easier to search, and easier to edit. In a blog post, the Wikimedia Foundation User Experience team wrote: "We've simplified the site navigation, relocated the search box to satisfy user expectations and to follow other web standards, reduced some of the clutter and made sure that the new features work with different resolutions, browser formats and window sizings."

Searching Wikipedia

According to Wired magazine, about 300 million people a month seek information using Wikipedia. And those curious people have some simple and intuitive tools to help them in their searches.

There are lots of ways to track down the information you're looking for on Wikipedia. The navigation menu is available from virtually every page, so you can start a keyword search from wherever you happen to be. Type in, say, "Star Trek," and you'll get a drop-down menu of likely choices that includes "Star Trek: The Original Series," "Star Trek: The Motion Picture," "Star Trek II: The Wrath of Khan," among others. You can click on one of these to go directly to an article with that title. Clicking on the Go button takes you to a page named "Star Trek." Clicking on the Search button brings up a page with a complete list of Star Trek-related articles with short summaries.

That navigation menu also lists a number of useful Wikipedia-created navigational links, including:

- **Main Page:** Takes you back to the Wikipedia home page.
- **Contents Portal:** Takes you to a page that's full of lists (glossaries, time-lines, and an alphabetical index, among others).
- **Featured Content:** Takes you to a page of content that the site considers "the best that Wikipedia has to offer." Includes articles, pictures, and other contributions that "showcase the polished result of the collaborative efforts that drive Wikipedia."
- **Current Events:** Takes you to a top-topics-in-the-news page.
- **Random Article:** Takes you to randomly selected pages. Clicking "Random article" repeatedly is an interesting way to browse Wikipedia's content.

Wikipedia's Toolbox menu also lists a couple of useful navigation tools, including: "What links here," which provides a list of links to other pages that link to the page you are viewing; and "Special pages," which takes you to a list of pages that are automatically generated and can't be edited, such as "Redirects," "Categories," and "Dead-end pages."

Wikipedia is known for its non-traditional, hyperlink-based organizational structure. But it also allows traditionalists to search its contents using old-fashioned library methodologies, including the Dewey Decimal system and the Library of Congress system.

Wikilinks and the Power of Hypertext

Wikipedia pages are *hypertext* documents, which means that they are bristling with links that take you to other pages within the website (called *wikilinks*) and to other websites. Just click on any word in the article rendered in blue text and you'll find yourself on a page related to that topic or concept. Go to Wikipedia's article on World War II, for example, and within the first paragraph you'll find hyperlinks on "military conflict," "most of the world's nations," "great powers," "Allies," "Axis," "total war," "Holocaust," "only use of nuclear weapons in warfare," "deadliest conflict in human history," and "seventy million casualties." There's also a linking form called hypermedia, which is a kind of graphical hyperlink that opens up an audio or video clip.

These are examples of internal links, but you'll also find external links, which take you to a website beyond Wikipedia. This kind of hyperlinking is a fairly common way to organize a website nowadays, and in Wikipedia, this feature enriches the usefulness of the site immeasurably. It builds a hypertext web of Wikipedia articles, and it integrates the website thoroughly into the World Wide Web. It's fair to say that it's one of the wiki's defining features. It's also consistent with the non-hierarchical culture of the Wikipedia community.

Among the site's most useful applications of hyperlinking are its "linked lists," which you'll see at the end of many of the articles. You can also find Wikipedia articles that are little more than hyperlinked lists. Clicking on "Contents" in the navigation bar on the side of the Wikipedia home page opens a Portal/Contents page. Click on "Topics" in the contents list and you'll open a page of Wikipedia lists.

Under the category "Culture and the Arts," for example, you can click on a hyperlinked category called "Celebrities on The Simpsons" to pull up a linked list of people who have guest starred on the animated *Simpsons* TV show. Dustin Hoffman, for example, guest starred as the character Mr. Bergstrom on an episode entitled "Lisa's Substitute." "Dustin Hoffman" is hyperlinked to the actor's Wikipedia bio page, which includes several links to pages about each of his movies, his career, other actors he's worked with, and acting and the movies in general. "Lisa's Substitute" is linked to a Wikipedia page that summarizes that episode of the show.

Hyperlinks on Wikipedia are rendered in blue text, but you'll also find links rendered in red. These "redlinks" are hyperlinks that don't yet lead to anything. If you click on a redlink, you'll end up on a page that needs content, which you're not only free to add, but encouraged to.

New Media Encyclopedias

Of course, Wikipedia isn't the only online encyclopedia you might want to search for information. The Encyclopedia Britannica, for example, publishes an online version that bundles its traditional content with articles from magazines and journals, as well as links to multimedia sources. The content is authority-written, not user-generated, so it's not social media. And it's not free. But it's published online, full of links and graphics, audio, and video, so it's fair to include it among the New Media.

The current roster of New Media encyclopedias and encyclopedia-like references includes the following:

Encyclopedia.com (*www.encyclopedia.com*)

Encyclopedia.com is a free encyclopedia with articles from more than 100 sources, including encyclopedias, dictionaries, and thesauruses. It includes facts, definitions, biographies, synonyms, pronunciation keys, word origins, and abbreviations.

Columbia Encyclopedia (*www.bartleby.com*)

The content of the Columbia Encyclopedia (Sixth Edition) is part of this free online website of the famous Bartleby's, which publishes the classics of literature, nonfiction, and reference sources. The site bills itself as the "pre-eminent Internet publisher of literature, reference, and verse for students, researchers, and the intellectually curious."

Infoplease (*www.infoplease.com*)

Infoplease is a free resource that combines an encyclopedia, a dictionary, a thesaurus, an atlas, and several almanacs loaded with statistics, facts, and historical records. The site is maintained by "a team of reference, entertainment, and sports editors." Infoplease also maintains a site for kids called Fact Monster (*www.factmonster.com/encyclopedia*).

Canadian Encyclopedia Online (*www.thecanadianencyclopedia.com*)

The free online encyclopedia of all things Canadian claims to provide "the most comprehensive, objective and accurate source of information on Canada for students, readers and scholars across Canada and throughout the world."

Autopedia (*http://autopedia.com*)

Autopedia is a free, comprehensive online encyclopedia of automotive resources. The site covers everything from auto maintenance, financing, and insurance to lemon laws listed by state.

Artcyclopedia (*www.artcyclopedia.com*)

A free online art encyclopedia, Artcyclopedia helps you to keep from getting "your Manets confused with your Monets, or your Carpaccios with your Caravaggios." It's mainly a searchable database of the world's artists throughout history. You can search by name, medium, subject, nationality, and gender. Artcyclopedia includes a list of the top thirty artists based on searches conducted by site visitors.

How Stuff Works (*www.howstuffworks.com*)

This is a free, very user-friendly site focused on a wide range of subjects. It's published by Discovery Communications. The articles are written by an "expert editorial staff," but the site also includes consumer opinions and expert ratings from Consumer Guide.

About.com (*www.about.com*)

This popular, free, expert-written site bills itself as an "online neighborhood of helpful experts, eager to share their wealth of knowledge with visitors." It covers a range of topics from TV characters to technology, and twentieth century history to teen fashion. Topics are divided into "channels," which users can browse. But the site is also easily searchable by keyword. It was purchased by the *New York Times* in 2005.

Wikipedians

On Wikipedia's first anniversary, a press release went out proudly announcing that it had generated more than 20,000 articles. By 2009, the English version alone had passed the 3-million mark. Which begs the question, who writes all that stuff?

As a public-facing wiki, Wikipedia is open to anyone who wants to contribute, and the people behind the project encourage all comers. In practice, there has probably always been a core group of a few hundred volunteers who write and edit most of the content of the site. Co-founder Jimmy Wales has alluded to this core group in public talks about Wikipedia. In a speech he gave in 2005, he said that most of the work was being done by a "close-knit group of editors," people he described as "semi-professionals at what they are doing." He added: "The types of people drawn to writing an encyclopedia for fun tend to be pretty smart people."

But even if it's true that a few hundred smart, volunteer Wikipedians have written the bulk of the site's content (and there's no final verdict on that question), it's also true that that content gets tweaked and re-tweaked by thousands.

A "Bureaucracy of Sorts"

"Wiki" is not synonymous with *anarchy*. Successful wiki projects usually operate under some kind of organization or structure. Wikipedia is no exception. It has what it defines as "a bureaucracy of sorts," which includes a "hierarchy of permissions and positions." It starts with the basic, non-registered contributor, who can edit most articles. That category includes, well, almost anyone. Further up the ladder are editors with access to articles that have been restricted because of vandalism or "edit-warring." And editors in good standing get access to additional editorial tools, including a "rollback" feature that helps them to undo edits.

Top editors get elected by the Wikipedia community to "administrator" status. According to Wikipedia, about 1,500 editors have administrator status, which includes "special powers to ensure that behavior conforms to Wikipedia guidelines and policies." You could say that the administrators are the editors' editors. Among other things, they can ban other editors from contributing to Wikipedia.

"Bureaucrats" are Wikipedians with permission (and the tools) to add or remove administrator rights, approve or revoke access to some tools, and rename user accounts. "Stewards" are the top techies who work on the site mainly in the background. There's also an arbitration committee, which settles disputes.

Registration Has Its Benefits

You don't have to be one of the big contributors to be called a "Wikipedian." You don't even have to register an account. Anyone who contributes earns that title. But at the time this book was written, Wikipedia had more than 12 million registered users.

Registering an account on Wikipedia is simple, and it gives you access to some tools for customizing your site preferences. Just open up the Wikipedia home page in your preferred language, and click on "Create an Account." Provide a username and a password, click "Create Account," and you're in.

Becoming a registered member of the Wikipedia community gives you access to tools that non-members don't have, which allows you to move articles, edit semi-protected articles, and vote in some elections. Your account has to be "autoconfirmed," which it is once it's at least four days old, and you have to have made at least ten edits.

Editing Articles

Members and non-members can edit articles in Wikipedia. Just click on the Edit tab at the top of an article page and you'll open an editing window that shows the article in *wikitext*, which is a simple version of the markup language HTML. There's also a formatting toolbar at the top of the window with a number of buttons for text formatting and other chores.

If you're not familiar with markup languages, this page can be a bit intimidating, but it's really not that complicated. The brackets and equal signs and other weird punctuation are used to define the formatting and purpose the words they surround. A word that should be rendered in italics, for example, has two apostrophes at each end. Make it three apostrophes, and you've got bold text. Add a colon to the front of a sentence to indent it.

To create an internal wikilink, enclose the name of the article in double brackets, like this: *[[The Beatles]]*. To create a link to an outside web page, enclose the URL in double brackets, like this: *[[http://www.the beatles.com]]*. If you want to turn a word or phrase in the article into an external link, insert the bracketed URL in the sentence, leave a space after it, and add the word or phrase, like this: *[[http://www.thebeatles.com the Beatles official webpage]]*.

Wikipedia offers lots more advice, tips, tricks, and general help with editing on its Help: Editing page at (*http://meta.wikimedia.org/wiki/ MediaWiki_User%27s_Guide:_Editing_overview*).

If you're just fixing a typo, all you have to do is double click on the word to select it, and then change the spelling. Click on "Show Preview" to get a look at your changes before they go live. Now click "Save this Page," and your changes appear immediately on the website. And your changes will be noted on the Recent Changes page and listed in the History section of the article page.

Wikipedia likes you to add a little explanation of what you've done, and it's best to get into the habit of doing this to stay in good standing with the community. You'll find a narrow Edit summary box below the edit window, in which you can briefly describe the changes you just made, something like: "changed 'aquired' to 'acquired.'" For this kind of tiny change, be sure also to check off the Minor edit button.

Wikipedia has a style guide for its articles, called the Manual of Style at (*http://en.wikipedia.org/wiki/Wikipedia:Manual_of_Style*). The style guide encourages contributors and editors to follow formatting rules and basic principles. You're considered a good contributor if, among other things, you follow this manual's recommendations.

What Do the Critics Say?

Wikipedia has plenty of critics. Proponents talk about "the wisdom of crowds"; critics talk about the dangers of favoring consensus over credentials; supporters emphasize the value of collaborative content; opponents warn about the dangers of reference works that are nonacademic and not expert-driven.

Amateurs and Vandals

Early in its evolution, Wikipedia was hit with two main criticisms: 1) the content isn't written by vetted experts, so it can't be trusted; 2) because it's a wide-open wiki, vandals are free to taint the content, so it can't be trusted.

The Wikipedian answer to these charges is that the site's openness makes it even more trustworthy, that its collaborative content is not a weakness, but a strength. There are so many people looking at the articles, edits, and activities on Wikipedia, they argue, that many more people monitor the content of the articles published than in traditional reference sources. As a result, mistakes and mischief are caught and corrected very quickly.

Another knock on Wikipedia is that the caliber of writing isn't the highest, because amateurs are generating the content. Wikipedians counter that the early "stub" entries might be amateurish, but eventually the articles published in Wikipedia are polished by hundreds of editors.

Systemic Bias

One current criticism is that Wikipedia exhibits systemic bias, because the content of the website is written by a cadre of hard-core Wikipedians. Far from the vaunted wisdom of crowds, the critics charge, Wikipedia actually represents the "wisdom" of a few, which results in systemic bias.

Defenders of Wikipedia counter that the statistics on this are misleading, that the active core of contributors are spending a lot of their time on technical chores and housekeeping, rather than actual contributions and direct editorial activities.

How this all shakes out in the Web 2.0 world remains to be seen, but Wikipedia has established itself as a go-to reference that's not going anywhere, and remains one of the most fascinating examples of social media on the web today.

CHAPTER 16

Virtual Worlds: A Different Kind of Avatar

And now we come to the bleeding edge of the social media universe: virtual worlds, those web-based, interactive, three-dimensional environments in which people assume the identities of video game-like characters in computer-generated landscapes populated by other characters operated by other people. Yikes! If you're new to all this, it might sound pretty weird, but you really have to give it a try. It's one of the coolest experiences on the social web, and as it turns out, incredibly useful. Here's what you need to know to dip your toe into the virtual pond.

What Is a Virtual World?

A virtual world is a three-dimensional computer environment designed to simulate the fundamental aspects of the real world, to mimic real life. There's an up and a down in a virtual world, a forward and a backward, a sky above and land below. It's true that a visitor to a virtual world might be able to fly around in that sky, but it's still a sky ruled by sky physics. Visitors (the flightless ones) must open doors, navigate stairs, and look both ways before crossing the street.

Virtual worlds can be elaborately realized environments, with detailed towns and cities, roads and rivers, shops and theaters. You might find a virtual museum, hotels, private homes, bars, strip joints, and just about any kind of place you can imagine. Denizens of virtual worlds hold conferences with real attendees, teach classes to real students, and set up businesses that make real money. And they just hang out and socialize with other users.

FACT

The definition is sure to change once Silicon Valley finally gets the bugs out of our total-immersion, sensory-surround body suits, but for now, a virtual world isn't quite the same thing as virtual reality, better known as VR. Virtual reality is an immersive artificial environment the user perceives as real. (Think *The Matrix*.) A computer scientist name Jaron Lanier is the guy who popularized the concept. In the 1980s, he developed those cool VR goggles and gloves that became emblematic of the concept.

Virtual worlds fit under the social media umbrella because of the critical role social networking plays in many of these environments, but also because the users of these computer-generated environments create a lot of content in the form of educational displays, user-planned tours, in-world games, and blogs, not to mention clothing, tools, and amenities for other users. In fact, the content virtual world users contribute is often part of the environment itself. By one estimate, users of *Second Life*, the best-known virtual world, have contributed around $500 million to its design and development. That's *real* money.

Virtual World Basics

All virtual worlds are not alike. Each one has its own rules, look, and feel. However, they do share some basic conventions:

- **Multiple Users:** You're not alone in a virtual world. In all their forms, these environments are occupied by many visitors and residents.
- **Persistence:** This is a techie term that means the virtual world exists whether you're walking around in it or not. In fact, nobody has to be logged in for a virtual world to exist. It persists.
- **Interactivity:** Users don't just look around in a virtual world, they interact with it—which means that they build shops, create communities, sponsor events, and even alter existing features.
- **Avatars:** All virtual worlds are populated by animated icons representing the users, called avatars.
- **Real Time:** Virtual worlds operate in real time, like chat rooms, which means that there's a real person behind that avatar at the very moment you interact with it. You can often blog, leave messages, and do some other things that communicate with other visitors and residents in a virtual world when you're away, but most of your interactions and experiences require you to be there, so to speak, behind your avatar.
- **Community:** In a persistent world that's occupied by lots of people interacting in real time, it's only natural to find social groups. Many virtual worlds provide tools and systems that make it easier to form online communities within those worlds—everything from a book club to a neighborhood.

Types of Virtual Worlds

There are hundreds of different virtual worlds out there in cyberspace, and several different types of virtual worlds, each designed to serve a different purpose or demographic segment of the user population. These include:

- **Online Communities:** When most of us think of a virtual world, chances are we're thinking of the online communities exemplified by *Second Life*. These are environments in which users gather for social purpose, to meet new people and hang out with old friends, to share activities, and to create and develop online personal spaces.

- **Games:** Another type of virtual world is a kind of computer game known as a massively multiplayer online role-playing game, or MMORPG. One of the best known examples of an MMORPG with a clear social networking component is *World of Warcraft* (*WoW*).

- **Education:** Some virtual worlds have educational components, such as *Second Life*'s Lakamaka Island, and some were specifically designed as educational environments, such as *Whyville*. They're used to expand classrooms, for collaboration, and for simulated field trips.

- **The Military:** It's not an application of virtual world technology that many of us get to see, but the military uses simulated worlds to train troops. They use them to rehearse missions, incident management exercises, and recruiting. In 2009, the U.S. Army's Research, Development and Engineering Command's simulation and training center launched the *Federal Virtual Worlds Challenge* to reach a global development community and explore innovative, interactive training and analysis solutions in virtual worlds.

- **Health Care:** This is an evolving use of virtual world technologies. Virtual worlds have been used to augment the training of medical personnel, to simulate emergency situations, and for professional collaboration. ESC's *Medical Nexus Environments* are an example of this application of virtual world technologies in health care.

- **Business:** Companies have been experimenting with creating corporate virtual worlds, but the success rate has been abysmal. Industry analysts at Gartner found in 2008 that nine of ten business forays into virtual worlds failed within eighteen months. But those same analysts predicted that, by 2012, corporations will have figured out what they're doing wrong and 70 percent will have established their own private virtual worlds. One example: Wells Fargo Bank's *Stagecoach Island* is an example of a company-generated and company-operated virtual world that is open to the public. It closely resembles *Second Life*.

- **Politics:** It's rare to find a virtual world with an entirely political purpose, but as this technology evolves, it seems likely that we'll see more. One current example that's still in the testing phase is *agoraXchange*, which was commissioned by the Tate Museum to become, as the website puts it, "a repository of ideas for a global politics game with four basic decrees that upend current institutions sustaining nationalism and inequality."

- **Kids:** There are virtual worlds designed specifically for children in different age groups. Many of these are educational sites, but not all. *Club Penguin* and *ToonTown*, for example, are aimed at little kids. *Whyville*, *Habbo Hotel*, and *Teen Second Life* are aimed at older kids.

Avatars

"Avatar" is a word that entered the popular lexicon in 2009, thanks to the success of James Cameron's 3D science-fiction epic of that name. Of course, virtual world isn't virtual reality, so when you visit one you don't actually need to pour your consciousness into a tank-grown meat puppet. In a virtual world, an avatar is the three-dimensional animated icon that represents you in that world. You use your avatar to explore the virtual world and interact with other avatars. In some virtual worlds, you can even speak through your avatar using a computer microphone; others communicate via texting.

A virtual-world avatar is a bit like a digital puppet, though hard-core virtual-world enthusiasts will insist that it's better defined as an *alter ego*. You can dress your avatar in any clothing you like, and customize it in a number of ways. You can make your avatar look like you, or someone—even some*thing*—completely different. You can be tall and thin like a supermodel, handsome and strong like a superhero, or cuddly and furry like a stuffed animal. In most of these worlds, you can choose to be animal, vegetable, or mineral.

Most of the virtual worlds that are open to the public provide customizable avatars to members for free. But the customization of avatars has become something of a cottage industry. If you want to create huge augmentations to your avatar, there's probably a vendor online or in-world with just what you need—for a price.

Virtual Goods

Commerce can be a big part of the virtual-world experience, especially in the more highly populated and mature worlds. What do you buy and sell in a virtual world? *Virtual goods*.

Wikipedia offers a succinct definition of virtual goods: "non-physical objects that are purchased for use in online communities or online games." These are things like the digital gifts you buy on Facebook, or the clothes with which you dress your avatar in *Second Life*. They can also include property in a virtual world, and attributes that enhance an avatar. These intangible items have no intrinsic value, but members of online communities spend real money on them as though they did.

MMORPGs

When the discussion turns to virtual worlds, it's usually about *Second Life*, *IMVU*, the *Habbo Hotel*, and the like. However, there are some straight up computer games that should really be added to that conversation—specifically, that genre of online games known as massively multiplayer online role-playing game, or MMORPG.

The first MMORPG with a persistent virtual world was a venerable game series called *Ultima Online*. Originally launched in 1997, by Origin Systems, Inc., it paved the way for all the others. Sony Online Entertainment's *Ever-Quest II*, a sequel to the enormously popular *EverQuest*, is another popular game that combines a persistent virtual world with social components. And there are many others.

ESSENTIAL

A growing number of social networks have emerged that focus exclusively on virtual worlds. For example, the membership of *Koinup*, an image- and video-hosting site and online community for users of virtual worlds, includes members of *Second Life*, *World of Warcraft*, *Frenzoo*, *IMVU*, *Twinity*, and *Blue Mars*, among others. They come together to network and talk about shared issues of life in a virtual world.

These and other MMORPGs support thousands of users, who play the games simultaneously (thus the "massively multiplayer" part of the gaming category). That simultaneous game play led to the game makers adding such social media features as blogs, forums, live chat, and virtual commerce along the lines of what you'd find in *Second Life*. *WoW* exemplifies this game-as-social-media model. It's one of the most popular MMORPGs, truly a phenomenon, and it's full of social components.

You maneuver avatars in the consistent world of *WOW* in the same way you would in a *Second Life*-type environment. You use your avatars to explore the world, but also to fight monsters and interact with so-called non-player characters that are part of the game. Those avatars also interact with other players' avatars, and even cooperate and work with them to pursue quests—and that requires conversation.

Second Life

Since it was launched in 2003 by San Francisco-based Linden Lab, *Second Life* (*www.secondlife.com*) has become an international phenomenon. Starting with one square kilometer of virtual real estate, the environment has grown into a 2073-square-kilometer world with 18 million registered users. This sprawling virtual space is filled with thousands of users who explore the environment in the form of avatars and participate in a wide range of individual and group activities. The virtual space contains woodlands, shopping malls, private residences, and all kinds of special-purpose areas, sometimes called islands or states. *Second Life* residents also buy and sell items, such as clothing, avatar attributes, and even property.

The idea to create a 360-degree immersive virtual world, the story goes, came to Linden Lab founder Philip Rosedale when he was a physics student at the University of San Diego. He founded Linden Lab in 1999, and reportedly worked for two years on creating his virtual world with hardware designed specifically for that purpose, before shifting gears and focusing on the software that led to the virtual world we know today.

Second Life offers a free membership, which permits a wide range of activities. But there's also a premium membership available, for which you pay a monthly fee; it allows you to build your own private home in the virtual world, bestows exclusive mainland building rights, provides instant access to adult-only areas, and shares advice from *Second Life* experts.

The range of *Second Life* activities is truly vast, and include entertainment, sports, travel, social events, and learning. People use the virtual world to visit places they could never go in real life, such as into the interior of a human skin cell or one of the Great Pyramids. They can sail to the Caribbean, even though they're frightened of water. They can visit virtual recreations of science-fiction author Frank Herbert's *Dune* or John Norman's *Gor.* And yes, they use it to try out activities that might have legal, social, or moral consequences, including what *Second Life* calls "biological" experiences.

QUESTION

What is a *Second Life* "pose ball?"
A pose ball is an object in the virtual world of *Second Life* that poses or animates your avatar. Originally, they took the form of a little sphere floating near, say, a chair. You'd click on the ball and your avatar would sit in the chair. But more often than not nowadays, you just click on the chair. Some of the more popular pose balls, *Second Life* tells us, are those that pose and animate romantic or sexual situations between characters.

The Grid and the Viewer

The virtual world of *Second Life* is known to users as The Grid or SL. The real world is known to the denizens of *Second Life* as First Life or FL. The virtual world is divided up into Regions or SIMS (Simulators), and each Region is given a unique name, content rating, and Internet address.

You can access *Second Life* through your web browser and do a lot of things, including shopping and exploring areas from a remote viewpoint. But to enter the world with your avatar, you need the three-dimensional browsing application, called the *Second Life* Viewer, that you download to your desktop. *Second Life* introduced a new version of its viewer in 2010. It's now a part of the default download for new users when they create a new account. The Viewer 2, as it's called, includes Shared Media, which is the ability to incorporate standard web-based media and content in *Second Life*, which Linden Lab says, enables content creators "to make more compelling, interactive experiences."

Second Life actually maintains a directory of viewers made by others (called third-party viewers), including the Snowglobe Viewer, which you may use instead of the official viewer. Downloading the viewer is simple, but your computer must be able to support it, so you'll want to check the system requirements. On the *Second Life* website, click on "Help" in the main menu, then click "System Requirements" to get a list of the minimum requirements and optimum recommendations for your Internet connection, your operating system, your computer's processors, your computer's memory, the screen resolution, and your system's graphics card. *Second Life* does a pretty good job of helping you get through all this techie stuff. If you've got an older machine, you might have to upgrade; if you bought your machine in the last couple of years, chances are you'll be okay.

Maturity Ratings

Second Life is a big world, populated by all kinds of people with all kinds of interests, some of which are spicier than others. You must be at least eighteen years of age to join *Second Life* proper, which residents refer to as "the main grid," so everyone visiting or residing in the space is a grownup. But *Second Life* gives you a heads-up about the adult level of the content you might find in different regions of this virtual world with what it calls "Maturity Ratings." *Second Life* changed its Maturity ratings in 2010 to the following for clearer guidance:

- **General:** Areas in SL rated General are the PG regions. They were actually rated PG until 2010, when *Second Life* decided that it was a confusing label for an area where no parental guidance was necessary. Nothing sexually explicit here, folks, no violence or depictions of nudity allowed. And no sexually oriented objects, please. As *Second Life* puts it, areas designated General "are areas where you'd feel free to say and do things that you'd be comfortable saying and doing in front of your grandmother, or a grade-school class." General areas are used by colleges and universities, conference organizers, and businesses users.
- **Moderate:** This rating covers areas that might not be suitable to your grade-school class, but not give your granny a heart attack. Areas designated Moderate include many common *Second Life* activities, such as social and dance clubs (not strip joints), pubs, stores and malls, galleries, music venues, beaches, and parks that, as *Second Life* says, "don't host publicly promoted adult activities or content." You might

find some sexy lingerie in a store in Moderate regions, or some burlesque acts in a club, but nothing that crosses any lines.

- **Adult:** Weird as it might sound, some areas of *Second Life* display content that is explicitly sexual, intensely violent, or depicts illicit drug use. You won't accidentally stumble into any of these areas, because you have to first verify that you want to enter.

Getting Around

In 2010, *Second Life* introduced a new environment called Welcome Island, where new users can go to learn the basic skills required to function in the virtual world. *Second Life* claims the intro takes about ten minutes, but you should expect a bit of a learning curve. You'll also find another environment called Discovery Island where new users can get starter experiences.

One of those basic user skills is the simple act of getting around. SL is such a sprawling environment it would be tough to get from place to place if the world didn't provide its users with a couple of different ways to move about. Using your keyboard and mouse, you move around SL very much as you would in a video game. Walking is the most basic means of travel, followed by running, flying (which is *very* cool, and is itself worth a visit to this virtual world), and teleporting (beam me over there, Scotty!). All four motility modes take some practice, but *Second Life* provides a bunch of tutorials, tips, and other hand holding to get you up and running (or flying).

But you can also put your avatar into a car, a boat, or other vehicle and travel that way. Vehicles provide a nice way to travel in group in SL.

Another way to get around is through SLURLs (*Second Life* URLs). *Second Life* allows you to copy the URL of a Region and save it for later retrieval—essentially, bookmarking that page. SLURLs are very useful for getting around quickly in this vast pseudo-space; you just click them and, poof, you're there.

The *Second Life* Economy

Second Life is widely regarded as the largest user-generated virtual economy. You don't have to spend money in *Second Life*. Not a dime. But if you want to, you can spend a bundle. Users shop in a company's store, explore their products and services, and even take them out for a virtual test drive. Clothing can even be tried on before you buy.

In case you're thinking that all of this is about a bunch of geeks playing with computer-generated puppets, keep in mind that, in 2010, Linden Lab reported that first-quarter user-to-user transactions in *Second Life* totaled $160 million. That's a 30 percent increase from the same period in 2009. The company also reported that the number of SL residents active in that virtual economy reached 517,349 in March 2010.

The currency used to shop and buy and sell property in SL is called Linden Dollars (L$). These virtual bucks can be exchanged for real world money through the *Second Life* Exchange and some other services. The exchange rate relies on market-based currency exchanges, but web watchers report that, over the last few years, that rate has hovered around L$250 to one U.S. dollar.

Parcels of land are bought and sold in SL among residents. The prices are determined by the local economy—in other words, the real estate crash in FL shouldn't have an impact on property values in SL. *Second Lifers* cannot designate an area their "home" without first buying it.

Second Life residents build beautiful homes, amusement parks, shops, and a host of other structures with three-dimensional modeling tools provided by Linden Lab. *Second Life* loves its builders, because they create the environment that is SL. You don't have to be a computer coder to use these tools, but there is a learning curve. You can build something by yourself, or collaborate with others. You can import graphics files to add to your structures. You can even imbue them with real-world physics with a gaming AI (artificial-intelligence engine) called Havok, so that you have things like gravity, inertia, and wind in your structures. And once you've built them, you can sell them to other residents.

The kinds of places you can build in SL vary widely, but along with the kinds of things that mirror the real world (shops, houses, bars, etc.), you can build ancient cities, historical recreations, and alternate realities that you might find in the *Twilight Zone*.

The virtual world also provides you with tools with which you can design, and then sell, clothing for avatars, including accessories, belts, glasses, etc. You can design furniture and accessories for homes, including houseplants, cars, and appliances. And because this is a virtual world, you can also design and sell hairstyles, skin, eyes, tails, fangs, wings, and other things you might not see at the FL mall. You can even design a complete avatar and watch it come to life.

ALERT

As of this writing, the Apple iPad tablet PC is only a few months old, but you should expect *Second Life* to come to that device very soon. Two applications for the iPhone, Sparkle by Genkii, and Touch Life by Pocket Metaverse, seem likely candidates.

Second Life is such a vast, multifaceted environment that a single chapter, let alone a section of a chapter on virtual worlds in a book about social media, couldn't give you more than a basic introduction. The good news is that *Second Life* provides extensive documentation and helpful tutorials. From the extensive FAQ page, to its searchable knowledge base, to its *Second Life* Answers Q&A service, this is one of the best documented social media services you find anywhere on the web.

Other Virtual Worlds

Second Life gets the lion's share of the virtual-world press, and it's well earned, but it's not the only game on the social web. Most of the popular virtual worlds utilize three-dimensional technologies, but some popular worlds are only two dimensional. Here's an overview of just a few of the many virtual worlds that you might like to visit as you explore this region of the social media landscape.

Active Worlds

Active Worlds (*www.activeworlds.com*) provides free software for constructing your own three-dimensional virtual world on the Internet. It provides the tools you need to build a world and create your own content, including avatars. *Active Worlds* hosts the virtual world you create, and provides access to about a thousand worlds created by its customers.

Kaneva

Kaneva (*www.kaneva.com*) is a free, three-dimensional virtual world that emphasizes social networking. Users create avatars, and all members get their own virtual loft. The world itself mirrors the real world, and serves primarily as a place to meet people, share photos, videos, and music, play games, and even watch TV, all in real time.

IMVU

IMVU (*www.imvu.com*) is another free, three-dimensional virtual world that emphasizes social networking. It provides the usual virtual-world amenities with a distinctly "singles" vibe. Most of its members are young adults between eighteen and twenty-four, the website claims. Users create avatars, shop for clothes and accessories, and furnish in-world personal spaces. It also boasts a virtual goods catalog with more than 3 million products.

Habbo Hotel

Habbo Hotel (*www.habbo.com*) is a virtual world aimed at teens. The company that created it, Finland-based Sulake Corporation, uses a hotel as a metaphor for the spaces in this world. There's a Lobby, which serves as the gateway. There are private and guest rooms. There are currently more than thirty hotels in the space. Membership is free, but there's a virtual economy based on Habbo Coins, which users purchase to buy clothing for their avatars and furnishings for their rooms.

Whyville

Whyville (*www.whyville.net*) is another virtual world aimed at teens. This is a two-dimensional world with a strong educational component. The world has millions of registered users, called "citizens," who come to "learn, create, and have fun together." *Whyville* has its own newspaper, its own Senators, its own beach, museum, City Hall, and town square. There's also an in-world economy based on "clams" that citizens earn by playing educational games.

Moove

Moove (*www.moove.com*) is a three-dimensional virtual world with a definite romantic slant. Basic membership is free; a full subscription provides access to additional features. It's based on a system called *Roomancer*. The website features busty and beefy avatars, and focuses on room building for online romantic encounters. Users develop their own avatars, which can be used for, according to the website, chatting, laughing, kissing, hugging, and "lifelike movements." But the site isn't aiming for a younger crowd. It boasts that the average age of *Moove* visitors is higher than most virtual worlds.

CHAPTER 17

Location Sharing: The *Who* Gets a *Where*

Over the past couple of years, the buzz has been growing steadily around a new generation of services designed to allow you to share your offline location with members of your online social network. The core concept isn't new, but new players have given it a spin that's winning fans, fast. Social media mavens see these services as evolutionary vehicles for extending the social web into the real world. But underneath the high-concept talk is simply a very cool social networking capability that you might want to try. Here's what all the fuss is about.

Location, Location, Location

When people talk about "location sharing," they're talking about technology that allows members of a web-based social network to tell each other where they are in the real world. It's pretty simple, really: social networking is about who you are; location sharing is about where you are.

This kind of interaction is called *location-based social networking*, *geo-social networking*, *social check-in*, or *social mapping*, depending on which expert you're talking to. To keep everyone's head from exploding, we'll be going with *location sharing* to cover the range of services in this category.

How Does It Work?

Approaches vary among the different location sharing services, but essentially, here's how they work: When you're out and about in the wide world and you stop for lunch, you take out your mobile phone and "check in" by posting your location to the service. You do it again when you stop at the Nature Mart to pick up some arugula, when you stop for gas, for a beer, or just to smell the roses. Others on your network have been doing the same thing, so you now have, literally, a real-time roadmap of your social connections.

It's a bit like posting regular status updates on Facebook or sending out tweets on Twitter.

Location sharing adds a distinctly real-world component to social networking. The services aim to facilitate easier connections among friends, offline and on the fly. They provide a way to say to your social network pals, "Hey guys! I'm *here*. Anybody else around?" Or "Hey guys! I was *there*. Here's what I think about that place." Or simply, "Been there; done that."

QUESTION

What's the "footstream?"
Jeff Holden, co-founder and CEO of Pelago, the company that owns Whrrl, often gets credit for coining this term, which he defined in a 2009 blog posting as "a digital record of the places a person goes in the real world."

Features vary among services, but most allow you to post notes at your check-in points ("This bar serves great nachos;" "This gas station has low prices"), to comment on other members' check-in points ("You were right about those nachos!"), and even to post photos of the places you've been.

How Location Sharing Is Used

Why would you want to do this? Among other reasons, it's fun. It facilitates a kind of engineered social serendipity, by allowing you to see, on a kind of social map, who's wandering around downtown or on campus near you, so you can bump into each other. And while you're connecting with your friends, you'll be meeting their friends, and maybe adding them to your social network.

But it's also a way of using your online social connections to find new places you might not have found on your own, while you're actually out and able to go there. Location sharing can help you to discover restaurants, pubs, parks, and shopping centers. It can help you to learn about nearby events, to explore your city in ways you might not have thought of, and to share your own knowledge and experiences of the places you frequent.

Location sharing makes it possible to discover busy and popular venues, places where lots of your friends are gathering or stopping by *right now*. Just as Twitter displays "trending" topics—things lots of people are twittering about—location sharing services show trending locations— places where lots of members of the service are gathering.

FACT

In early 2010, the microblogging service Twitter added a feature that appends geographical info to your tweets. Twitterers can now add their current location to their 140-word messages.

Local merchants have begun to exploit the great-places-in-your-town aspect of location sharing, offering special deals to patrons who check-in at their places of business regularly and promote to their social circle. And if you're using a service, such as Foursquare, that provides access to your "check-in" history, you have an automatic daily activity diary, map of where you've been, who you met there, and where you've been spending your money.

Oversharing

Critics of location sharing argue that letting everyone know you're out can be dangerous. A prank website launched in 2010, called PleaseRobMe. com, used Twitter and the Foursquare location sharing service to figure out when users of those services weren't home, and then publish the names and addresses of those people. The site's developer, a Dutch citizen named Boy Van Amstel, said at the time that he did it to raise awareness of "the danger in publicly telling people where you are." The site was actively posting addresses for only a short while, though it's still up as of this writing with the aim of "raising awareness about over-sharing."

Defenders of location sharing argue that only your social network friends get to learn your whereabouts, and your friends aren't going to rob you. (We sincerely hope.) Tech journalist Mathew Homan also pointed out in a blog posting that if you've got a nine-to-five job, people already know when you're out of the house, so "the Foursquare as robbery accomplice" assertion doesn't hold water.

The effect of location sharing on the national burglary rate has yet to be measured, but location information is sensitive data, and common sense tells us to share it only with people we trust. Location sharing marries "place" with social networking, and some have argued that it's not a marriage made in heaven. It causes users to abandon their privacy at an even deeper level. Be sure to take control of your privacy settings when you sign on to a location-sharing service, and check those settings regularly.

Major Providers

The biggest headline getters in the location-sharing space right now are Foursquare and Gowalla, two start-up companies that made big splashes at recent tech trade shows and are the subjects of intense speculation by the tech press. Their competition for users in this space is being reported variously as a location-based "War," "Battle," "Throwdown," and "Face-off."

FACT

In 2010, PepsiCo entered a partnership with Foursquare. The location sharing service provides the beverage company with live notifications when its users are close to any place that sells soft drinks—grocery store, gas station, restaurant. PepsiCo then has the opportunity to send those Foursquare users an advertisement to entice them to buy.

But there are several other similar services with loyal memberships, some that pre-date the two current superstars. And a number of other social media services—most notably Facebook and Twitter—are adding or have already added location-sharing features of their own. Other social-media services have caught the location sharing bug—or "gone geo," as the insiders say. Yelp rolled out a check-in feature for its iPhone app in 2010. Google has gotten into the game with its Latitude application. And Yahoo! joined the fray with Fire Eagle. And we're likely to see more.

Foursquare

By the time you read this, Foursquare (*www.foursquare.com*) may already have hit the million-member mark. In early 2010, the service was claiming 725,000 users and 22 million check-ins, but it was also adding 10–20 thousand new members daily. And rumors were flying that Yahoo! might acquire it. Not bad for a service not yet two years old.

Foursquare debuted at the 2009 South by Southwest Interactive (SXSWi) technology conference (where Twitter was launched two years earlier), and reportedly took the event by storm. It was founded by Dennis Crowley and Naveen Selvadurai. Back in 2000, when Crowley was a student at New York University, he and classmate Alex Rainert started a location-sharing service called Dodgeball, which was a text-message-based social-networking service that earned a respectable following. Google acquired Dodgeball in 2005, but discontinued the service in 2009, and later launched its own location sharing service.

Friend Finder Meets City Guide Meets Game

The Foursquare website describes the free service as "a cross between a friend-finder, a social city guide, and a game that rewards you for doing interesting things." Users can access the Foursquare website from their desktop computers, but the service also provides applications that can be downloaded into an iPhone, BlackBerry, Android device, or a Palm Pre. You can also access the Foursquare mobile website from another type of phone and check in with a text message (sent to 50500). Mobile phones play a critical role in location sharing. They are, in fact, the preferred computing platform for this type of application.

Once you've joined the Foursquare community, you register your locations by "checking in" when you arrive somewhere. The service then uses the Global Positioning System (GPS) on your phone to verify your locale and let your friends know where you are. The service also uses GPS to show a list of nearby places that might be of interest—everything from movie theaters to coffee shops to dentists' offices.

Originally, the Foursquare service was limited to a few major cities, but it now claims to be available from anywhere in the world. Keep in mind that Foursquare doesn't actually track your location via satellite. It's not following you around like Big Brother or Skynet. It only knows where you are when you check in. The service even allows you to check in "off the grid," which means you use the service without sharing your location.

Tips and To-Dos

Location sharing services are part of the social media landscape because they add an important capability to social networking. But even if you ignored the social component, these services would fit securely under the social media umbrella, because their users are also adding *content* to the web. On Foursquare, that content takes the form of "Tips" and "To-Dos."

All Foursquare users are free—make that encouraged—to comment on the places from which they check in. These comments generally come in two forms. Tips are recommendations along the lines of: "Rent a paddle boat and swing around the lake during lunch!" or "Be sure to try the chicken kabobs." When you arrive at a place, the service displays tips related to that venue. And there are To-Dos, which Foursquare describes as "notes to self." These might be: "Remember to rent a paddle boat next time."

Turning Real Life Into a Game

After its debut, the service took off like a rocket in a product category that had previously seen only modest growth and user interest. Social-media mavens suspect that it's Foursquare's gaming component that sparked its warp-speed growth. In April 2010, Crowley told Tim Adams of *The Observer*, "A lot of our group had grown up with Super Mario, and they wondered about the possibility of turning life into a game. Getting rewards for adventures just like Mario did on screen."

The service adds up your checkins and uses them to calculate points. You get five points each time you check-in at a place for the first time. If you checkin at a place that no one else using the service has been to, effectively adding a new venue, you get five points. You also get one point per check-in for every place you register, and one additional point with each check-in at that venue.

Points also earn "badges." Everyone gets a badge for their first check-in (it's called a Newbie Badge), but you can also earn an Adventurer Badge for checking in at ten different places; an Explorer Badges for checking in at twenty-five different places; and a Superstar Badge, for checking in at fifty different places. You get the Bender Badge for checking in at the same place four nights in a row; the Crunked Badge for checking in four times in one night; the Player Please! Badge for checking in with three members of the opposite sex; the Gym Rat Badge for checking in to a gym ten times in thirty days; the Jetsetter Badge for checking in at five different airports; and so on.

FACT

In the spring of 2010, Foursquare joined forces with the *Wall Street Journal* to offer users of the location-sharing service New York-specific badges. At about the same time, Gowalla teamed up with the *Kentucky Courier-Journal* to create special tours designed to help celebrants make the most of the annual Kentucky Derby.

Think of badges as stickers on your travel trunk. And Foursquare is always adding new ones.

And if you check-in from a place more than anyone else has—even if it's only once or twice—you become "mayor" of that venue. Bars, cafes, restaurants, and other businesses hoping to attract customer traffic through

Foursquare are beginning to offer "Mayor Discounts," or "Mayor Specials"—things like a free slice of pizza or discounts on lattes. As of this writing, Foursquare is "experimenting with how points can turn into real-world rewards," and soliciting suggestions from its members.

Gowalla

Just as Foursquare had done in 2009, the Gowalla (*www.gowalla.com*) location sharing service made a big splash at the 2010 SXSWi conference, and it has been riding a wave of press that can't seem to stop speculating about the rivalry between the two services. Gowalla actually debuted at SXSWi in 2009, but was overshadowed by Foursquare. In 2010, however, the free service won the event's Mobile category that year.

Gowalla was founded by Josh Williams and Scott Raymond, whose Austin, Texas-based company, Alamofire, makes digital collectibles. Alamofire created the popular card-collecting game, PackRat, which was designed for Facebook. By mid-2010, the service had accumulated 250,000 members and was claiming a month-to-month growth rate of more than 50 percent.

Gowalla and Foursquare have a lot in common. They're both game-oriented location-sharing services. They both provide downloadable applications for the iPhone, the BlackBerry, Android devices, and the Palm Pre. They both leverage GPS technologies. And they both run on check-ins.

Items

One big difference between the two services: Foursquare leverages gaming elements to promote social networking; Gowalla leverages virtual goods in a gaming context to complement the location sharing. Gowalla's virtual goods are called "Items." Members acquire items when they check in at a location, and they're available for swapping or "dropping" (leaving one behind for a friend to discover).

This virtual-goods component of Gowalla really sets it apart from other location sharing services, and it's a pretty big part of the experience. The icons are thoughtfully designed by Alamofire. The company's website talks about "the intersection of friendship and beautiful design." Gowalla items range from Kio fish to espresso machines.

Each user has the option of keeping his items in a vault, but once they go into your vault, they can't come out. They become part of your personal collection. One-of-a-kind items show up in Gowalla Land, as well as unique items created for special events, such as the Olympics. Alamofire also partners with other companies to provide real-world items as prizes.

Spots and Trips

Gowalla calls the places where its users check in "Spots," and it maintains a large and growing spot database. Click on the "Spots" tab and you'll see a group of featured spots and new spots.

Gowalla users can create collections of spots they've visited, which the service calls "Trips." A trip could be a sight-seeing tour or a pub crawl, or an exploration of your city's bookstores. Once your trip is assembled, Gowalla publishes it so that other members can see it—and *take* it. People who finish featured trips and invites can earn "trip pins."

Trips are easy to create: When you arrive at a destination and check in, you simply click the "Add to Trip" button to begin assembling your spots. Gowalla allows you to create up to five trips, to name them, describe them, and add up to twenty spots to each one. As of this writing, the service was planning to allow users to create more trips. Gowalla also posts the names of the top ten visitors to a spot.

Creators and Founders

If you're the first person to check in with Gowalla at a spot, you are acknowledged by the service as that spot's "Creator." Unlike the mayors of Foursquare world, who can be deposed if someone else visits a location more often than they have, a creator is a lifetime appointment. Foursquare's approach drives traffic to a venue; Gowalla's approach encourages exploration.

A "Founder" is a Gowalla member who drops an item at a spot without swapping it out for another one. You essentially pay for founder status with your item. But it might also earn you a "Pin."

Pins and Stamps

On Foursquare, it's badges; on Gowalla, it's pins. Members who complete a specific task or trip earn recognition in the form of a pin. The first pin you earn is your "I Installed Gowalla" pin. You earn additional pins by checking in at different locations.

All your pins and items are recorded on your Gowalla Passport, which is similar to a profile page on a social network. There's even a place for a photo and a friends list. Your passport also tracks all the places you've visited with "Stamps." Every time a Gowalla user checks in at a spot, the service adds a stamp to her passport.

Accumulating stamps is how you acquire pins. For example, you get the Wanderer pin for checking in at five different spots; the Discoverer pin for checking in at fifty different spots; and the Epic Voyager pin for checking in at a 1000 different spots.

Street Team Elite

Gowalla users can also become members of the Street Team Elite (STE), which is a group of members with additional privileges. STE members can edit and move spots, merge identical spots, re-categorize them, add information to their descriptions, and fix misspellings and incorrect categorizations.

Other "Geos"

Foursquare and Gowalla are grabbing the spotlight right now, but the social web is home to lots of location sharing services. And a growing number of other social media are adding this type of capability. They're all free, so there's no reason not to take as many as you like for a test drive. If this type of social media interests you, you'll definitely want to check out some of the following location-sharing services.

Loopt

Loopt (*www.loopt.com*) is a free location sharing service based in Mountain View, California, and founded in 2005. Loopt calls itself a "mobile social-mapping service" that lets you use the location of your phone to discover the world around you. Users check in at locations via their cell phones and share tips, comments, and photos. The service claims around 3 million registered members, and works on more than 100 types of mobile devices, including the iPhone, the iPod Touch, the Blackberry, and Android devices.

Loopt shows its members where friends are located with map displays on their mobile phones—something along the lines of MapQuest and Google Maps. It also gives its members access to detailed information on local events and places from Zagat, Citysearch, Bing, TastingTable, Zvents, Metromix, and SonicLiving. It's also integrated with Facebook and Twitter.

The Loopt Mix version is designed specifically to help members meet new people. It provides access to profile, real-time chat features, and the ability to post status updates. In 2010, the service began offering a special version of its software, Loopt Pulse, designed for the Apple iPad device.

Whrrl

Whrrl (*http://whrrl.com*) is a free service based in Seattle, Washington, launched in 2007 at SXSWi. Whrrl resembles Loopt's map interface and provides similar functionality. Users check in at locations, share tips and comments, and follow each other's progress through the real world. The Whrrl mobile app is currently only available on the iPhone, but if your phone can open a web browser, you'll have access to the service's mobile website. The service was expected to release an application for Android devices sometime in 2010.

There's a big emphasis on community at Whrrl. The service supports what it calls "Whrrl Societies," which are micro communities of members with similar interests who visit the same places. Checking in often at a particular place automatically earns you membership in that locale's micro community.

Whrrl has also been described as a storytelling application that lets its users "share life's moments in real-time through location, photos and text updates." Several people can contribute content to a single shared story.

Brightkite

Brightkite (*http://brightkite.com*) is a free location sharing service based in Denver, Colorado, founded in 2007. The service allows users to check in from their favorite places from their mobile phones, and see who else is there, who's been there, and who's nearby. Users post notes and photos at places that others nearby can see.

The service provides mobile applications for iPhones, BlackBerrys, Nokia phones, Android Devices, and the Palm Pre. Users can also access Brightkite features from the website. In fact, you can check in via the web, text messaging, and mobile e-mail. The mobile phone apps allow users to post 140 character notes, and photos of the location.

Brightkite resembles Gowalla and Foursquare. One distinctive feature: The Brightkite Wall, which allows you to turn your desktop monitor into an interactive, live display of events, bars, trade shows, retailers and other gatherings. It's also integrated with Facebook, Twitter, and Flickr.

Buzzd

Buzzd (*http://buzzd.com*) is a free location sharing service based in New York City, founded in 2008. It's billed as a location-aware city guide aimed at mobile devices. It supports iPhones, BlackBerries, and Android devices, or you can access it through a mobile website.

The service has a great slogan: "Your city. real time." And its "buzzdmeter" is a useful, if goofily named, tool. It shows users the "real-time buzz" around a location emanating from Twitter, Foursquare, Gowalla, Yelp, and other social media. Users rate a location with a thumbs up or down, comments, and photos posted from a mobile phone.

There is no real gaming element to this location-sharing service, but users can earn "influence" points by contributing ratings. The more places you rate, the more points you earn. Big point getters win prizes, such as gift cards, plane tickets, and concert tickets.

The service nurtures a lot of partnerships with supporting content providers, including Helio, Virgin Mobile, Flavorpill, Time Out, Zagat, CitySearch, MyOpenBar, Metromix, and Buy Your Friend A Drink. Buzzed is integrated with Facebook and Twitter.

Google Latitude

The search engine giant's entry into the location sharing space (after dumping Foursquare precursor Dodgeball), Google Latitude (*www.google.com/latitude*), is a free, location-aware mobile application that essentially functions as a feature of Google Maps for Mobile. Users add willing contacts from their Gmail accounts, and the locations of those friends pop up in little boxes on the map interface.

The service, which was launched in 2009, is aimed at mobile devices (iPhone, Blackberry, Android, Nokia, etc.), but there's also a desktop interface available through iGoogle. It uses GPS and cell phone tower proximities to pinpoint a user's location. Seems like a natural for keeping track of friends and family at big conferences, state fairs, and shopping malls.

One standout feature of this service: People can share their exact or general location, such as the city or town they're in. And they can opt out anytime. The service also allows you to "hide" from specific people; you won't appear on their map at all.

Yahoo!'s Fire Eagle

Yahoo! got into the location-sharing business in 2008 with a free service called Fire Eagle (*http://fireeagle.yahoo.net*). This isn't so much about location sharing as it is management of your location data. Fire Eagle is a kind of storehouse/platform, from which registered users can authorize other services to access their information. You could, say, allow Facebook to update your location on your home page.

Yahoo! opened up the platform so that software developers can include location-based features in their programs. Brightkite was one of the services built on it. So were the location-based services Diplity, Dopplr, Lightpole, Pownce, and Loki, among others.

CHAPTER 18

Social Media and Education: Teaching the Digital Natives

Social media are playing an increasingly important role in education. More and more educational applications, especially those that are web-based, incorporate social networking, blogging, wikis and other genres of social media. And educators are exploring the potential of social media to engage a generation of students who grew up surrounded by it, for whom "friend" and "text" have always been verbs. Where this exploration will lead remains to be seen, but here's what's happening at the intersection of social media and education.

Reading, Writing, and . . . Twittering?

Facebook, Twitter, and YouTube aren't yet an integral part of twenty-first century education, but they're no longer viewed strictly as distractions. Few educators who are paying attention are still rolling their eyes at this "fad." Social media is simply a fact of life for all of us, they realize, and for modern students, the "digital natives" populating today's classrooms, it's an essential part of how they deal with information and with each other.

Digital Literacy

Until very recently, schools that banned students from using social media in the classroom were commonplace. But in the last few years, that attitude has begun to seem quaint, old fashioned, and downright counterproductive. In fact, a growing number of educators are integrating social media into their curriculum, and some are even suggesting that it's their responsibility to teach students how to use it, to help them develop a kind of digital literacy.

Palo Alto, California, high school teacher Esther Wojcicki, who also serves as Chair of the Board of Creative Commons, said it best in a 2010 interview with the author of this book for *The Technology Horizons in Education Journal*:

People worry about online predators and they forget that students are already putting everything about themselves on Facebook. Their fears are preventing us from teaching students the appropriate use of technology in the schools. They grow to be adults and they get ripped off left and right, because they can't distinguish between an advertising website and an information website. They can't distinguish between fact and fiction. These schools are abdicating their responsibility for teaching kids how to deal with the web.

QUESTION

What's a Digital Native?
The term was coined in 2001 by author, game designer, and educational thought leader Marc Prensky in an article entitled "Digital Natives, Digital Immigrants." He wrote: "Our students today are all 'native speakers' of the digital language of computers, video games, and the Internet."

Self-Directed Learning

In a 2009 study of youth and new media sponsored by the MacArthur Foundation ("Kids' Informal Learning with Digital Media: An Ethnographic Investigation of Innovative Knowledge Cultures"), researchers found that it's not a waste of time for kids to hang out online. In fact, their research showed that the Internet is actually empowering a generation of students that grew up with technology to pursue self-directed learning on their own terms and time schedules.

For the majority of youth in the United States today, social media are now part of their everyday lives, the researchers found. "Ten years ago, if I had stood in this room and said that most kids in the U.S. will have made a personal homepage, I probably would have been laughed out of the room," said Dr. Mimi Ito, the report's lead author, in a presentation at Stanford University. "Now, in an era of MySpace, that statement is completely unremarkable."

The ubiquitousness of social media allows students to pursue learning in self-directed ways, the researchers concluded. Students have greater access to information, as well as other people who share their interests, but are not part of their local communities.

ESSENTIAL

The "Millennials" are the members of the post–Generation-X generation. Gen-Xers were born after the Baby Boom between 1980 and 2000. The Millennials are sometimes called Generation Y or Generation Next. This is the generation that is the most comfortable with computer technology, because it has always been a part of their lives.

Offline Values

Parents and teachers might find another of the study's conclusions comforting: As weird and unintelligible as kids' online expressions may be, the basic values those kids learned in the offline world follow them into their new media practices.

"We do not believe that educators and parents need to bear down on kids with complicated rules and restrictions and heavy-handed norms about how they should engage online," the researchers write in the study's conclusion. "For the most part, the existing mainstream strategies that parents are mobilizing to structure their kids' media ecologies, informed by our ongoing public discourse on these issues, are more than adequate in ensuring that their kids do not stray too far from home."

Social Media in the Classroom

Social media are making their way into the classroom, whether we like it or not, but educators are finding ways to use it to support their teaching objectives. Social networking activities, for example, can be focused on research, data gathering, and communicating with experts. Blogs can be used to stimulate debate and discussion. Wikis can be used for collaboration. And microblogs can be used to reach out to famous experts. All of these social media can also provide educators with access to support, collaboration, professional development, and community-generated best practices.

Social Networks and the Schools

Social networks, such as Facebook and MySpace, probably aren't the first online services that come to mind when you're considering education technologies. But many educators attempting to make their classrooms reflect the real world of the digital natives they're teaching are trying out some strategies that incorporate these social networks into their teaching plans.

Facebook, for example, can serve as home base for a class project. Students can track news feeds from the social network, share book recommendations, post assignments for their instructors to grade, and collaborate with fellow students.

University and college students are generally ahead of K–12 on social networking, but school districts such as Fairfax County Public Schools in Virginia are catching up. The suburban Washington, D.C., district is the largest in Virginia and twelfth largest in the nation. It's also known for being ahead of the tech curve. It's not surprising to see that it has a big Facebook presence.

Colleges and universities have set up Facebook pages by the thousands, mainly for recruiting purposes. An application called Schools on Facebook, designed to make Facebook pages and groups "work for your institution's needs," is aimed at higher education. Its creator, Ingral, promises to leverage "the Facebook platform across the student lifecycle" for admissions marketing, student engagement, and alumni involvement. The company bills Schools on Facebook as a "lifecycle engagement platform" that will serve students from application through graduation and beyond."

One popular social network created especially for educators, administrators, and those interested in Web 2.0 and social media in education is Classroom 2.0. Developed by social learning consultant Steve Hargadon using the Ning platform, Classroom 2.0 is a free, community-supported network. The network includes the usual social-networking components, such as profiles and a central display of status updates. But it also provides its members with blogging tools, wikis, chat features, forums, and sponsored events.

Classroom 2.0 supports a number of groups, including "Elementary Math," "Middle School Science," Elementary School 2.0," and "Google Apps for Education," among others.

Twitter in the Classroom

Microblogging is the newest type of social media to find its way into the classroom because, among other reasons, it's the newest type of social media. Cutting-edge educators are allowing their students to use Twitter to reach out to experts for research, as a source of information on real-time events, and to network among classmates.

Social polling is emerging as a dynamic use of Twitter in the classroom. Students construct a 140-character question on a controversial topic, a scientific issue, or a current or historical event, hashtag it, and send it out over the microblogging service. They then track the answers.

In colleges and universities, educators are beginning to use Twitter as a tool to improve student engagement during lectures. This is something that radio talk show hosts and tech conference keynote speakers have been doing, too. Writing for the Read Write Web website in 2009 (*www .readwriteweb.com*), Marshall Kirkpatrick reported on an experiment by Dr. Monica Rankin of the University of Texas at Dallas, who began allowing her students to send tweets during a lecture. The experiment began pulling more students into the discussion, and she eventually began using a weekly hashtag to organize comments and questions, Kirkpatrick reported. Other teachers have tried this experiment, with largely positive results.

Interest in this use of Twitter is growing—as is skepticism. But the last two years have seen a plethora of articles on the subject, along the lines of "10 Things to Do with Twitter in the Classroom," and "A Teacher's Guide to Classroom Tweets."

Wikis for Collaborative Education

Of all the social media discussed in this book, nothing is as education-friendly as the collaborative websites called wikis. Wikis have become the gotta-have-it enhancement for a range of educational software and websites. Wikispaces provides a version of its product specially designed for teachers. Learning-management systems, ePortfolios (discussed later), and other educational software are sporting wikis these days.

Wikis provide the right collaboration tool for students of every age. Middle schoolers use them to brainstorm science-fair-project ideas. High school students use them for collaborative writing projects. Teachers use them to share and develop teaching materials.

Virtual Worlds

The potential of virtual worlds to support education is enormous, but the logistics of keeping children safe in these three-dimensional environments has proved to be something of a stumbling block. *Second Life*, for example, would seem to be a natural for teaching and learning. Imagine being able to take students on a virtual field trip to the Sistine Chapel, Chateaux Versailles, The Alamo, the Holocaust Museum, Virtual Harlem, 1920s Paris, Capitol Hill North, or a living coral reef—all of which have been recreated in that world.

But all of those recreations exist on the Main Grid. *Second Life* is a bifurcated world where thirteen- to seventeen-year-olds don't mix with eighteen-and-overs; it's kind of a tough space in which to get teachers and students together. Colleges and universities can take advantage, but K–12 students are relegated to *Teen Second Life*, which is a great space, but no adults allowed.

But *Second Life* isn't the only virtual world in cyberspace, and even if it were, teaching students isn't the only reason educators might want to go there. A few kinks notwithstanding, virtual worlds are providing students and teachers with an interesting and evolving resource.

Professional Development

Second Life, for example, has proved to be a rich and productive environment for teacher education, professional development, and networking. One of the strengths of the growing education community in *Second Life* is what John Lester has called its "fundamental predisposition to collaborate." Lester was a technology evangelist at Linden Lab, where he led that company's education and health-care market development group. His *Second Life* avatar, "Pathfinder Linden," is one of SL's best-known residents. He maintains that teachers bring a built-in culture of collaboration to that virtual world. It is, he says, "in their DNA."

Teachers find other teachers to work with on projects in *Second Life*. They develop best practices and leverage the content, events, and tools that have already been created in the virtual world. "At its core, *Second Life* is a rich ecosystem of learning experiences that are open to the public," Lester said in a 2009 interview. "Teachers don't have to create everything from scratch."

Second Life has proved to be especially fertile ground for professional-learning communities for K–12 educators. One highly respected example is the *Lighthouse Learning Island*. Founded by Kathy Schrock, Administrator for Technology at the Nauset Public Schools, *Lighthouse Learning* was created by four school districts in southeastern Massachusetts, including Nauset, Barnstable, Dennis-Yarmouth Regional School District, and Plymouth Public Schools.

In her blog on the launch of the virtual island, Schrock wrote that its purpose was twofold: to serve as an "engaging venue for traditional professional development and collaboration, including staff meetings, presentations on topics of interest to the educators in our district, and training materials" and to "ramp up the *Second Life* skills of the teachers in the four districts, in order to move ahead, in year two, with content-specific Teen Grid islands."

Lighthouse Learning member districts lead tours of the virtual world and host seminars and "learning opportunities" at in-world venues—virtual meeting rooms and auditoriums constructed for that purpose. Attendees' avatars gather at these venues, where they can listen to lectures and watch slides and video. They participate through their avatars, very much as they would in a real-world session, and they can interact with other attendees before and after a presentation.

Language Immersion

Researchers at Stanford Research Institute International (SRI) have been experimenting with virtual worlds as environments for English-language learners. SRI is an independent, nonprofit research institute, conducting client-sponsored research and development for government agencies, commercial businesses, foundations, and other organizations.

In 2007, SRI's Center for Technology in Learning (CTL) launched a test project called Lakamaka Island, named for some virtual real estate—a tropical island—that the institute had purchased in *Second Life*. Principal investigators Valerie Crawford and Phil Vahey and their team used the virtual island as a staging ground for language-learning studies.

Participants in the project checked into hotels, ordered meals, and engaged in many of the activities they might face during a trip to another country, interacting exclusively in the language being learned. According to John Brecht, a learning technology engineer on the project, the idea was to provide language learning in context, and to provide an immersive environment in which to practice language skills—the kind of environment students could only get by moving to a foreign country or logging on to *Second Life*.

MMORPGs

Believe it or not, MMORPGs are also potential facilitators of language learning. Researchers Edd Schneider and Kai Zheng conducted a study in 2007 in which a group of graduate students tutored a group of Chinese middle-schoolers in English through online computer games. They found that the social environment of *WoW*, for example, presented language learning in a context that motivated rapid acquisition, similar to the experience of total immersion in a foreign culture.

It turns out that the competitive, monster-hunting, sword-and-sorcery environment of a MMORPG is less threatening than a classroom, where a student might be embarrassed in front of peers, and the questing and cooperation necessary among players is highly motivating.

In the spring of 2006, researchers Bruce Gooch, Yolanda Rankin, and Rachel Gold put together a pilot study to evaluate second-language acquisition in the context of MMORPGs. They focused on Sony Online Entertainment's *EverQuest II (EQII)*. The eight-week study involved six English-language learners—two native speakers of Korean, two of Chinese, and two of Castilian Spanish. The subjects played the game for at least four hours per week.

The researchers found that the game reinforced language acquisition, because the players became "active learners" who had to engage with other players and the gaming environment to pursue quests, which is inherently motivating.

The *EQII* research was first suggested to Gooch by John Nordlinger, program manager for the Microsoft Research group. In response to the suggestion that *WoW* and *EQII* are likely to infect players' vocabularies with odd terms not found in most classroom language texts ("sword," "elf," "wizard"), he observed that many students in American English classes are now reading the Harry Potter novels, which operate from a similarly exotic lexicon. "Yes, there are skeletons and vampires in *EverQuest*, but don't think they're not already in English class," he says.

ePortfolios

The education sector has also been fertile ground for the development of a unique type of user-generated content not previously discussed in this book. It's called an electronic portfolio or ePortfolio, and it actually predates much of the social media mentioned here.

Back in 2003, the National Learning Infrastructure Initiative defined an electronic portfolio as "a collection of authentic and diverse evidence, drawn from a larger archive representing what a person or organization has learned over time, on which the person or organization has reflected, and designed for presentation to one or more audiences for a particular rhetorical purpose."

That's a long-winded definition, but it's held up pretty well, even as ePortfolios have evolved from simple digital storehouses for browser-accessed copies of student work into sophisticated multimedia environments that can integrate with a range of electronic-learning technologies.

Not a Scrapbook

An ePortfolio shouldn't be confused with a blog or an online scrapbook. These collections can contain similar content, but the purpose of an ePortfolio is to highlight a set of skills, represent work, and organize information. Both teachers and students use them to collect audio, video, graphics, and textual "artifacts," including things like work samples, formal and informal assessments, resumes, teaching/learning philosophies, lesson plans, course projects, and personal reflections. An ePortfolio also provides educators with a means of organizing and storing teaching resources for later use; for facilitating professional development through evidence collection, reflection, self-study, and classroom analysis; and even help with a job search.

Types of ePortfolios

These systems for gathering, storing, and presenting digital evidence of the academic accomplishments of students and the professional credentials of educators have been around for more than a decade. But this is very much an evolving form of social media. Many of the tools and technologies for creating and maintaining online portfolios now integrate social networking, blogging, and social tagging. And many ePortfolio vendors are taking a much longer view, with products designed to follow the student from K–12 through higher education and on into the workplace.

Keep in mind that this is still a lively space with evolving definitions and research. That said, some social-media mavens have divided ePortfolios into three main types:

- **Developmental,** which provide a record of things that an individual has done over a period of time, and may be directly tied to learner outcomes
- **Reflective,** which include personal reflections on the content and what it means for the individual's development
- **Representational,** which show an individual's achievements in relation to particular work or developmental goals and is, therefore, selective.

ePortfolio Providers

The ePortfolio products in use today come with the same basic ability to collect and organize artifacts in a range of digital file types to demonstrate the achievement of specific goals and objectives. Most support storage and presentation of text files, spreadsheets, audio files, photos, graphics, and video clips. Most live on the web on systems accessed through a web browser. Following is a list of some ePortfolio products you might want to investigate.

Epsilen

The Epsilen ePortfolio (*www.epsilen.com*) is one of the most feature-rich ePortfolio products on the market. It's a centrally managed system that provides an online repository in which students collect a range of examples of their work, including photos, videos, and text. Epsilen also supports a number of social media, including blogging tools and a wiki application. Few ePortfolio vendors have embraced social networking as ardently as Epsilen. One unique feature of this system is its connection to the archives of the *New York Times*. The newspaper provides Epsilen users with access to 150 years of articles and interactive features in its own online content repository.

Desire2Learn

Desire2Learn (*www.desire2learn.com*) is another ePortfolio provider with some useful Web 2.0-based features. The system is web-based, and it stores a diverse range of file types—documents, audio and video, and graphics. It also comes with a set of Web 2.0-standard-interface components, including a browser-based dashboard and social tagging tools. The tagging tools, which allow users to attach so-called metadata to their files in the form of keywords, are something of a differentiator among ePortfolio providers. The repository can be managed manually or dynamically populated with artifacts, and the artifacts can be grouped into collections that share tags to facilitate the sharing of content.

Digication

Digication (*www.digication.com*) is an ePortfolio provider with an eye on the future of this technology. Along with editions designed for K–12 and higher education users, the company offers a Personal edition of its ePortfolio systems. The Digication product provides the essential ePortfolio features—hosted repository, browser-based dashboard, multimedia file storage, customizable templates and menus—along with several Web 2.0 tools, such as tagging. Users can also link directly to content from YouTube, Google Video, TeacherTube, SchoolTube, Photobucket, and Brightcove.

ANGEL Learning

The e-learning solutions provider ANGEL Learning's ePortfolio (*www.angellearning.com/community/k_12.html*) supports the collection and storage of the usual range of file types—documents, spreadsheets, audio, photos, video clips, etc.—collected via drag-and-drop and accessed though a browser. The system provides blogging capabilities, RSS feeds to stream blog postings which instructors and others can subscribe to, rubrics, customizable templates and themes for publishing student work, a password-protected document-sharing feature, and an HTML editor.

Chalk & Wire

Chalk & Wire (*www.chalkandwire.com*) is a frills-free ePortfolio authoring system, essentially a suite of tools designed to allow educators and students to build customized ePortfolios. Student work samples and assessment data can be collected and stored on the web in a hosted environment, or stored locally on a district's own servers. There's a browser-based dashboard, tools for editing and commenting on work directly in the student's ePortfolio, artifact annotation tools for markup, and an audio commenting feature that records comments and stores them in the ePortfolio as audio files connected to specific assessment records.

LiveText

LiveText (*www.livetext.com*) is a web-based e-learning solution with a simple ePortfolio development toolset for students. There's a browser-based dashboard, a digital repository, and an online workspace for document authoring and ePortfolio assembly. C1 is essentially a service that can be integrated with the company's learning- and course-management solutions.

ePortfolio.org

Designed and supported by the Connecticut Distance Learning Consortium, ePortfolio.org (*www.eportfolio.org*) is billed as a "student-centered platform." The product provides students and teachers with tools for creating and customizing electronic portfolios for academics, but also for career and personal use. The repository supports a range of file formats, including audio, graphics, and text. And it's all web-based, so access is gained through a browser.

Elgg

Elgg (*www.elgg.org*) is one of a handful of open-source ePortfolio products currently available. It's been around since 2004, and benefitting from a growing community of contributors since then. According to the community, "The emphasis with Elgg is very much on the learner. Elgg looks to give learners the means to control and own their own development and growth through the use of everyday web technologies." Elgg supports an online repository, and comes with blogging and tagging tools, social networking capabilities, a profile feature for linking to other learners, fine-grained access controls in the hands of the users, and a lightweight connection to a wiki space.

Mahara

The other well-known open-source ePortfolio project is Mahara (*www.mahara.org*). It was originally sponsored by New Zealand's Tertiary Education Commission's e-learning Collaborative Development Fund, and then contributed to several of that country's universities.

Like Elgg, Mahara is a stand-alone ePortfolio system designed to be integrated into a learning-management system. According to the project maintainers, the product's architecture was inspired by the modular and extensible architecture of the Moodle learning-management system. The system provides for the typical web-based repository for user artifacts. Stored files can be structured into sub folders. A range of file formats are supported.

Foliotek

Foliotek (*www.foliotek.com*) was developed in 2003 by the University of Missouri for Lanit Consulting. The company now offers both a student ePortfolio solution for the education market and an institutional solution aimed at commercial enterprises. The company's Student Portfolio product provides many of the features of the other ePortfolio solutions described previously, but organized in a three-part bundle that includes an Assessment Portfolio, a Presentation Portfolio, and a Scrapbook Portfolio.

iWebfolio

Developed by software maker Nuventive, iWebfolio (*www.iwebfolio.com*) is another ePortfolio management system with a trifold model. Users can create Learning Portfolios for reflection and formative evaluations; Assessment Portfolios based on accrediting or local standards; and Presentation Portfolios for showcasing achievements. All three portfolio types may contain a range of digital content, including audio and video files, Word documents, PowerPoint presentations, and even animated GIFs. The product also comes with a rich-text content editor designed to allow users to include links to files, URLs, graphics, tables, and Flash content.

Adobe Systems PDF Portfolios

Adobe's entry into the ePortfolio market, PDF Portfolio, is based on the company's ubiquitous Portable Document Format (PDF) (*www.adobe.com/education/instruction/teach/acrobat-curriculum.html*). So-called PDF Packages offer an electronic wrapper for rich media content, including text documents, e-mail messages, spreadsheets, CAD drawings, and PowerPoint presentations. Users can organize different source files into what the company calls "logical collections" that can be linked for customized navigation and search. Each file can be opened, read, edited, and formatted independently of the others in the PDF Portfolio. The free Adobe Reader, version 9, is required to view the content.

CHAPTER 19

Social Media Marketing: Creating Buzz with the Social Web

Social media marketing is all the rage these days. More and more companies and individuals are turning to the social web to promote their products and services and to build and maintain customer relationships. But leveraging platforms of user-generated content for marketing purposes is still a new game with its own evolving rules and best practices. Even the experts are still figuring them out; an awful lot of people are still experimenting. Still, some basic principles and strategies have emerged. Here's what the pioneers in this area have come up with so far.

What Is Social Media Marketing?

"Social media marketing" is a truly hype-soaked buzz phrase, but what does it really mean? To state the obvious, it's marketing through social media. What's not so obvious is that it's a discipline and a methodology for developing a reputation and brand within social media communities, and cultivating influence among potential customers, fans, and supporters.

It's not *advertising*, which you see plenty of on social media sites cycling through side panels on the main page. It's the *promotion* of a product, service, company, cause, or person through the use of social media pretty much the way everyone else uses it. You blog, share photos, create a profile page, add status updates, and just generally join the conversation.

Anyone can engage in social media marketing. All you need is an account with a network or service. But it's tricky to do well.

FACT

In 2010, Pepsi did something that should prove at least somewhat validating for proponents of social media marketing. Instead of advertising on the Super Bowl, as the company had for many years, Pepsi went with a $20 million interactive Internet campaign that included a big Facebook promotion.

How Is It Being Used?

Companies use social media to promote brands and products, to post corporate materials, and to connect users to the company's home page through hyperlinks. To a certain extent (though the jury is still out on this), they use them to generate leads and even to help make sales. They also use them to monitor what is being said about them on the Internet so that they can address issues and correct misinformation. And if they're smart, they use it to *listen* to what their customers are telling them about the products and their organization.

Specifically, social media marketing is currently being used by organizations and individuals to:

- Build product and brand awareness
- Develop and nurture relationships

- Maintain and enhance reputation
- Increase traffic to a website
- Create buzz about a company, product, or person
- Learn what customers, fans, and supporters want
- Generate leads
- Connect people to offline events

Not all forms of social media are right for every type of organization or marketing campaign. How much bang are you going to get for your virtual buck launching a *"Twilight* Team Edward" campaign on LinkedIn? How many fans would even the most helpful and content-rich home page for a retirement planning service draw on MySpace?

Who's Using Social Media?

Quite a few companies seem to be making the social web work for branding and promotion. The makers of the movie *Avatar,* for example, established a wildly successful Facebook fan page to promote the movie and respond to fans. It reportedly drew 700,000 fans, and it was still going strong months after the movie premiered. The author Neil Gaimen twitters frequently about his adventures on book tours and readings at local book stores, and he responds to his readers through the microblog. At last count, he had nearly 1.5 million followers. Mark Cuban, owner of the Dallas Mavericks pro basketball team, blogs regularly, holding forth on a range of topics, and speaking directly to fans of the team; Cuban's blog consistently appears on all the major top-blog lists. The University of Phoenix promotes its online classes through YouTube by posting beautiful mini-documentaries about its graduates. Automaker Toyota released a virtual version of its Scion line of cars in the virtual world *Second Life.* And a range of companies have established accounts on Flickr to share photos of their facilities and employees.

The range of companies currently engaged in social media marketing is wide, but it's worth noting that most haven't been at it for very long. Corporate blogs, of course, are old hat, but full-fledged social media marketing plans hit the front burner in the marketing department only recently.

In 2008, social marketing guru Peter Kim (*www.beingpeterkim.com*) compiled a widely circulated list of companies engaged in social media marketing. That list included, among many others: AT&T, which had a fan page on

Facebook, a microblogging presence on Twitter, a YouTube video channel, and a Flickr photo-stream page. Coca Cola made Kim's list, with a corporate blog, a "virtual thirst" contest on *Second Life*, and two Facebook applications. Wells Fargo Bank had a blog, a YouTube channel, a MySpace page, a Facebook application and fan page, and its own virtual world called *Stagecoach Island*. Dunkin' Donuts and CNN both got by with just a Twitter account.

A year later, researcher Michael A. Stelzner revealed the results of a survey of nearly 900 marketers. Among those results: The majority of those surveyed (81 percent) said the number one advantage of social media marketing was its power to generate exposure for the business.

What It's Really Going to Cost

When they begin implementing a social media marketing initiative, many companies discover that they save some money. After all, an account on Facebook or Twitter is free, so it shouldn't come as a surprise that, when social media are added to the marketing mix, expenditures can decline. But they also discover that making those accounts work for them isn't free. What it costs is *time*.

You can't just set up a social media account and walk away. These aren't billboards. Social media accounts need *tending*. If you want to grow an audience, you have to add content to your account that other users consider valuable, and you have to add it regularly. And if you want to keep those users coming back, you have to nurture the relationships you create there.

If you set up an account on a social network, for example, you might need to update your status about once a day. If you're using Twitter, it's more like *several times* a day. These are what social media marketing mavens call the realities of the media. And you have to respond to your visitors' comments and questions, too.

How much time should you expect to spend? Depending on which social media maven you ask, and what your campaign involves, anywhere from five to twenty hours per week. The bottom line: The accounts you set up for social media marketing require ongoing attention.

There's really nothing less interesting to the denizens of social media sites than an account that hasn't been updated in a while, or that doesn't respond to user input. Think about it: Would you return to an unresponsive site with stale content?

Keeping up with their social media marketing accounts has proved to be so time-consuming that some companies are outsourcing the job, the way a landlord might hire a property manager to run her apartment buildings. The result is a cottage industry of specialists who manage your social media accounts.

Social Media Marketing Plans

Another core principle the experts seem to agree on is that successful social media marketing efforts start with a plan. The truth is, all effective marketing efforts start with a plan, whatever the medium. As you begin thinking about social media marketing, ask yourself a few questions. Start with: What am I promoting? Is it a product with broad appeal, or a specialty item? Is it a service aimed at an age group or demographic, or the general public? Is this something brand new for which I'll need to create a market, or something with a household name?

Next ask yourself: What do I hope to accomplish? What are my goals here? Am I trying to promote product awareness? Company visibility? Brand recognition? How about creating a new community around products or services? Am I trying to generate sales leads? Foster better customer relationships? Improve our organization's reputation? Am I trying to increase traffic to my website? Boost page views? Engagement with customers for surveys and feedback? All of the above?

There may be moments when lightning strikes and your YouTube video goes viral (spreads by word of mouth), or the twitter stream chirps with a hash-tagged topic that you initiated. But those are merely results. Social media marketing is a practice and a method of establishing your influence, reputation, and brand within communities of potential customers, fans, and supporters.

Sociability

Because you're planning to promote your brand or product on social media sites, it also makes sense to consider whether there's anything inherently "social" about it. Movies, of course, attract communities of fans. But communities form around a vast number of areas. If you're promoting, say, a chain saw, you immediately fall into the do-it-yourself (DIY) community. If it's your new cookbook, you're instantly part of the foodie community. Gamers, bikers, sailors, knitters, and hobbyists of every stripe are part of a community. People don't really care about your business, but if your home improvement company can help members of the DIY community fix a leaky faucet, you bring value to the conversation beyond your interest in selling some pipe wrenches.

ESSENTIAL

A 2009 study conducted by Wetpaint (*www.wetpaint.com*) and the Altimeter Group (*www.altimetergroup.com*) found, among other things, that successful social media marketing campaigns at the corporate level involved dedicated teams within the company. They didn't have to be large teams, but they had to be focused on social media.

This sociability factor matters because the key to successful social media marking isn't in the presentation, but the conversation. That's not to say you don't need compelling content. The important point is to remember that this is a social environment, the guts of which have been generated by the users, and it's all about interaction.

Listen In

When the talk turns to social media marketing, the focus tends to be on the content you create, or the message your company sends. That's critical, of course, but more and more companies are discovering the value of the social media two-way street. Engaging in social media marketing offers a unique opportunity to have a conversation with your customers, to hear what they really care about and what interests them.

Before you launch yourself onto the social web, take some time to listen to what they're saying about you online. Use a search engine to pull up blog postings. Sign up for a social network or other service and keep a low profile while you search for mentions of you or your company. You could also start a topical conversation and follow the responses. Pay attention to how you or your company is perceived, how people feel about you, whether they like or trust your brand.

While you're listening in, take some time to identify the "influencers" out there, the bloggers and twitterers whose opinions hold sway with the communities. These are the people who will drive traffic to your website, your Facebook page, or your blog. These are the valuable people you want to recommend you.

You'll also want to track mentions of your brand or your name, and even your industry. It's perfectly possible that you won't find anything, but it's a good idea to know what kind of environment you're stepping into.

Strike Up a Conversation

The participatory platform that is the social web requires would-be marketers to participate in the online conversation. Okay, it's not exactly a requirement, but most web watchers and marketing gurus see it as a unique opportunity to get to know and better understand their customers, fans, and supporters. You can have direct interactions with these folks in a way that was never possible before. You can provide them with the very latest information about your products or services. You can make and maintain connections with existing customers, and reach out to potential new ones.

This two-way street will be invaluable going forward. You'll be able to catch misinformation before it spreads far and wide, and take steps to correct it. And you can discover what your customers are really interested in and what they really think about you.

QUESTION

What is Voice Share?
"Voice Share" or "Share of Voice" is a marketing term for how much of the online conversation about a particular industry or topic mentions you, your brand, your product, or your company. A greater Share of Voice is better, as long as the mentions aren't negative.

When it comes to running your social media marketing accounts, forget automation. If you can't manage well yourself, hire somebody, but don't click the cruise control and fire off scheduled posts. You might be able to get away with it on Twitter, which has a fat and flowing tweet stream. But on social networks like Facebook and MySpace, you're expected to show up.

Most social media sites offer some kind of demographic information, which is very useful when you begin to target your audience. But it's also worthwhile just to spend some time on a site, interacting with its members, getting to know them one-on-one. The big numbers matter, but it's also useful to get a sense of the community from firsthand experience with it.

You'll also get to know the "personality" of the network or service. Twitter is a microblog and naturally has little in common with the Flickr photo-sharing site. But even social media in the same categories have their own rhythms and quirks. Facebook, MySpace, and LinkedIn are all social networks, but they're different worlds.

FACT

Brand advocates are members of a social network or other service who recommend products and services just because they like them. These folks have no axe to grind and no sponsorships. They just call 'em like they see 'em, and others respect them for it. Brand advocates are also considered "influencers," because their recommendations carry a lot of weight on the social web.

And while you're at it, get to know the rules of the community. These things may seem like free-for-alls, but many have definite dos and don'ts, which you can usually find in the help menu. If you try to sell anything on Flickr, for example, your account will be deleted. This is no place to cross any lines or violate social conventions.

Marketer-Generated Content

What you publish matters just as much as how often you publish it. If the content you create is perceived by the community as purely promotional, it won't be welcomed, and you could turn off potential customers and supporters. If the community decides that the content you're offering is "spammy" or just an advertisement, or worse, unreliable, your credibility and brand could actually be damaged. They won't mind some promotional stuff, as long as it's mixed in with genuinely valuable content.

You want other users of the social media site to recommend your content and link to it, which will ultimately drive traffic to your site. The best way to make this happen is to publish compelling content that is related to your company, but doesn't push a particular product or service. If you're a hotel, for example, publish status updates and tweets about recreational activities in your city. Include photos and videos of the sites. Mention restaurants and shows. But don't mention room rates.

ESSENTIAL

When you engage with other members of a social media community, lose the formality. Make your messages conversational and personal. If you use marketing speak or canned responses, you'll sound like a robot.

Once a reputation is lost on the social web, it's very difficult to get it back. This is an environment in which you can get a lot of attention very fast and cause a lot of damage if you don't stop to think things through.

Compelling Content

You can approach the challenge of creating compelling social media marketing content in a couple of ways:

- **Demonstrate Expertise:** Blog on a topic you know very well. Post tips and tricks on your Facebook page. Recommend good products on Epinions—if you want extra credibility, recommend competing products. Do it because they're good, and you're the expert who knows. Offer free advice on your area of expertise that users will find helpful.
- **Become a Real Resource:** One of the best examples here is Home Depot's YouTube channel. It provides a wealth of free videos on topics ranging from "What's new in Outdoor Gardening" to "How To Save Energy by Installing Ceiling Fans." There's a forum for user comments, some social networking features, and a subscription option. There are also links to the "Weekly Ad," a "Store Finder," and "Great Online Deals," all of which promote the company directly. But the home page is just full of helpful stuff for visitors.

- **Provide Real-Time Information:** Give other members of the social media community the inside scoop on breaking news that only you can provide, and that's about as compelling as content gets. Think Apple giving YouTube subscribers a sneak peek of a new iPad feature, or a pop star giving MySpace fans a heads up about an upcoming concert.
- **Talk to People:** If you find that people are responding to something you've posted, get back to them. Today! Pose a provocative question. Invite others to join in. Get the conversational ball rolling.
- **Create a Group:** You don't have to be the only one adding valuable content to a social media site if you start a group. Groups can give you a leadership position and provide even richer customer feedback. They can also provide focus. If you're a nonprofit, for example, a Facebook group can provide a platform and virtual gathering place. Like-minded people who share your views could become supporters.

Estimates of the number of active blogs vary, but the BlogPulse search engine tracked down nearly 127 million active blogs in mid 2010. And that number keeps growing. Standing out in that crowd requires truly great *original* content. The junk and the me-too stuff simply gets ignored.

The Conversation

The marvel of social media as a marketing tool is its ability, not only to deliver your message to customers and potential customers, but its ability to allow them to speak to you. The social web, remember, is a two-way street, so the content you create in that environment is actually part of an ongoing conversation. This is where a lot of people new to social media marketing seem to drop the ball. They forget that these are participatory software platforms, that this demographic are not passive consumers of content, but active creators of it. Social media marketing, therefore, is less about getting your message out than it is about joining the conversation.

And here's the thing about conversations: they're not the place for a sales pitch. The best social media marketing content is open and authentic, and free of product or brand hype. It's a very different type of marketing than many people are used to, but those out there blazing the trail consistently warn about this potential pothole.

What is Linkbait?
"Linkbait" is an online-marketing term. It refers to an article or blog posting created specifically to generate links to a website. The basic idea is, if a posting is thought-provoking, entertaining, controversial, or valuable in some way, readers will want to share it with friends or recommend it. Consequently, they link to it from their blogs, social networking accounts, and/or webpages, creating more doorways to the originating website.

Effective social media marketers don't actually talk about themselves very much. They talk about and recommend others. A lot. Blowing your own horn is fine in a job interview, but on the social web it's a sign that you're there to sell something, and that turns people off. Instead, be useful, friendly, funny, and a resource for reliable links and recommendations that fit your profile, but don't necessarily pitch your products.

Multiple Media

When it comes to promoting your brand, your products, or yourself, there's really no single service or community that can meet all your marketing needs. There is no "best" type of social media, no single most effective network or service that can reach all the people you want to reach. Consequently, the experts tell us, an effective social media marketing campaign often requires your presence on more than one.

That situation is unlikely to change in the short term, but keep in mind that the social media space is shifting and evolving at a breezy clip. Different services work together to expand and combine their features. Some services are being acquired by others so that their technologies become integrated. Some larger services are adding features that might make the smaller services obsolete.

Although it's clear that the hyperbolic claims about social media marketing should be ignored, you'll be hard pressed to find a marketing professional not taking this phenomenon seriously.

CHAPTER 20

What's Next on the Horizon for Social Media

The tech world has been making bad predictions for decades. In 1943, IBM's Chairman Thomas Watson said, "I think there is a world market for maybe five computers." In 1977, Digital Equipment's founder Ken Olsen said, "There is no reason anyone would want a computer in their home." In 2007, Microsoft's CEO Steve Ballmer reportedly said: "There's no chance that the iPhone is going to get any significant market share." What follows are a few predictions about the social media that seem likely today, but which you should probably take with a grain of salt.

We Get Used to the Idea

As this book is being written, the percentage of Americans age twelve and older who have created a profile on at least one social networking service is nearing half the population. According to a national survey from Arbitron Inc. and Edison Research ("The Infinite Dial 2010: Digital Platforms and the Future of Radio") published in 2010, 48 percent of the population has already signed up. That's up from 24 percent in 2009.

It's seems clear that the digital immigrants are warming up to social media. And the number of digital natives, who were already pretty darned comfy with it, is growing, fast. It's safe to say that regular people can and do generate online content that's valuable. And that's likely to lead to decreased dependence on mainstream media for many things.

QUESTION

Did social media decide the U.S. presidential election in favor of Barack Obama?
There's no doubt that the Obama campaign's use of social media helped the candidate to defeat his democratic rival, Hilary Clinton. It has been argued that Ron Paul was the only other candidate in that race who understood social media as well as Obama.

Traditional and Social Media Become Symbiotic

Traditional media and social media appear to be evolving as interdependent content creators. In fact, it's already happening. In early 2010, George Washington University and Cision, a media-relations software firm, released a study of how journalists use social media and online tools. The survey found that 56 percent of journalists overall consider social media to be important to some degree. Among journalists writing for online publications, 69 percent thought it was important, while 48 percent of writers for mainstream magazines found social media to be important.

Even if you've never twittered a tweet or friended a friend—even if you'd never be caught dead joining a social network or posting your family photos online—you're being inculcated with social media. How? Through traditional mainstream media, which is increasingly finding sources among the generators of that content.

Newspapers, magazines, and broadcast news are now routinely quoting bloggers and twitterers. And scarcely a week goes by without a YouTube video making it to the nightly news or the late-night talk shows.

Social Media Marketing Explodes

As of this writing, Facebook has nearly 500 million members and Twitter has moved beyond its 10 billionth tweet. Even though much of the worst hype around social media marketing is already dwindling, the audiences made available for marketing campaigns by social networks and other social-media services will just keep getting bigger.

Social media is transforming the way companies communicate with their customers, and that's not a fad, but a trend. The big social networking players are sorting out the market. Niche players are emerging. And the companies that figure out how to deliver their marketing messages though these networks will kick the competition's butt.

QUESTION

What Does Stephen Colbert have against Wikipedia?
Probably nothing, but the comedian and star of *The Colbert Report* got a lot of mileage out of a bit of mischief, when, in 2006, he made changes to Wikipedia articles during his show and urged his viewers to change entries on the site to say that elephant populations had tripled. Wikipedians locked out these changes as soon as they became aware of them, and reportedly banned the account "Stephencolbert." Colbert was moved to create his own wiki called Wikiality.com, the Truthiness Encyclopedia, which is currently hosted by Wikia (*http://wikiality.wikia.com*).

And that means that best practices and standard approaches will be established. Users have already seen the nascent rules of thumb for social media marketing surfacing and establishing guideposts.

The downside for users is that the networks are going to be stacking up a staggering volume of company and product pages in the future. Or maybe that's a good thing, because it'll give us access to the products and companies that matter to us. Time will tell.

Integration and Acquisition

In 2010, the loudest buzz in the social-media universe was around location-sharing services, in particular Foursquare and Gowalla, both of which killed at the annual South by Southwest Interactive conference. But as cool and interesting as those companies are, it's their capabilities that matter in the long run. That's why unconfirmed reports that Facebook might be adding location sharing to the features of its social network came as no surprise and caused a lot of heads to nod. It's a logical arrow to add to that service's quiver. Of course, Twitter did the same thing earlier in the year.

2010 also saw Twitter acquiring a company called Tweetie, which provided a very popular Twitter application for the iPhone. Tweetie is now called Twitter for the iPhone. Twitter also partnered with RIM, the company that makes the Blackberry smartphone, to launch the "official" Twitter for Blackberry application. The company later announced plans to release an official Twitter app for Android mobile devices.

Rumors were also circulating at about that time that Twitter was set to release its own URL shortening feature. But companies such as TinyURL, bit.ly, goo.gl, and tr.im, already provide URL-shortening tools. Twitter CEO Evan Williams said at the time, "Much of the early work on the Twitter Platform has been filling holes in the Twitter product . . . . Some of the most popular third-party services on Twitter are like that. Mobile clients come to mind. Photo-sharing services come to mind. URL shorteners come to mind. Search comes to mind. Twitter really should have had all of that when it launched or it should have built those services right into the Twitter experience."

These developments are probably harbingers of things to come. This is bad news for third-party developers, but good news for end users who are weary of shuffling multiple social-media accounts. The downside, of course, is that we'll almost certainly have fewer choices. Consolidation tends to slow innovation. Even if Twitter's URL-shortener isn't as good as TinyURL, lots of people will use it just because it's there. Your social network is going to be able to do more of the things you go to other social-media services for, and that is going to make your social-media activities much easier to manage.

More People Roll Their Own

As the number of tools and platforms for building social networks evolves, more and more people are going to build their own focused, special purpose networks. The development of Classroom 2.0 is a perfect example. Ning, which was used to build that social network for teachers, and Active Worlds, which is used to build virtual worlds, and other tools like them are putting serious horsepower into the hands of users.

As the creators of user-generated content become the creators of user-generated environments, we'll see more social networks emerge around narrow interests. That's good news for users; even if no one develops an exclusive network for fans of *Red Dwarf*, or a virtual world for fly casters, chances are they'll come up with something new, and something that's good for everyone.

Social Networking Becomes a Business Tool

Salesforce.com, a leading provider of a platform and tools for building and running business applications in "the cloud" (marketing/techspeak for the Internet), unveiled its own social networking application in 2010. Called "Chatter," the application was billed as "a brand-new way to collaborate with people at work."

It wasn't exactly brand new, but Chatter signaled that social networking for business had arrived. The application brought the standard social networking components into a business context. Users will be able to use the application to create profiles that go into company directories. They'll be able to post status updates, just as you would on Facebook or MySpace, though these updates are meant to be about work—literal updates on the status of a project, for example. Users will be able to use the app to form project groups.

And it will even integrate with popular social networking sites, such as Twitter and Facebook, as the company puts it, "to form stronger connections with customers, prospects, and colleagues."

Chatter is an example of something called an "internal social media platform," which allows companies to take advantage of the collaboration potential of a social network. Companies like Jive, blueKiwi, Remindo, and even Microsoft's SharePoint support these kinds of services. NASA has one called "Spacebook." And others are beginning to appear.

Company blogs have been around for a while, but the enterprise (what techies call companies and corporations) is likely to at least take newly emerging internal microblogging services for a test drive. A company called Yammer, for example, specializes in providing "enterprise microblogging."

Mobility and New Devices

Social media are going to be appearing on a growing number of mobile devices. There are already numerous iPhone, Blackberry, and Android social media apps. You can expect that trend to continue, if for no other reason than the inescapable fact that everything is showing up on these and other mobile devices.

Mobile phones have become the new computing platform, and for some social media, such as location sharing, they're essential. For microblogs, such as Twitter, Tumblr, and Jaiku, mobile devices are almost the preferred platform. Facebook has reported that 25 percent of its users, or about 100 million people, access the social network primarily through mobile devices.

But it's not just the cell phones that will tapping into the social web. In 2010, Amazon.com announced that it would upgrade its popular Kindle e-book reader to allow users to access Facebook and Twitter. And despite its rejection of Flash, Apple's iPad seems like a likely candidate for social media. The enterprise will probably drive some of this development, as untethered workers find themselves needing to link with the company social network while on the road.

Augmented Reality

It's sounds like science fiction, but "augmented reality" is real technology that superimposes computer images and some audio over the real world in real time. It's sort of like the POV of *Iron Man* we saw in the movies.

If you're a football or hockey fan, you saw the tech used to show how far up the field your team needed to go for a first down, and as colored trails that followed the pucks shooting across the ice. This technology enhances your view of the world with computer images and text. You're laying real-time digital information over the real world. The U.S. Postal service is using it to help customers use their webcams to find the right sized shipping box. BMW mechanics wear special glasses that provide an enhanced view of a car engine, and play audio instructions through a set of integrated headphones. (Very *Terminator.*)

The Layar Reality Browser, for example, combines real-time computer data with geo tagging information from location-sharing service Brightkite, on images you see of the real world through your camera phone. The camera displays the view, but also superimposed photos, location markers, and real-time comments from other uses in the area. You can even see real estate listings for the nearby buildings.

The opinion-sharing service, Yelp, supports an iPhone application called Monocle, which combines the phone's camera view with the tags that identify landmarks, bars, and restaurants in that view, and pairs them with Yelp's user reviews. We're at the bleeding edge with this technology, but it is too cool not to go mainstream, fast.

Privacy Concerns Grow

This book is full of admonitions to check your privacy settings regularly in the social networks you belong to and the social-media services you use. Protecting your privacy isn't likely to become much more convenient in the near future, because the social-media providers have too much to gain by reaching deeper into your identity, both from a genuine concern about performance and features, but also with a little profit in mind.

Facebook came under harsh criticism in 2010 for its apparent nobody-cares-about-privacy-anymore attitude. There's no doubt that the changes the company implemented in its privacy policies would have helped to personalize the social-networking experience of its members, but those members felt that they were being asked to give up too much privacy by default, and Facebook was forced to backtrack.

This kind of stuff is inevitable, and as these networks grow and proliferate, we're only going to see more of it. In the spirit of the social web, it's really up to the users to take charge of their privacy, and to provide some user-generated feedback to social networks and other social-media services who force them to share too much.

Glossary

Adobe Reader:
A free program from Adobe Systems that allows you to read documents in the PDF format.

Aggregator:
A collector of web content, generally news and blogs, often for distribution via RSS feeds.

Android:
Mobile phone platform developed by Google, who released it to the Open Handset Alliance.

AOL:
America Online; one of the world's largest online service providers.

App:
Short for application. A software program.

Applet:
A small software application.

Artifact:
Audio, video, graphics, and textual files saved in an ePortfolio.

Asynchronously:
Literally, not synchronized; not at the same time.

Augmented reality:
Technology that superimposes computer images and some audio over the real world in real time.

Avatar:
An animated icon representing a member of a virtual world. Operated by that member in real time.

BBS:
Bulletin Board System; an Internet forum that allows groups of users to log onto a computer network and interact with each other.

Blog:
Short for "web log," a type of shared online journal, written by an individual published on a web page, and available for anyone to read.

Blog search engine:
Used to surf the Blogosphere. Technorati is one of the most popular. Google and Yahoo! also provide blog search engines.

Blogosphere:
The entire world's blogs taken as a whole, along with reader comments and any links or connections. Sometimes called "the blogging community."

Blogroll:
A list of links to other blogs, typically shown in a sidebar on a blog index page.

Bookmarking:
Saving a web page address in your browser so you can return easily to that page.

Bookmarklet:
A small software application or "applet" designed to allow users to send bookmarks directly to a social bookmarking service from a web browser.

Brand advocate:
Member of a social network or other service who recommends products and services just because he

likes them. No connections to the vendor. Considered an "influencer" because his recommendations carry a lot of weight on the social web.

Browser:
A web browser is a software program that lives on your desktop or laptop, and retrieves and displays web pages from the Internet.

CAD:
Computer aided design. Used by architects and engineers.

Chatter:
Salesforce.com's new social media application for business.

Chrome:
A web browser developed by Google.

Citizen journalism:
Average people using blogs and other social media to engage in reporting and commentary on current events.

Classroom 2.0:
A social network for educators.

Clone:
Another version of a software program that is very similar or heavily inspired by the original.

Cloud:
Essentially, the Internet. "In the cloud," usually means an online service or storage, or some computing activity that once took place on a company server, but now takes place on servers outside the company.

CompuServe:
The first major online service in the U.S. Similar to AOL.

ConnectU:
A social network developed by Harvard students. An early Facebook rival.

Consumer-generated media:
Social media content generated by consumers sharing experiences with products and services they've bought or tried.

CSS:
Cascading Style Sheets; web-page developers use it to control designs and layouts across multiple web pages.

Digital immigrants:
Author Marc Prensky's term for anyone not born into a world in which personal-computing technologies weren't already part of daily life.

Digital natives:
Term coined by author Marc Prensky for modern students who grew up surrounded by computer technology. The term is now widely used.

Download:
To receive computer files on your desktop or laptop computer from a remote computer.

EFF:
Electronic Frontier Foundation, the leading civil liberties group focused on digital rights.

ePortfolio:
Electronic portfolio; a collection of evidence representing a person's educational or career progress.

Extension:
The part of the file name that comes after the "dot" near the end and indicates the type of information in the file. Some examples are docx, WMV, MPEG, and FLV.

fan wiki:
A wiki with user-generated and user-edited articles about the popular TV shows, movies, pop stars, and other fan-oriented topics.

FAQ:
Frequently asked questions.

FarmVille:
A very popular social game.

Favorites:
A list of bookmarks.

Firefox:
An open source web browser

FL:
First life; what users of the *Second Life* virtual world call the real world.

Flash:
Adobe's nearly ubiquitous platform for displaying multimedia on web pages.

Footstream:
A digital record of the places a person goes in the real world. Jeff Holden, co-founder and CEO of Pelago, the company that owns Whrrl, often gets credit for coining this term.

Fork:
To use a legal copy of an open-source technology or content for the development of a different version.

Forum:
An online discussion site.

Freemium:
A subscription model that combines a basic free membership with fee-based premium services.

Friending:
Adding someone to your list of contacts in a social network.

Galeon:
A web browser.

GIF:
A graphics file format. Stands for Graphics Interchange Format. Many banner ads on the web are created as GIFs.

Google:
The world's leading web search engine. Provides other services, including e-mail, online mapping, and social networking.

GPS:
Global Positioning System; a satellite-based navigation system.

Grid:
The name insiders use for the *Second Life* virtual world.

Hashtag:
A tag in the Twitter microblogging service, consisting of a # sign in front of a single word.

Hosting:
A service that provides space on its web servers (big computers permanently connected to the Internet) to store the content of your website, blog, or wiki, and from which you and others can access that content with a web browser. It's the home of your website.

HTML:
Hypertext Markup Language; a simple, tag-based language used to create web pages.

Hypermedia:
A kind of graphical hyperlink that opens up an audio or video clip.

Hyperlink:
A link from one web page to another, typically in the form of text in a different color (usually blue). Click on the text and you open a new web page.

IM:
Instant messaging.

Internet:
The public-facing global system of interconnected computers and networks that allow for the sharing of content, technology, and services; "the Net."

Internet Explorer:
Microsoft's web browser.

Intranet:
Internal company computer network.

Klingon:
An alien race from the *Star Trek* television series and movies.

Konqueror:
A freeware web browser based on Linux.

Layar Reality Browser:
Example of augmented reality. An app that combines real-time computer data with geo-tagging info from location-sharing service Brightkite, on images of the real world seen through a camera phone.

Linden Dollars (L$):
The virtual currency of the *Second Life* virtual world.

Linkbait:
Online-marketing term for a thought-provoking or entertaining blog posting or article created to get others to visit the site.

Linklog:
A blog that is mainly a collection of hyperlinks to other websites.

LMS:
Learning management systems.

Location sharing:
Technology that allows members of a web-based social network to share their locations in real time. Also called location-based social networking, geosocial networking, social check-in, and social mapping.

Mafia Wars:
A popular social networking game.

Mainstream media:
The news from television, newspapers, and radio, even when it's published online.

MediaWiki:
The wiki engine originally developed for the Wikia Foundation and used to run Wikipedia.

Microblog:
A blog allowing very short text updates. Twitter is an example.

Millennials:
Members of the post–Generation-X generation, sometimes called Generation Y or Generation Next. This is the generation that is the most comfortable with computer technology, because it has always been a part of their lives.

MMORPG:
Massively multiplayer online role-playing game. Blizzard Entertainment's *World of Warcraft* is a popular example.

MP3:
A compressed audio file format. Short for MPEG layer 3.

Netscape:
A web browser.

Newbie:
Slang for someone new to a social network or virtual world. A newcomer with few skills.

Newsgroup:
One group in the worldwide network of online discussion groups called Usenet. Generally focused on a specific topic.

Ning:
A platform for creating social networks. Classroom 2.0, for example.

Open source:
Software that is developed and maintained by communities of software developers and freely available. The Linux operating system is one example. The OpenOffice alternative to Microsoft Office is another.

Opera:
A web browser.

Opt in:
A system that requires you to say "Yes, I want to do this." If you do nothing, the default choice is "no."

Opt out:
A system that requires you to say "No, I don't want to do this." If you do nothing, the default choice is "yes."

PDF:
Portable Document Format.

Permalink:
A link that points to a specific blog posting. The link is "permanent" because it remains intact even after the posting has slipped off the front page and into the blog archive.

Persistence:
A techie term that means the virtual world exists whether or not anyone is logged in. It persists.

Photoblog:
A blog consisting primarily of photographs, with commentary.

PHP:
A popular dynamic scripting language often used in social media.

Phreaking:
Breaking into phone systems.

Ping:
A notification to another blogger that you have linked to, or commented on, something in that person's blog. ("Ping" is an acronym for Packet Internet Grouper.)

Plug-in:
A computer module that you add to another program, say, a web browser, to add a feature or capability.

Podcast:
An audio or video file made for distribution on the Internet. Gets its name from Apple's iPod player.

Portal:
A point of access to a group of web pages and websites. Companies provide them as starting points for their corporate websites. Yahoo! is a well-known public portal.

Pose ball:
An object in the virtual world of *Second Life* that poses or animates your avatar.

Real time:
Happening right now.

Reputation:
The part of your online identity defined by others. Your standing among your peers on the web.

RSS:
Real Simple Syndication; a method of distributing aggregated web content that changes frequently. If you subscribe to an RSS feed, the aggregated content gets sent to you automatically.

Safari:
Apple's web browser.

Scrapbook:
A feature of a photo-sharing service. Allows you to combine your photos with text and a range of decorative backgrounds.

Search engine:
A computer program running in your web browser that helps you find web pages. Google and Bing are examples.

SEO:
Search engine optimization. Techniques for improving your website's ranking in the leading search engines.

Shared-authorship model:
An approach to developing web content that allows users to add new content and revise existing content without asking for permission to do so.

SL:
Short for *Second Life*.

SLURL:
The web address of a *Second Life* destination.

SMO:
Social Media Optimization. Like SEO only for social media.

Social bookmarking:
Saving web page bookmarks to a special-purpose website that allows you to organize and share them.

Social game:
Game specifically designed for social networks or virtual worlds. *FarmVille* and *Mafia Wars* are examples.

Social media marketing:
The promotion of a product, service, company, cause, or person through the use of social media by blogging, sharing photos, creating a profile page, adding status updates, and just generally joining the conversation.

Social media:
Umbrella term for all user-generated content. Includes blogs, wikis, social networks, location sharing, social bookmarking, social news, photo and video sharing, and virtual worlds.

Social network:
A web-based service through which people interact socially, creating a kind of online community. Facebook and MySpace are examples.

Social news:
Services that allow users to recommend news stories, articles, images, blogs, and videos. Digg and Slashdot are examples.

Spam:
Junk e-mail, or any undesired electronic content, typically automatically generated by marketers. Bulk e-mail.

Status update:
The message you post in a social network telling people what you're up to.

Stubs:
Brief starter Wikipedia articles, summaries of the topic in about 500 words; most Wikipedia articles start out as stubs.

Tag cloud:
A visual organization of tags into a "cloud" of words; the more important, popular, and relevant tags are displayed in large text, in striking colors, near the center of the cloud.

Tagging:
The act of attaching a keyword to a piece of web content to make it easier to find and organize.

Thefacebook:
A student-oriented social networking website, developed in a Harvard dorm room, which evolved into Facebook.

Trackback:
A system that notifies you that another blogger has mentioned your blog posting in her blog.

Trending locations:
Just as Twitter displays "trending" topics—things lots of people are twittering about—location-sharing services show trending locations—places where lots of members of the service are gathering.

Trolling:
A form of wiki sabotage in which a user inserts intentionally offensive, misleading, or inflammatory content.

Tweet:
A 140-character message sent over the Twitter micro-blogging service.

Twitter:
The act of sending a tweet.

Upload:
To transfer a computer file from your desktop or laptop machine to a central computer at a different location.

URL:
Universal Resource Locator; the address of a web page.

User-generated content:
Content on the web produced by members of the population of end users of that content. Includes blogs, wikis, recommendations, critiques, virtual world elements, advice, videos, photos, etc. Not created by professionals.

Usenet:
A worldwide network of online discussion groups, called newsgroups, which are generally focused on a specific topic.

Video compression:
The process of reducing the number of bits required to store and transmit a video file.

Video-hosting service:
Services that allow users to upload videos for display and sharing on a website. These websites function as distribution platforms. Most are free, paid for by advertising, but some offer paid memberships that include additional storage and services for the video makers.

Viral video:
Video clips posted to the web that gain rapid popularity by word of mouth. The "Star Wars Kid" is an example.

Virtual goods:
Non-physical items you purchase in an online community, social network, online game, or virtual world.

Virtual reality:
An immersive artificial environment the user perceives as real. Computer scientist Jaron Lanier popularized the concept. Also known as VR.

Virtual world:
A three-dimensional computer environment designed to simulate the fundamental aspects of the real world, to mimic real life.

Vlog:
Video blog; a blog in the form of a video.

Voice Share:
Marketing term for how much of the online conversation about a particular industry or topic mentions you, your brand, your product, or your company.

Web 2.0:
The second generation of the web, which is a highly interactive environment full of user-generated content. Coined by tech-book publisher Tim O'Reilly.

Web crawlers:
Computer programs that relentlessly browse the web. Used to index websites.

Website:
A collection of web pages on the World Wide Web.

WELL:
Whole Earth 'Lectronic Link; one of the most successful BBSs in history.

Widget:
A small, portable web application or piece of dynamic content that can be installed and executed on a web page.

Wiki engine:
The software package used to build and run a wiki.

Wiki farm:
A wiki-hosting service that provides space for multiple wikis.

Wiki:
A website designed to allow visitors to freely add, edit, remove, comment on, and just generally change the content stored there.

Wikiblog:
A hybrid of the blog and the wiki. Also known as "wikiweblogs," "wikilogs," "blikis," and even "wogs," wikiblogs combine the features of the two models. The content can be edited like a wiki.

Wikification:
The process of turning a page of text or a web page into a Wikipedia page using the wikitext markup language. It also refers to the process of adding lots of hyperlinks to a Wikipedia page.

Wikilinks:
Links within a Wikipedia article to other pages on the website.

Wikipedian:
Someone who contributes content or editing to the Wikipedia online encyclopedia.

Wikitext:
A simple version of the markup language HTML used to write articles for Wikipedia.

World Wide Web:
All the web pages on the Internet connected with hyperlinks and accessed with a web browser.

WoW:
Short for *World of Warcraft*, a popular massively multiplayer online role-playing game.

WYSIWYG:
Stands for "what you see is what you get;" the web page being edited will be displayed on the web exactly the same way.

Additional Resources

140 Characters
Dom Sagolla's must-read guide to the art of the tweet. Available online and on the iPhone.
www.140characters.com

About.com
Useful online collection of expert-written articles on a broad range of topics. An "online neighborhood of experts."
www.about.com

Active Worlds
Provides free software for constructing your own three-dimensional virtual world on the Internet.
www.activeworlds.com

Adobe Systems
Software company behind Flash, Flex, PDF, and Acrobat Reader. Headquartered in San Jose, California.
www.adobe.com

Adobe Systems PDF Portfolios
Adobe's ePortfolio product. Based on the company's Portable Document Format (PDF).
www.adobe.com/education/instruction/teach/acrobat-curriculum.html

agoraXchange
A repository of ideas for a global politics game. Currently in beta.
www.agoraxchange.net

Alamofire
Austin, Texas-based company behind Gowalla. Makes digital collectibles. Created the popular card-collecting game, PackRat.
http://alamofire.com

Alexa.com
Excellent source for web traffic and trends. Calls itself "The Web Information Company." Indispensible resource for web watchers.
www.alexa.com

Amazon.com
Electronic commerce company originally known as a bookseller. Now features a massive catalog of products, including the Kindle e-book reader.
www.amazon.com

ANGEL Learning
A maker of learning management systems. Merged with rival Blackboard in 2009.
www.blackboard.com/Teaching-Learning/Learn-Resources/ANGEL-Edition.aspx

Angie's List
A subscription-based aggregator of consumer reviews. Focused on local services.
www.angieslist.com

Apple, Inc.
Formerly Apple Computer. Maker of the Mac, the iPod, the iPhone, and the iPad.
www.apple.com

Arbitron
A media research firm. Based in the U.S.
www.arbitron.com

Artcyclopedia
Free online art encyclopedia.
www.artcyclopedia.com

Autopedia
Free online encyclopedia of automotive resources. Covers auto maintenance, financing, insurance, lemon laws, and more, by state.
http://autopedia.com

Autospies
A social network of industry employees, analysts, dealers and car fanatics who leak information about cars. Headquartered in San Diego.
www.autospies.com

Avatar Facebook fan page
The Facebook fan page of the James Cameron hit movie. Good example of a fan page.
www.facebook.com/pages/ AVATAR-MOVIE-FAN- SITE205508540822

Badoo
Social network founded in London in 2006, now owned by a Greek company. Free, multi-lingual. Popular in Europe.
http://badoo.com

Bebo
Social network popular in the UK. Owned by AOL.
www.bebo.com

Beeing
Microblogging service.
www.beeing.com

Bit.ly
URL shortening service.
http://bit.ly

Blackplanet
Free social network aimed at African Americans. Founded in 1999. Billed as the largest black community online.
www.blackplanet.com

BlinkList
Free social bookmarking service claiming 450,000 users in 2010.
http://blinklist.com

Blip.TV
Video-hosting service. Claims 50,000- plus independently produced, original web shows, developed by 44,000-plus creators.
www.blip.tv

Blizzard Entertainment
Computer-game company, creator of *World of Warcraft*, *Diablo*, *Starcraft*, and other major hits.
http://us.blizzard.com

Blogger
Free hosting service maintained by search engine giant, Google. Launched in 1999, it's one of the best-known blog-hosting services.
www.blogger.com

Bloggers' FAQ on Intellectual Property
A must-read article from the Electronic Frontier Foundation's Bloggers' Legal Guide. Covers questions about copyright.
www.eff.org/issues/bloggers/legal/ liability/IP

Bloggers' FAQ on Online Defamation Law
A must-read article from the Electronic Frontier Foundation's

Bloggers' Legal Guide. Covers online defamation law.
www.eff.org/issues/bloggers/legal/ liability/defamation

Blue Mars
Free virtual world and platform. Users terraform whole planets. Some third-party developers offer subscription-based games and services.
www.bluemarsonline.com

blueKiwi
An example of an internal social media platform. Aimed at companies and organizations.
www.bluekiwi-software.com

Brightcove
Internet TV service for adding video to a website.
www.brightcove.com

Brightkite
Free location-sharing service based in Denver, Colorado, founded in 2007. Provides mobile apps for top smart phones.
http://brightkite.com

Buzzd
Free location-sharing service based in New York City, founded in 2008. Billed as a location-aware city guide aimed at mobile devices.
www.buzzd.com

Buzznet
Music-focused network with about 10,000 members. Members share photos, videos, and blog posts about their favorite bands.
www.buzznet.com

Canadian Encyclopedia Online
Free online encyclopedia about Canada. Provides "the most comprehensive, objective and accurate source of information on Canada."
www.thecanadianencyclopedia.com

Care2 (formerly C2NN)
Social network focused on green lifestyle and health issues.
www.care2.com/news

Chalk & Wire
A suite of tools designed to allow educators and students to build customized ePortfolios.
www.chalkandwire.com

Chatter
An example of an "internal social media platform." Being developed as enterprise-collaboration software by Salesforce.com, a provider of distributed business software.
www.salesforce.com/chatter

Citizendium
Free, wiki-type online encyclopedia, launched in 2007. Started as a "fork" of Wikipedia, but now publishes only articles written by known contributors.
http://en.citizendium.org

Classmates.com
Founded in 1995, one of the earliest services considered a social network by modern standards. Helps members connect with long-lost friends from school, work, and the military.
www.classmates.com

Classroom 2.0
Free social network for educators. Developed with the Ning platform.
www.classroom20.com

Club Penguin
MMORPG and virtual world for kids. Created in 2005. Now owned by Disney.
www.clubpenguin.com

CNet
One of the top online news sites covering the high-tech industry. A must-read for product reviews and news.
www.cnet.com

CNN.com
The cable news network's website. Packed with breaking news and features.
www.cnn.com

Columbia Encyclopedia
The content of the Columbia Encyclopedia (Sixth Edition) is part of this free online website of the famous Bartleby's, which publishes the classics of literature, nonfiction, and reference sources.
www.bartleby.com

comScore, Inc.
Great source of digital-marketing research, including online-audience measurement, e-commerce, advertising, search, video, and mobile. Offers dedicated analysts with digital-marketing and vertical-specific industry expertise.
www.comscore.com

Conservapedia
Wiki-based web encyclopedia with a conservative Christian point of view.
www.conservapedia.com

Cookbook Wiki
A wiki filled with user-generated recipes and articles about food.
http://recipes.wikia.com/wiki/Recipes_Wiki

Craig's List
Centralized network of online classified advertisements and job listings.
www.craigslist.org

Creative Commons
Nonprofit organization "dedicated to making it easier for people to share and build upon the work of others, consistent with the rules of copyright." Terrific resource for legal issues around user-generated content.
http://creativecommons.org

Criminal Minds wiki

A fan wiki focused on the television show *Criminal Minds*. Good example of a fan wiki.

http://criminalmindswiki.wetpaint .com

Daily Beast

Online magazine publishing news and opinion. Published by Tina Brown, former editor of *Vanity Fair* and *The New Yorker*.

www.thedailybeast.com

Daily Kos

A political blog with a progressive point of view. "Kos" is the U.S.-Army/screen nickname of the founder, Markos Zúniga.

www.dailykos.com

Delicious

One of the original social bookmarking services. Originally "del.icio.us." Claims to have reached 9.5 million users with more than 180 million bookmarks.

http://delicious.com

Desire2Learn

ePortfolio provider with useful, well-designed Web 2.0-based features.

www.desire2learn.com

deviantART

Social network for art lovers founded in 2000. Claims more than 11 million members. Provides a gallery where members display their art. Home to 80 million pieces of art in 2,000 categories.

www.deviantart.com

Diabetes Wikia

Wiki focused on diabetes. Features articles about diabetic treatments and products, as well as "stories of personal triumph."

http://diabetes.wikia.com

Digg

The web's most popular social news community at the start of 2010, with more than 40 million users. Launched in 2004.

http://digg.com

Digication

Provider of ePortfolios for K–12 and higher education users. Also offers a Personal edition. Lots of social media features.

www.digication.com

"Digital Natives, Digital Immigrants" by Marc Prensky

A must-read paper published in *On the Horizon* (MCB University Press, Vol. 9 No. 5, October 2001). Prensky coined "digital native" to describe modern students who grew up surrounded by computer technology. The term is now widely used.

www.marcprensky.com/writing/ Prensky%20-%20Digital%20Natives, %20Digital%20Immigrants%20-%20 Part1.pdf

DOE's Open Energy Information wiki

The Department of Energy's planned free, editable, and evolving wiki-platform for helping to deploy clean-energy technologies across the country and the world. Expected to make data available to the public.

www.openei.org

eBay Neighborhoods

Social network of the popular online marketplace. Introduced in 2007.

www.ebay.com

Edison Research

Conducts market research and exit polling, providing strategic information for businesses and media organizations worldwide.

www.edisonresearch.com

EditThis.Info

A no-frills, free wiki farm. Registered members get unlimited pages, an unlimited number of users, wiki spam protection, and RSS feeds.

http://editthis.info/wiki

Electronic Frontier Foundation (EFF)

Nonprofit organization founded in 1990 to defend free speech, privacy, innovation, and consumer rights in a digital world. Great source on legal issues for bloggers and anyone interested in social media.

www.eff.org

Elgg
One of a handful of open-source ePortfolio products. Available since 2004 with a growing community of contributors. Provides learners with means to control and own their own growth through the use of everyday web technologies.
http://elgg.org

Encyclopedia.com
Free encyclopedia with articles from more than 100 sources, including encyclopedias, dictionaries, and thesauruses.
www.encyclopedia.com

Engage Digital Media (formerly Virtual Worlds Management)
A leading provider of specialized trade events and media. Focuses on games, toys, social media, virtual worlds, and user engagement. Tracks the virtual-worlds industry.
www.engagedigitalmedia.com

Epinions
A popular general-interest opinion-sharing website currently owned by Shopping.com (which is owned by eBay). Founded in 1999. Considers itself to be a platform for shared user experiences.
www.epinions.com

ePortfolio.org
A student-centered ePortfolio platform. Provides students and teachers with tools for creating and customizing electronic portfolios for academic, career, and personal use.
www.eportfolio.org

Epsilen
One of the most feature-rich ePortfolio products on the market. Provides an online repository for collecting examples of student work, including photos, videos, and text. Includes blogging tools and a wiki application.
www.epsilen.com

EverQuest II
Popular MMORPG developed by Sony Online Entertainment. Sequel to EverQuest.
http://everquest2.station.sony.com

ExpressionEngine
Powerful web-publishing solution that comes with a "weblog module." Supports unlimited number of blogs, RSS and Atom syndication, a template library, and mobile blogging.
http://expressionengine.com

Facebook
The world's largest social network. Founded in 2006; by 2010 it had claimed nearly 500 million members.
www.facebook.com

Fark
Social news site with satirical slant.
www.fark.com

Faves (formerly Blue Dot)
A bright and lively bookmark-sharing site with a big social component.
http://faves.com

Federal Virtual Worlds Challenge
A contest for virtual world developers. Focused on training or analysis capabilities conducted wholly in a virtual world. Led by the U.S. Army Research, Development, and Engineering Command's Simulation and Training Technology Center.
http://fvwc.army.mil/FVWC-Main.html

FishbowlDC
A feature of the Media Bistro website focused on news and gossip about politics and media in Washington, D.C.
www.mediabistro.com/fishbowldc

Flickr
Popular image hosting and photo sharing service. Claims to host more than 4 billion images. Debuted in 2004. Bought by Yahoo! in 2005.
www.flickr.com

Flixter
Social network for movie lovers. Founded in 2006, the service allows members to create profiles, chat with friends, and rate movies. Features movie clips and celebrity photos.
www.flixter.com

Foliotek

Developed in 2003 by the University of Missouri for Lanit Consulting. Provides typical ePortfolio features organized in a three-part bundle that includes an Assessment Portfolio, a Presentation Portfolio, and a Scrapbook Portfolio.
www.foliotek.com

Fotki

Photo-sharing service with a social network. Founded in 1998 by a married couple who wanted to share their photos with friends and family. Commercial version launched in 2003.
www.fotki.com

Foursquare

Leading location-sharing service competing head-to-head with Gowalla. In early 2010, the service was claiming 725,000 users and 22 million check-ins, but it was also adding 10,000 to 20,000 new members daily.
http://foursquare.com

Fox Interactive Media

Bills itself as "an interactive services company dedicated to connecting, informing, entertaining and empowering consumers with the most compelling online media experiences." Owns MySpace and Photobucket. Headquartered in Beverly Hills.
www.fimcareers.com

Frenzoo

A browser-based three-dimensional virtual world, currently in beta.
www.frenzoo.com

Friendster

One of the first of the modern social networks. Founded in 2002. Reportedly the model for MySpace. Currently claims approximately 115 million members, with 90 percent of its traffic in Asia.
www.friendster.com

Gartner, Inc.

Leading information technology, research, and advisory company. Essential information and insights on high-tech and telecom.
www.gartner.com

Goo.gl

Google's URL shortener.
http://goo.gl/

Google Analytics

One of the top web-traffic tracking tools, and it's free. Provides reports in detail about the visitors to your blog or website.
www.google.com/analytics

Google Buzz

Social networking service launched in 2010 by Internet search giant Google. Offers the usual social networking features, but also tools from Google, such as Gmail, Picasa, Google Reader, and Blogger.
www.google.com/buzz

Google Latitude

Google's free location-aware mobile application that essentially functions as a feature of Google Maps for Mobile.
www.google.com/latitude

Gowalla

Top location-sharing service, competing head-to-head with Foursquare. By mid-2010, the service had accumulated 250,000 members and was claiming a month-to-month growth rate of more than 50 percent.
http://gowalla.com

Guardian.co.uk

The online version of the *Guardian* newspaper, which is published in the UK. Great technology section.
http://observer.guardian.co.uk

Habbo Hotel

Free virtual world aimed at teens. Uses a hotel as a metaphor for the spaces in this world. There are currently more than 30 "hotels" in the space.
www.habbo.com

Hi5

Social network founded in 2003. Claims around 50 million active members, most of them in Latin America.
http://hi5.com

Hitwise

A must-consult provider of online intelligence; "providing daily insights on how 25 million Internet users around the world interact with more than 1 million websites."

www.hitwise.com

How Stuff Works

Free, user-friendly information site focused on a wide range of subjects, from animals to entertainment, computers to gardening. Published by Discovery Communications. Articles are expert-written.

www.howstuffworks.com

How to Change the World

Guy Kawasaki's blog. A must-read blog from one of Silicon Valley's most tech-savvy venture capitalists. He's the managing director of Garage Technology Ventures, an early stage venture capital firm, and a columnist for Entrepreneur Magazine.

http://blog.guykawasaki.com

Huffington Post

American news website. Aggregates blogs. Generally thought to be liberal-leaning.

www.huffingtonpost.com

Hulu

Website showing commercial TV shows from NBC, Fox, ABC and others.

www.hulu.com

IDC

One of the leading providers of market intelligence and advice on high tech. Great source for a ton of information and insights.

www.idc.com

IMVU

A free, three-dimensional virtual world that emphasizes social networking. Provides the usual virtual-world amenities with a distinctly "singles" vibe. Most members are between eighteen and twenty-four.

www.imvu.com

IndianPad

A social news site aimed primarily at Indian-American users.

www.indianpad.com

Infinite Dial 2010: Digital Platforms and the Future of Radio

A study originally delivered as a webcast on April 8th, 2010, derived from an Edison Research/Arbitron Internet and Multimedia Study. Represents an overview of American media and technology usage and habits. The PDF file of the principal findings is available as a free download.

www.edisonresearch.com/home/archives/2010/04/the_infinite_dial_2010_digital_platforms_and_the_future_of_r.php

Infoplease

Free resource combining an encyclopedia, a dictionary, a thesaurus, an atlas, and several almanacs.

www.infoplease.com

Inside Facebook

A website dedicated to all things Facebook. Not connected to Facebook, but a service of Inside Network. Great independent source for news and market research on America's favorite social network.

www.insidefacebook.com

iWebfolio

ePortfolio management system with a trifold model. Users can create Learning Portfolios for reflection and formative evaluations; Assessment Portfolios based on accrediting or local standards; and Presentation Portfolios for showcasing achievements.

www.nuventive.com/products_iwebfolio.html

Jaiku

Microblogging service maintained by volunteer Google engineers.

www.jaiku.com

Jive

An example of an internal social media platform. Aimed at companies and organizations.

www.jivesoftware.com

Just Tweet It

Twitter tool that searches for twitterers with common interests in database of subject-specific directories.

http://justtweetit.com

Kaneva

Free, three-dimensional virtual world that emphasizes social networking. Bills itself as a combination of the two.

www.kaneva.com

Kids' Informal Learning with Digital Media

A 2009 ethnographic investigation of "innovative knowledge cultures." The conclusions are published online. A must read for anyone interested in kids and social media.

http://digitalyouth.ischool.berkeley.edu

Kirsty

Social news site.

www.kirtsy.com

Knol

An online encyclopedia launched in 2008 by Google. Widely seen as the Wikipedia Killer. Instead of a wiki, Knol is written by experts paid through ad-revenue-sharing. By 2009, Knol had grown to include about 100,000 articles.

http://knol.google.com/k

Kodak Gallery

Online photo-sharing site from old-school photo-film provider. Originally launched in 1999 as Ofoto. Acquired by Kodak in 2001. It's a mainstream photo-finishing service with a social component.

www.kodakgallery.com/gallery/welcome.jsp

Koinup

An image- and video-hosting site and online community for users of virtual worlds.

www.koinup.com

latimes.com

Online version of the Los Angeles Times. Lots of tech coverage.

www.latimes.com

Layar

Creator of an augmented-reality browser that combines real-time computer data with geo-tagging info from location-sharing service Brightkite, on images you see of the real world through your camera phone.

www.layar.com

Lighthouse Learning Island

A *Second Life* community for the professional development of teachers.

http://lighthouselearning.blogspot.com

Linden Lab

San Francisco-based creator of *Second Life* virtual world.

http://lindenlab.com

LingWiki

A wiki for language experts.

http://lingwiki.com

LinkedIn

Business oriented social network. Launched in 2003. Claims more than 65 million registered users around the world.

www.linkedin.com

Linkroll

Free social bookmarking service that bills itself as a "link blogging" service.

www.linkroll.com

LiveJournal

A free blog-hosting service that emphasizes the personal journal aspect of blogging. Provides design templates, privacy controls, integration with YouTube, Photobucket, and Slide. Fee-based upgrades available.

www.livejournal.com

LiveText

Web-based e-learning solution with a simple ePortfolio development toolset for students.

www.livetext.com

Loopt

Free location-sharing service based in Mountain View, California, and founded in 2005. Calls itself a "mobile social-mapping service." Claims around 3 million registered members, and works on more than 100 types of mobile devices.

www.loopt.com

LyricWiki

A wiki that publishes the lyrics to more than a million songs.

www.lyricwiki.com

Mahara

Open-source ePortfolio project from New Zealand. Stand-alone ePortfolio system designed to be integrated into a learning management system. Modular architecture.

www.mahara.org

Mark Cuban's Blog

An example of a well-maintained and content-packed blog from a business executive.

http://blogmaverick.com

Marvel Database

A wiki devoted to Marvel comics and the Marvel Universe.

http://marvel.wikia.com

Mashable.com

Billed as the Social Media Guide. An online magazine devoted to social media. Lots of news, trend updates, and how-tos. A must-read for those interested in social media.

www.mashable.com

Mighty Girl

A great example of a personal blog that went beyond its creator's expectations to become highly influential and revenue generating.

www.mightygirl.net

Mixx

A top social news site. Launched in 2007. Has content partnerships with *USA Today*, Reuters, The Weather Channel, *Los Angeles Times*, and CNN.

www.mixx.com

MobyPictures

A tool for adding photos, audio, and video to your tweets.

www.mobypictures.com

Moove

Three-dimensional free virtual world with a romantic slant. Based on a system called Roomancer.

www.moove.com

MoTwit

A mobile Twitter client for Palm smartphones.

www.mitreo.com/motwit_twitter_palm_os

MouthShut

Consumer-generated-review site based in India. Has a substantial U.S. following among both Indian-American consumers and Indian residents.

www.mouthshut.com

Movable Type

Free, open-source blog-publishing system. Provides customizable templates, tagging features, access management, TrackBack, and support for multiple blogs.

www.movabletype.com

Multiply

A social network built around media sharing. Big emphasis on family. Supports photos and videos. Promises to store your media "permanently and in full resolution."

www.multiply.com

Muti

Free social bookmarking service is "dedicated to content of interest to Africans or those interested in Africa."

www.muti.co.za

MyOuterSpace

Social network launched in 2010 by actor William Shatner. Targets science-fiction fans who'd like to pursue careers as writers, game designers, animators, or actors specializing in science fiction, horror, and/or fantasy.

www.myouterspace.com

MySpace

Social network founded in 2003. Was the largest from 2006 to 2008. Claims more than 100 million members today.

www.myspace.com

National Institute for Technology in Liberal Education

Community-based, nonprofit initiative helping liberal arts colleges and universities explore and implement digital technologies.

www.nitle.org

Newsvine

Social news site. Draws content from users and mainstream sources.

www.newsvine.com

Nielsen Company

Service that, among other things, monitors and measures more than 90 percent of global Internet activity. Great source for trends and statistics.

http://en-us.nielsen.com

Ning

A platform for creating other social networks. Co-founded by Marc Andreessen (co-creator of the first web browser) and Gina Bianchini in 2004. Claims there are nearly 2 million Ning Networks with around 40 million registered users.

www.ning.com

Nowpublic

Lively social news site. Great slogan: "crowd powered media."

www.nowpublic.com

NYtimes.com

The *New York Times* online.

www.nytimes.com

Open Diary

Founded in 1998 by computer programmer Bruce Abelson. Probably the first blogger. Blog-like service, but billed as a personal diary; you write for yourself and share or not with others in the community.

www.opendiary.com

Origin Systems

Computer game developer based in Austin. Creator of Ultima Online. Play the game here:

www.uoherald.com/news

PackRat on Facebook

This is the Facebook page for the popular PackRat collectible card game.

www.facebook.com/playpackrat

Palm

Palm is the maker of the Palm Pre smart phone. At the time this book was being written the company was being acquired by HP.

www.palm.com

PayPal

An online payment service (e-commerce) used by many of the services that sell virtual goods.

www.paypal.com

PBworks

A wiki-hosting service focused on business and legal communities.

www.pbworks.com

Photobucket

The world's most popular photo-sharing service. Claims to host around 7 billion images. Launched in 2003, it's sometimes recognized as the first big photo-sharing service. Owned by Fox Interactive Media.

www.photobucket.com

Picasa Web Albums

Google acquired the Picasa photo organizer in 2004, and then came out with this free photo-sharing component. Offers geotagging, standard editing tools, and photo sharing options.

www.picasa.com

PleaseRobMe.com

A prank website launched in 2010 to put a spotlight on the potential dangers of oversharing locations on social networks.

www.pleaserobme.com

Plime

Social news site, but billed as a wiki community "where users can

add and edit weird and interesting links." Users earn "karma" when other users vote on their actions.
www.plime.com

Plurk

A microblogging service billed as "a social journal for your life."
www.plurk.com

Pocket Metaverse

An iPhone app for Second Life.
www.pocketmetaverse.com

Politico.com

Online publication covering politics. Some interesting writing on political aspects of technology trends.
www.politico.com

Politics Wikia

A wiki that assembles a range of political opinion articles.
http://opinion.wikia.com

Propeller

Well-organized social news site. A very good example of social news.
www.propeller.com

QuitSmoking wiki

A wiki where former smokers and smokers who are trying to quit share their experiences, advice, and opinions on things like nicotine withdrawal, cancer, and asthma.
http://quitsmoking.wikia.com/wiki/Quit_Smoking

RDECOM

U.S. Army Research, Development, and Engineering Command. The Army's technology leader and largest technology developer. Interesting work on virtual worlds.
www.army.mil/info/organization/unitsandcommands/command structure/rdecom

Read Write Web

A must-read blog that includes web technology news, reviews, analysis, and trends. Lots of information about social networking.
www.readwriteweb.com

Reddit

One of the top social news sites. Launched in 2005. A no-frills site, with a very simple and almost graphics-free design. Also, it's an open-source project.
www.reddit.com

Remindo

An example of an internal social media platform. Aimed at companies and organizations.
www.remindo.com

Research in Motion (RIM)

Makers of the Blackberry smart phone.
www.rim.com

Reuters.com

Online version of the international news service. Great source for news about social media.
www.reuters.com

Revver

Launched in 2005, one of the first user-generated video-hosting services to offer revenue sharing with its contributors. Famous for hosting early user-generated video stars like LonleyGirl15 and Ask a Ninja.
www.revver.com

Ryze

This free, business-focused social network was founded in 2001, and now claims a global membership of 500,000.
www.ryze.com

Salon.com

Online magazine. Often a source for insights on social web.
www.salon.com

Schooltube

A video-sharing site for students and the classroom.
www.schooltube.com

Second Life

The leading virtual world. Launched in 2003 by Linden Lab. Offers free and premium memberships.
www.secondlife.com

Seesmic
A desktop Twitter client.
http://seesmic.com

Shoutwire
A social news site with a big emphasis on community.
http://shoutwire.com

Shutterfly
Photo-sharing service that calls itself a "social expression and personal publishing." Founded in 1999. Provides free online storage for members for life. Claims a community of nearly 3 million members.
www.shutterfly.com

Simpy
Free, no-frills social bookmarking service launched in 2004.
www.simpy.com

Slashdot
The granddaddy of social news communities. Founded in 1997. Features user-submitted summaries of stories published on other sites. Also offers opinions and comments on technology and science related web content.
www.slashdot.org

SmugMug
A leading fee-based image hosting services. Emphasis on high-quality photos.
www.smugmug.com

Snapfish
Combines free photo-sharing and fee-based photo printing services. Launched in 2000, now owned by Hewlett-Packard. Claims about 70 million members.
www.snapfish.com

Snaptweet
A tool for sharing Flickr photos on Twitter.
www.snaptweet.com

Social Media Marketing Industry Report
Michael Stelzner's excellent report on the social media marketing industry. Must-read if you're interested in this topic.
www.whitepapersource.com/socialmediamarketing/report

Sony Online Entertainment (SOE)
Creator of the popular MMORPG *EverQuest II*.
www.soe.com/soe.vm

South by Southwest Interactive (SXSWi)
Austin, Texas-based technology conference where Twitter, Foursquare, and Gowalla first gained media attention.
http://sxsw.com/interactive

Sparkle
Second Life app for the iPhone.
http://sparkle.genkii.com

Squeelr
Microblogging service.
www.squeelr.com

SRI International
An independent, nonprofit research institute conducting client-sponsored research and development for government agencies, commercial businesses, foundations, and other organizations. Provides access to several publications.
www.sri.com

SRI's Center for Technology in Learning (CTL)
Research and development arm of SRI focused on learning and teaching. If you're interested in social media and schools, you'll want to keep track of this group's reports.
http://ctl.sri.com

StumbleUpon
Popular social news site. Emphasis on sharing websites you "stumble upon." Toolbar feature for your browser.
www.stumbleupon.com

Talking Points Memo
Political commentary site with a liberal perspective. Occasionally offers useful coverage of impact of tech trends on politics.
www.talkingpointsmemo.com

TeacherTube
Video sharing site for educators, launched in 2007. Emphasis

on instructional videos. Strong community aspects. User contributed videos encouraged.

www.teachertube.com

Tech Crunch

Must-read online technology publication. Follows all things digital and Internet. Breaking news, trends, and reviews.

www.techcrunch.com

Technorati

A must-read blog indexer. Lists top 100 blogs, popular videos, top articles, and "hottest" posts from the blogosphere. If it's an audience you want for your blog, this is the place you want to be listed.

www.technorati.com

Teen Second Life

The area of the *Second Life* virtual world reserved for users ages thireen to seventeen. No one eighteen and older is allowed into this space; and users under eighteen are not allowed in the *Second Life* main grid.

http://teen.secondlife.com

Telegraph.com

Online version of the UK newspaper. Worth checking for a look at tech issues from outside the U.S.

www.telegraph.co.uk

The Technology Horizons in Education Journal (T.H.E. Journal)

Great online publication and paper magazine about technology and education.

www.thejournal.com

Tiny Twitter

A mobile Twitter client for Java-enabled devices and Windows Mobile Pocket PC or Smartphone.

www.tinytwitter.com

TinyURL

A leading URL shortening service.

www.tinyurl.com

Tip'd

Social news site emphasizing financial news and money tips.

http://tipd.com

Toontown

Disney's massively multiplayer online game for kids and families. It's also a virtual three-dimensional world. Award winning. Lots for kids to do.

http://toontown.go.com

Treehugger

Social news site with an environmental emphasis. Billed as "a one-stop shop for green news, solutions, and product information."

www.treehugger.com

TripAdvisor

Opinion and user review site focused on travel, hotels, and vacations.

www.tripadvisor.com

Tumblr

Microblogging service. Users post text, photos, quotes, links, music, and videos, from their browsers, phones, desktops, e-mails, "or wherever you happen to be."

www.tumblr.com

Tweako

Social news site that publishes links to guides, tutorials, service reviews, new software, general information, how-tos, and user-written articles.

http://tweako.com

Tweet Scan

A Twitter search tool that looks for keywords.

www.tweetscan.com

TweetDeck

A desktop Twitter client.

www.tweetdeck.com

Tweetie

A mobile Twitter client for the iPhone.

www.tweetie.com

Tweetmeme

A trend-watching tool that aggregates popular links on Twitter.

www.tweetmeme.com

Twellow

A directory billed as a yellow pages for Twitter.

www.twellow.com

Twhrl
A desktop Twitter client.
www.twhirl.org

Twiddeo
A tool for adding video to your tweets.
www.twideo.com

Twinity
Virtual world launched in 2008. Billed as a "3D mirror world based on real cities." First cities: Berlin, Singapore, London.
www.twinity.com

Twippera
A browser plug in for the Opera web browser.
www.twippera.com

Twitdir
A search tool for words in user names, locations, and descriptions.
www.twitdir.com

Twiterriffic
A desktop Twitter client.
www.twitterrific.com

Twitpic
One of the most popular tools for adding pictures to your tweets.
www.twitpic.com

Twitscoop
A trend-watching tool for Twitter. Tracks trends and events.
www.twitscoop.com

Twitter
The world's leading microblogging service. A web-based messaging service that allows its users to share short text updates about the moments of their lives. Answers the question: "What are you doing?" Messages, called tweets, are limited to 140 characters.
www.twitter.com

Twitterbar
A browser plug-in that allows you to post to Twitter via the address bar of your Firefox web browser.
https://addons.mozilla.org/en-US/firefox/addon/4664

Twitterberry
A mobile Twitter client for the BlackBerry.
www.twitterberry.com

Twitterfox
A browser plug-in that updates the status of your follow list on the Firefox web browser.
www.echofon.com/twitter/firefox

Twitaholic
A tool that scans the Twitter public timeline a few times a day and calculates individual statistics "for each twittering twit in our database."
www.twitaholic.com

Twitterline
A browser plug-in that displays the public timelines of the people you follow on your Firefox browser toolbar.
www.greenspace.info/twitter/line/en.html

Twitterment
A topics-based search tool for Twitter.
www.twitterment.com

Twittie Me
Tool billed as "a place for twitter users to advertise their profiles and get followed by other people who share their interests."
www.twittieme.com

Twittorati
Tracks the tweets from the highest authority bloggers, starting with the Technorati Top 100. Planning to include more. Slogan: "Where the blogosphere meets the twittersphere."
http://twittorati.com

Twitturly
A tool for tracking and ranking links on Twitter.
www.twitturly.com

Typepad
Fee-based service that is Search Engine Optimized. Provides customizable design templates, mobile support, a widget catalog, podcasting support, spam control, revenue opportunities, and traffic tracker, among others.
www.typepad.com

Ultima Online
Venerable MMORPG, originally launched in 1997 by Origin Systems. Paved the way for *World of Warcraft* and *EverQuest*.
www.uoherald.com

USAtoday.com
Online version of the daily newspaper. Worth checking for coverage of popular consumer tech and trends.
www.usatoday.com

Vimeo
Video hosting service launched in 2004. No commercial video and no games. A true user-generated video site. Claims more than 3.4 million members and an average of more than 20,000 new videos uploaded daily.
www.vimeo.com

Vox
A free personal blog-hosting service with a neighborhood feel. Provides a built-in blog editor, privacy controls, e-mail, and support for photos and videos.
www.vox.com

Washington Post
Online version of the daily newspaper.
www.washingtonpost.com

Webshots
Launched in 1999 as an online community, it's one of the oldest photo-sharing services on the web. In 2010, it claimed 23 million visitors per month.
www.webshots.com

WELL
The first online community.
www.thewell.com

Wells Fargo Bank's Stagecoach Island
A good example of a corporate virtual world.
http://blog.wellsfargo.com/ stagecoachisland

Whrrl
Free location-sharing service based in Seattle, Washington. Provides a map interface similar to Loopt. Supports "Whrrl Societies," which are micro communities of members with similar interests who visit the same places.
http://whrrl.com

Whyville
Virtual world aimed at teens. A two-dimensional world with a strong educational component.
www.whyville.net

Wikia
Free wiki-hosting service aimed at communities. Founded in 2004 by Jimmy Wales, co-creator of Wikipedia, and Angela Beesley Starling, Wikimedia Foundation advisory board member and longtime Wikipedia volunteer editor. According to Starling, the service was hosting more than 80,000 wikis in 188 different languages by 2010.
www.wikia.com

Wikiality, the Truthiness Encyclopedia
A encyclopedia wiki created by Stephen Colbert, host of *The Colbert Report*. Filled with tongue-in-cheek articles.
http://wikiality.wikia.com

WikiAnswers
Community-generated "social knowledge" question-and-answer platform.
www.answers.com

Wikibooks
A wiki for generating free textbook content.
www.wikibooks.com

WikiDoc
A medical wiki. Bills itself as "the original medical wiki/ encyclopedia."
www.wikidoc.org

Wikidot
Bills itself as the world's third-largest wiki farm, and claims 500,000 users running 120,000 sites and serving about 40 million unique visitors per year. Launched in 2006. Developed in Poland and headquartered there.
www.wikidot.com

Wikidweb

An online directory of wikis.

www.wikidweb.com

Wikimedia Foundation

Nonprofit organization that owns Wikipedia. Established in 2003 and based in San Francisco. Emphasized hands-off policy toward Wikipedia. Sponsors many other wiki projects.

http://wikimediafoundation.org/wiki/Home

Wikimedia Incubator

A wiki-testing platform. Sponsored by the Wikimedia Foundation.

http://incubator.wikimedia.org/wiki/Main_Page

Wikinews

Free news source wiki. Sponsored by the Wikimedia Foundation.

http://en.wikinews.org/wiki/Main_Page

Wikipedia

The world's largest wiki. A combination of a wiki and an online encyclopedia. Launched in 2001 by Jimmy Wales and Larry Sanger. More than 3.2 million articles and nearly 20 million web pages in the English version.

www.wikipedia.org

Wikipedia Manual of Style

The style guide for articles published in Wikipedia.

http://en.wikipedia.org/wiki/Wikipedia:Manual_of_Style

Wikipedia Signpost

The Wikipedia community newspaper. Covers news and events of special interest to Wikipedians, and Wikimedia Foundation projects.

http://en.wikipedia.org/wiki/Wikipedia_Signpost

Wikiquote

A quotations reference wiki. Sponsored by the Wikimedia Foundation.

www.wikiquote.com

WikiRoots

A grassroots political-action wiki.

http://grassroots.wikia.com

Wikisource

An online library of free reference books. Sponsored by the Wikimedia Foundation.

http://wikisource.org

Wikispaces

A wiki-hosting service emphasizing ease of use. Claims nearly 5 million members and 1.6 million wikis.

www.wikispaces.com

WikiWikiWeb

The first wiki. Came online in 1995. Created by Ward Cunningham. Still exists as a techie site focused on software development.

http://c2.com/cgi-bin/wiki

Wiktionary

Free, Wikipedia-style online dictionary. Sponsored by the Wikimedia Foundation.

www.wiktionary.org

Wired

Popular magazine of technology. A must read for anyone interested in cutting-edge tech and tends.

www.wired.com

WordPress

One of the blogging world's most popular publishing platforms. Free and available on WordPress.org (not to be confused with WordPress.com). Powered by PHP and MySQL.

http://wordpress.org

World of Warcraft

One of the world's most popular MMORPG, with more than 10 million subscribers.

www.wow.com

WoW Wiki

A wiki for players of the *World of Warcraft* MMORPG.

www.wowwiki.com/Portal:Main

Xanga

A blogging service built on a community/journaling model. Very user-friendly. Offers free and fee-based premium services. Provides templates, comments, photo manager, video-blogs, tracking, and other features.

www.xanga.com

Xing

Leading business-oriented social network in Europe. Claims more than 8 million users.

www.xing.com

Yahoo!

The well-known Internet-services provider.

www.yahoo.com

Yahoo! Fire Eagle

Yahoo!'s free location-sharing service. Launched in 2008.

http://fireeagle.yahoo.net

Yammer

Microblogging service for the enterprise. Billed as a "real time communications platform."

www.yammer.com

Yelp

One of the best known consumer-review-based communities. Founded in 2004 and based in San Francisco.

www.yelp.com

YouTube

By far the most well-known video hosting service/community.

Founded in 2005. In 2008 accounted for one-third of the 9.8 billion online videos viewed by U.S. web surfers that month.

www.youtube.com

Zooomr

Photo-sharing site with a strong community component.

www.zooomr.com

Zynga

Social gaming company. Maker of the popular *Mafia Wars* Facebook/MySpace game.

www.zynga.com

Index

Earl & Mooch

a MUTTS™ treasury
by Patrick McDonnell

Andrews McMeel
Publishing, LLC

Kansas City · Sydney · London

Other Books by Patrick McDonnell

The Best of Mutts

Mutts
Cats and Dogs: Mutts II
More Shtuff: Mutts III
Yesh!: Mutts IV
Our Mutts: Five
A Little Look-See: Mutts VI
What Now: Mutts VII
I Want to Be the Kitty: Mutts VIII
Dog-Eared: Mutts IX
Who Let the Cat Out: Mutts X
Everyday Mutts
Animal Friendly
Call of the Wild
Stop and Smell the Roses

Mutts Sundays
Sunday Mornings
Sunday Afternoons
Sunday Evenings

Shelter Stories

Mutts is distributed internationally by King Features Syndicate, Inc. For information, please write to: King Features Syndicate, Inc., 300 West Fifty-Seventh Street, New York, New York 10019, or visit www.KingFeatures.com.

10 11 12 13 14 BAM 10 9 8 7 6 5 4 3 2 1

ISBN-13: 978-0-7407-9768-2
ISBN-10: 0-7407-9768-9

Library of Congress Control Number: 2010921945

Earl & Mooch is printed on recycled paper.

Mutts can be found on the Internet at
www.muttscomics.com

Cover design by Jeff Schulz.